ROUTLEDGE LIBRARY
ADULT EDUCAT

Volume 16

USING THE MEDIA FOR ADULT BASIC EDUCATION

USING THE MEDIA FOR ADULT BASIC EDUCATION

Edited by
ANTHONY KAYE AND KEITH HARRY

Routledge
Taylor & Francis Group

LONDON AND NEW YORK

First published in 1982 by Croom Helm Ltd

This edition first published in 2019
by Routledge
2 Park Square, Milton Park, Abingdon, Oxon OX14 4RN

and by Routledge
52 Vanderbilt Avenue, New York, NY 10017

Routledge is an imprint of the Taylor & Francis Group, an informa business

British Library Cataloguing in Publication Data
A catalogue record for this book is available from the British Library

ISBN: 978-1-138-32224-0 (Set)
ISBN: 978-0-429-43000-8 (Set) (ebk)
ISBN: 978-0-367-00078-3 (Volume 16) (hbk)
ISBN: 978-0-367-00088-2 (Volume 16) (pbk)
ISBN: 978-0-429-44461-6 (Volume 16) (ebk)

Publisher's Note
The publisher has gone to great lengths to ensure the quality of this reprint but points out that some imperfections in the original copies may be apparent.

Disclaimer
The publisher has made every effort to trace copyright holders and would welcome correspondence from those they have been unable to trace.

Using the Media
for Adult Basic Education

EDITED BY ANTHONY KAYE AND KEITH HARRY

CROOM HELM LONDON

ISBN 0-7099-1506-3

Printed and bound in Great Britain by
Biddles Ltd, Guildford and King's Lynn

CONTENTS

FOREWORD

This book is a product of an exploratory Study carried out by the Distance Education Research Group at the Open University (U.K.) on behalf of the Directorate of Education and Vocational Training of the Commission of the European Communities. The Study reviews recent attempts at using the mass media and distance teaching methods for adult basic education in the member states of the European Community.

When commissioning this Study, the Commission felt it would contibute towards meeting a widely felt need amongst practitioners and decision-makers within the ten member states as well as the two applicant countries, Portugal and Spain, for information about innovatory practices in the use of such methods and thus break down the isolation which some of the practitioners in particular seem to experience.

The book examines some of the major themes and issues involved in the combined use of broadcasting, distance teaching methods, and local tutorial or counselling provision for adult basic education. Particular emphasis is laid on identifying means of reaching groups and individuals with special needs in literacy, numeracy and social skills. It demonstrates clearly that broadcasting, be it through radio or TV, in conjunction with local provision, with tutors and counsellors, can be a most effective way of reaching groups that might not otherwise be reached.

Detailed case-studies of seven particularly important projects in this field are presented, drawn from five different European countries. Each of these projects makes significant use of broadcasting, associated print materials, and local provision.

The experiences described in this book are of particular relevance to three specific risk groups of special concern throughout the Community in respect of adult basic education provision: the unemployed (both school-leavers and older adults), the members of ethnic and cultural minorities, including migrant workers and their families, and the adult population living in economically disadvantaged (peripheral, sparsely populated or otherwise) regions of the Community.

This book also has a wider relevance in illustrating some of the ways in which closer links can be established between formal and informal education, and in pointing out the essential role of basic adult education in policies for continuing education and training related to employment. In this respect, we hope that this book will stimulate reflection and contribute to policy development and innovation in the educational field in the years to come.

We should like to take this opportunity to thank all those who have contributed to the preparation of the present book.

Ivor Richard, Commissioner for Employment, Social Affairs
and Education

Hywel C. Jones, Director for Education, Vocational Training
and Youth Policy

Commission of the European Communities

EDITORS' PREFACE AND ACKNOWLEDGEMENTS

We hope that this book will be useful to practitioners and decision-makers interested in exploiting the potential of the mass media and of distance learning methods for adult basic education. Multi-media methods, using distance learning and independent study as their main thrusts, have already proved successful in a wide range of countries and contexts for formal education - even at degree level. We believe, however, that there are urgent needs, even in the economically developed countries of Europe, for a wider and more accessible provision for basic education opportunities which have been largely ignored until recently. We have tried to sketch out some of these needs in the first chapter of this book, before going on to present the reader with a particularly interesting set of case-studies of projects which have attempted to use multi-media methods to meet some of these needs. A noticeable feature which emerges from these studies is the importance of linking personal contact opportunities (counselling, tuition, group animation) with mass media and distance methods in adult basic education programmes. This is in contrast to the greater emphasis on independent self-study methods in projects orientated more towards formal educational curricula at secondary, degree, or professional training levels.

The case-studies are followed by a final chapter which we hope will be useful in helping the reader follow up in more detail the various points raised too briefly in this short book. The chapter comprises a directory of projects and initiatives in this field in Europe, with some more general information on adult education and broadcasting provision, together with a selective bibliography on projects and initiatives.

This book is based on a Study carried out for the Commission of the European Communities, which was very much a collective effort. We have listed in Appendix I the names of all those involved in the Study, and in Appendix II can be found references to a number of detailed reports and case-studies produced as part of the Study, some of which space did not permit us to include in the book. We would like to acknowledge our gratitude to all those who have contributed reports and comments during the conduct of the original Study.

Special acknowledgement is due to our colleague on the Study Team from the Open University, Dr. Kevin Wilson, who played a major role with us in planning and executing the original work on which this book is based. We are also very grateful for the help and advice received from Karen Fogg and Henriette Bastrup-Birk, of the European Commission.

Finally, we would particularly like to thank Nazira Ismail, of the Open University, for her competence in supervising and organising the typing of successive drafts of this book, and Gwen Green, of Stantonbury Parish Print, for preparing the camera-ready copy.

Anthony Kaye   Keith Harry
St. Bauzille-de-Putois   Milton Keynes

Chapter 1

USING THE MEDIA
FOR ADULT BASIC EDUCATION

Anthony Kaye

ADULT BASIC EDUCATION

What is 'adult basic education'? It is perhaps easier to start by describing what it is not. It is not the scholastic or academic education as represented by the major part of what is currently taught in secondary schools, colleges, and universities. Nor is it strictly professional or vocational training in specific fields of expertise. Nor is it only the use of existing opportunities in these areas - through full-time or part-time study - by groups and individuals as a 'second-chance' route to achieve upwards social mobility. The latter point is important, as the notion of adult basic education should encompass that of education for, and by, the groups involved - not merely the opening of new channels of access to a form of knowledge and culture designed by the privileged groups in society for those of a less privileged status, but the encouragement of the less privileged to 'produce for themselves the knowledge and skills which they need in their struggle'.[1] Thus, in a wider sense, adult basic education should encompass not only the development of a 'toolkit' of social skills, but also the application of the tools to the acquisition, use, and production of relevant and useful knowledge which can help bring about changes in society itself.

What might comprise the toolkit of basic education skills? It would seem that the following areas are of relevance:

1. functional literacy and numeracy skills, related in the first instance to everyday needs of a practical sort (reading newspapers, following instructions, filling in forms, keeping account of household expenditure, shopping etc.)

2. social coping skills needed to survive in, and overcome the complexities of modern society (in, for example, seeking employment, finding out one's rights in housing, social services, health care, and taking action to obtain them)

3. parental and family education aimed, for example, at helping parents understand and participate in the educational, physical, and psychological development of their children

4. consumer education and domestic economy, aimed at helping people to learn for themselves how to go about getting the 'best buy' for the goods and services which they require, and at providing information and guidance on, for example, balancing a housekeeping budget, and on carrying out basic repair and maintenance tasks in the home.

5. community education: provision of help and information which will enable members of a community as a group to take actions to improve their situation through mutual co-operation (e.g. action to obtain improved health, educational, and employment provision)

6. the raising of levels of awareness about existing opportunities for formal and non-formal education and for professional and vocational training, including the breaking down of any psychological barriers which seem to prevent many members of disadvantaged groups from using such provision as does exist

7. preparation for vocational and professional training associated, for example, with re-conversion to new or different employment sectors

8. provision of elementary and seconday education equivalent facilities in specific subjects for adults who, for whatever reason, missed out on schooling provision during their childhood.

The seven case-studies included in subsequent chapters of this book, as well as the various European projects and initiatives referred to in Chapter 9, each cater for one or more of the areas of provision listed above. Table 1.1 indicates schematically the princpal themes of 1-8 above covered by each of the seven case-studies.

The development of skills and knowledge of the sorts covered in the eight categories above is a fair representation of the concept of 'adult basic education' in the English language and within an Anglo-Saxon cultural context. However, it should be borne in mind that in a wider, European, context a ready equivalent of the term 'basic education' does not always exist. For example, in French the expression 'éducation

Table 1.1. Areas of Provision Covered in the Case-Studies

Case Studies	Areas of Provision (see list above)							
	1	2	3	4	5	6	7	8
Télé-Promotion Rurale						†	†	
Just the Job		†				†		
OU Community Ed'n			†	†	†			
UK Adult Literacy	†							
Danish for Adults	†							†
Dutch Open School		†				†		
Radio ECCA			†				†	†

de base' has little meaning, and the Spanish 'educacion general basica' refers predominantly to the primary school curriculum. In the context of the Study for the European Commission on which this book is based, it was therefore important to ensure that a common meaning can be assigned to this term. After lengthy discussions with colleagues from other European countries involved in the original Study, we have come to believe that 'adult basic education' is a meaningful concept in each of our cultures, and that it can be briefly defined as:

'the provision of educational facilities and resources outside the contexts of both the formal schooling system and the professional/vocational training sector, for educationally and socially disadvantaged adults; adult basic education should provide what is needed to help people live better lives, and to enable them to make full use of existing social, economic, and educational facilities as equal members of society'.

THE EDUCATIONALLY DISADVANTAGED

Most of the public educational and vocational training provision for adults in Western Europe is aimed at, or taken up by, the articulate, motivated and advantaged groups in society. Large sums are set aside for full-time higher education for - usually - a minority of young adults who have already been subject in their school years to relatively rigorous selection procedures. For example, in the UK in 1978, £1500 per student per annum was spent from public funds for the fortunate few (425,000) young adults following full-time higher education courses. The equivalent figure per student per annum for all other publicly provided further and adult education courses was £115, for over four million adults, of all ages.[2] And within this latter group, only a small proportion of funding goes into education and training specifically aimed at disadvantaged groups, or for provision of basic education opportunities. Similarly, in France, and in the West German Lander that have introduced a right to paid educational leave, that right has been made much more readily available to skilled manual workers. For unskilled manual workers and for the unemployed, it is virtually not available at all.

And yet there would seem to be evidence of fairly specific needs for basic educational opportunities for a variety of different groups of adults in many of our modern, developed, societies.

Firstly, there are those adults with no formal qualifications of any value on the labour market, and with only minimal competencies in basic literacy and numeracy (which will probably have deteriorated rapidly within a few years of leaving school). Such people are generally from poor and disadvantaged milieux, have either experienced a repeated sense of failure during their school years or have not been to school at all, and are particularly at risk in times of rising unemployment. It is not always easy to gain accurate, official, information on the numbers of adults with only minimal literacy and numeracy skills, and there are evident problems of definition of levels of literacy and numeracy. However, in the UK, Start and Wells demonstrated that in 1971, 3.18% of 15 year-olds in England and Wales could be classified as 'semi-literate' (defined as having a reading age of 'less than the mean 9 year-old in 1938').[3] In France, 0.6% of the 400,000 men called for military service each year are found to be illiterate, unable even to form letters of the alphabet in response to Armed Services selection tests.[4] In 1976, 17,500 conscripts were participating in primary education courses. Data showing similar tendencies could probably be identified for other northern European countries. When such figures are cumulated over a period of many years in succession, it is not difficult to see that the much-quoted unofficial estimate of about two million adult 'functional illiterates' in Britain at the present time might well be fairly accurate.

And if the situation of adult literacy and semi-literacy is bad in European countries that have enjoyed compulsory schooling for several generations, it is much worse in those European countries whose mass schooling provision is more recent, as the figures in Table 1.2 below show:

Table 1.2. Illiterate Population of 15 Years of Age and Over, and Percentage Illiteracy, by sex

Country	Year	Illiterate Population			% Illiterates		
		Total	male	female	total	male	female
Greece	1971	1,030,040	217,480	812,560	15.6%	6.7%	23.7%
Italy	1971	2,487,142	928,403	1,558,739	6.1%	4.7%	7.4%
Portugal	1970	1,786,170	636,530	1,149,640	29.0%	22.4%	34.7%
Spain	1970	2,413,209	671,470	1,741,739	9.8%	5.7%	13.6%

Source: 'Unesco Statistical Yearbook' (1980)

Secondly, there are those adults, again often from deprived sectors of society, who would welcome the opportunity to learn new skills and to train for new jobs, but who have in a very real sense been conditioned to believe that such formal and non-formal opportunities that do exist are 'not for the likes of them'. Many such people have, once again, been classed as failures at school, and the last thing they want is to have to return to the scholastic and schoolroom-like atmosphere of much of the existing part-time educational provision for adults. Such surroundings and such an ethos bring back only too vividly the memories of unhappy school years. And even when this is not the case, the available provision may not be relevant to the needs of these groups - maybe it is too academic, not sufficiently vocationally-oriented, or even deliberately 'recreational'. And the locus of such provision, when it does exist, does not always correspond geographically to the areas of greatest need. People living in poorer rural areas (e.g. Eire or in Southern Italy), or in regions of industrial decline (e.g. the mining and steel communities in Eastern France, Belgium, Wales) are doubly disadvantaged in this respect.

A third category of adults containing significant numbers in need of basic education programmes and facilities is composed of the different ethnic minorities in a given society. Within this category can be grouped:

- migrant workers (from Turkey, Portugal, North and West Africa etc.)
- members of immigrant communities (such as Asians and West Indians in Britain)
- nomads and gypsies.

The problems and needs of these three groups are quite specific and different in many ways. However, both migrants and first generation immigrants will often need basic language and literacy training in the tongue of their host country, as well as the provision of a range of facilities to help in the development of social survival and coping skills in a new and strange environment.

It should be pointed out that many of the families in the groups referred to above, form part of a 'fourth world' sub-proletariat living in extreme poverty and under conditions of effective exclusion from many of the benefits of modern society. The total population of this 'fourth world' in the current member states of the European Economic Community is estimated by ATD - Quart Monde as being of the order of eight million people - men, women and children. Such families accumulate difficulties and problems in effectively every domain - health, education, employment, housing, access to social services - and transmit their problems from generation to generation through the hostility and poverty of the environments in which their children are raised. It is not altogether naive to hope that provision of better, more relevant, and more accessible educational provision to such families might help them to develop the arms which they need to climb out of this poverty trap.

Finally, there are at first sight less obviously disadvantaged groups whose needs for a range of basic educational facilities are not always adequately met:

- working adults wishing to re-train for new jobs, and requiring some pre-vocational help and guidance before embarking on specialist training programmes
- those running the risk of redundancy in years to come, and needing preparation now for a changed, and probably worsening, personal situation in the future

- married women who are about to return to work after childbirth and the early care of young children
- parents wanting to understand, help and participate in the psychological and educational development of their own children
- members of isolated rural communities, far from the facilities taken for granted by those living in urban and well provided regions
- families moving to new industrial development areas and to new towns and cities
- entire families without a wage-earner in the household and likely to remain so during years of unemployment.

The members of these diverse groups can all be said to share a common characteristic basic to their state of disadvantage: the inability - for whatever reasons - to satisfy their educational needs through the formal educational system. To this can be linked the fact that many members of these groups can be said to be victims of social (and schooling) systems which are not only failing to eliminate social and economic stratification, but can even be claimed to be reproducing it from generation to generation. It is well known that the chances of a child of working-class or peasant origin going on to University are far less than those of a child from a middle-class or professional family background. In France, for example, the ratio of 'chance' was estimated as 16 to 1 in favour of children from middle-class backgrounds in 1975, and large proportions of children leave school with no educational qualifications at all: French Government statistics for 1973 show that, of 817,000 school leavers that year, 500,000 (61%) left without any sort of diploma or certificate.[5]

Furthermore, most European societies are currently experiencing an economic recession, which is affecting the already disadvantaged groups most severely. At the time of writing this chapter (June 1981) figures for the unemployed on official registers in the European Economic Community number 8,500,000. By 1985, it is estimated that, at current rates, the numbers of registered unemployed in the existing states of the EEC will exceed 12 million.[6] Public funds for education and social provision are being squeezed, and the little that is available for adult education provision tends, in many European countries, to be directed towards professional and other job-related training linked to the needs of the production system.

Given the above situation, it would seem naive to expect that basic education programmes - using whatever methods - are going to eliminate educational disadvantage amongst adults. The problem can only be solved in its entirety by action on a whole range of conditions - action which would effectively amount to a fundamental restructuring of society. Compulsory full-time schooling has failed to eliminate educational and social disadvantage: voluntary part-time adult education, even with new objectives and new methods, is unlikely to provide a comprehensive solution without other changes occurring.

However, this does not imply that nothing can or should be done in terms of developing new initiatives in the field of basic education for adults, and in applying new methods to extend and enhance existing initiatives. But these developments should be put in the context of an overall problem of educational disadvantage which is of serious dimensions, and which needs to be tackled on a wide range of fronts - not only the educational.

We have tried in this book to pick out some of the more interesting and innovative attempts to use the mass media in conjunction with other, more traditional methods, to approach the problem of educational disadvantage. The scale of the problem - or rather of the problems, because one is not concerned here with a homogeneous group of people or of needs - seems to demand responses at regional and national levels. The press and broadcast media can be demonstrably effective in modifying peoples' behaviour and attitudes - the success of commercial advertising and of popular television programmes show this. Therefore, it would seem appropriate and sensible to use these methods, at national and regional levels, for educational purposes, both for developing public awareness of the problems of educational disadvantage, and for providing help in developing appropriate skills, i.e. in providing learning resources. Additionally, in a gloomy economic situation, there may be a cost-effectiveness argument for using the mass media for reaching diverse and scattered disadvantaged groups.

However, before discussing the application of such methods, it is appropriate to briefly review some of the more traditional methods of provision, for new and integrated approaches will always need to take account of the lessons to be learned from earlier experiences.

METHODS TRADITIONALLY USED FOR ADULT BASIC EDUCATION

Many of the existing basic education facilities for adults, where they exist, are provided through a variety of channels, both publicly and privately financed:
-   voluntary organisations of various types, working essentially at a local and community level, even when represented on a national basis (e.g. the movement ATD-Quart Monde in France)
-   trade union organisations
-   churches and religious organisations of various denominations
-   official Government departments and parastatal organisations and councils
-   pressure groups of differing kinds (e.g. consumer groups, community action groups)
-   in some countries, public broadcasting organisations
-   public educational institutions providing part-time classes and courses

The methods used by these various organisations differ widely - ranging from individual person-to-person activities, the running of study groups at local and community level, the dissemination of printed information, the use of community and local media facilities where these exist (cable-TV, local radio), and the broadcasting of radio and television programmes on a regional or national basis. Each of these methods has its strong points, but taken separately, each also has serious limitations.

Inter-personal activities can take a variety of forms: direct individual and group meetings, self-help groups, action groups, as well as indirect contact through post or telephone. Such contacts have important pedagogical and motivational functions. They can be used as an occasion for learning specific skills, from either a local volunteer, a specialist tutor, or a skilled practitioner. Such meetings do not need to take place in formal or classroom-like surroundings, but might be arranged in peoples' homes, in bars, or in community centres. The motivational functions of such face-to-face encounters are equally, if not more, important, than the pedagogical ones. It is a chance for people to discuss their problems, should they wish, either in confidence, or in a group atmosphere where experience can be pooled and mutual support be forthcoming. It is a chance to share learning experiences with other people, and eventually maybe to work together on concrete actions: setting up a play-group, organising a tenants' association, building up a pressure group for better health or school facilities.

But there are drawbacks. Group meetings of more than a few people can be difficult to organise at times which will suit all the people involved. One-to-one personal 'tutorial' meetings (e.g. to teach literacy skills) require potentially large numbers of volunteers and tutors. In sparsely populated communities problems are magnified, and time and money will be needed for getting to and from meetings. Some people are either natural loners or wish in any case to learn new skills on their own in a setting in which they will not run the risk of feeling threatened or of being ridiculed. For programmes which might involve large numbers of people, the unit costs of organising and running meetings can become very high (travel, meeting rooms, payments to tutors and other resource personnel involved, and their training and briefing, overhead costs of administration and organisation . . .). Perhaps the greatest drawback, from the user's point of view, is the potential inflexibility imposed by constraints of time and place, when meetings run the risk of being missed because of other unpredictable and more pressing demands on time.

Self-study print materials. One way of overcoming some of these drawbacks - not without creating new ones - is to opt for using self-study print materials to provide a proportion of the basic learning medium. Such materials can take the form of leaflets, newspaper or magazine supplements, or more extensive self-instructional texts. To be effective, it helps if they are prepared in an attractive and stimulating style and format, possibly derived from that used in the newspapers, magazines, or publicity materials which will be familiar to the intended audience. They should be 'student-active', containing ideas and suggestions for practical activities and exercises which will not only allow the learner to test newly acquired knowledge, but also to apply this knowledge to real-life situations which are important and relevant to him. And they should be developed and designed with the active participation of a sub-set of the intended future audience. This implies the need for some form of 'piloting' of draft materials, so that potential learning difficulties can be identified and ironed out at an early stage, and before any mass production printing is set in motion. Such materials, properly

18

developed and presented, can prove very effective for imparting a range of basic knowledge and skills, provided that there is sufficient motivation amongst the target group for them to develop, with appropriate guidance if needed, the necessary self-study skills. Print materials have the advantage of being infinitely flexible in use - no fixed time or place is needed to study from them, they provide a permanent record which can be returned to time and again, and the student can work from them at his or her own pace. Print materials of a different sort can also form a resource for group learning and discussion, with or without the presence of a tutor or animateur.

The disadvantages of a strong reliance on the use of self-study materials, especially in the field of adult basic education, are, however, fairly evident. Even with a popular and attractive presentation, print does demand both a reading habit amongst the target group, and the motivation to build up, and persist with, the habit of studying independently over extended periods of time. Other drawbacks include the fairly long leadtime needed to develop and prepare suitable materials, and the costs and difficulties associated with improving, modifying, and up-dating them. Furthermore, it is not always easy to identify, or train, people with the necessary skills in preparing attractive self-study materials.

Television and radio broadcasting. A third medium often used in some countries for providing inputs to a basic adult education provision is that of television and radio broadcasting, at national, regional, and, where the facilities exist, community level. The advantages of using broadcasting in this field are numerous. Attractively presented broadcasts can provide valuable publicity for a learning project or related social issue if transmitted at appropriate hours. They can be an invaluable domestic learning asset in certain areas - such as the development of language skills. But, perhaps more importantly, television and radio broadcasts can stimulate the viewers and listeners, and develop their motivation and confidence to a point at which they want to start a learning project or embark on a course of action. It is not difficult to find instances of such programmes (for example, in Britain, the television series 'Parosi', intended to stimulate Asian women to seek local help in learning English). At a local and community level, radio phone-ins and cable TV facilities which provide public access (e.g. Canal-Emploi in Liège, Belgium) can encourage and develop popular participation, deal with listeners' and viewers' problems, and provide valuable feedback to programme producers. However, broadcasting also has severe limitations. To some extent, broadcasts solve the 'space' problem inherent to group meetings: the broadcasts can be received at home, without the need to go out and travel to a centre. However, broadcasts are transmitted at fixed times which, for educational programmes, are not usually the most convenient ones, because of commercial and other pressures on peak viewing and listening hours. Broadcasts are in essence transient, and often received in a home environment with competing demands on the viewer or listener. Finally, because of the accepted norms of broadcasting in many European countries, organised broadcast series, especially television ones, tend not to be repeated from year to year: their ethos, in the educational field, is more that of a campaign than of a continuing provision or resource.

Many of the current and the past actions in the field of adult basic education have been limited to the use of one or two media (broadcasts plus printed back-up materials, or classes and study groups alone). Such programmes, by their nature, have not been able, on the one hand, to exploit the best points of each medium, nor to counterbalance the specific disadvantages of one or other particular medium. However, there have been a small number of projects which have used, or are planning to use, the different media in varying 'mixes' or combinations and it is this integrated use of broadcasting, distance and self-study methods, and local resources, that forms the principal theme of this book .

MULTI-MEDIA AND DISTANCE EDUCATION METHODS

One paradigm for the integrated use of a variety of different media and learning methods for adult basic education is that of distance learning. Distance learning methods, as they have developed over the last ten years or so, have perhaps become best known in the fields of higher and advanced education (for example, in Europe: Britain's Open University, the Fernuniversität in Western Germany and the Universidad Nacional de Educacion a Distancia in Spain). But in many developing countries, such methods have been successfully used for many years for basic education.

The essence of distance learning is the separation, in space and time, of the teacher/producer of information from the student/user of information. This does not necessarily imply the absence of face-to-face contacts between learners and tutors, animateurs, or other resource personnel at a local level. It does, however, imply a significant change in the role of such mediators: much of the brunt of providing information and 'teaching' is taken up in distance learning systems by other media (print, broadcasts, etc.).

The role of the local mediator becomes one of guidance, help and problem-solving, as well as the provision of feedback to learners on their progress. Such systems can liberate the learner from the constraints of space, time, and often, age, associated with much conventional provision and thus permit a much greater degree of flexibility as to the regularity, timing, and location of his or her study activities. The principal general features of distance education methods have been summarised by Kaye and Rumble (1981) [7] as :

"Concerning students . . .
–   an enlargement or 'opening' of educational opportunity to new target populations, previously deprived either through geographical isolation, lack of formal academic requirements, or employment conditions;
–   the identification of particular target groups and their key characteristics (needs, age, distribution, time available for study, local facilities, etc.) to enable appropriate courses, learning methods and delivery systems to be designed on a systematic basis.
Concerning the learning materials and teaching methods which characterise the courses, the notable features are:
–   a flexibility in the curriculum and content of the learning materials through, for example, modular structures or credit systems;
–   the conscious and systematic design of learning materials for independent study, incorporating, for example, clearly formulated learning objectives, self-assessment devices, student activities and the provision of feedback from students to learning system staff and vice versa;
–   the planned use of a wide range of media and other resources, selected from those available in the context of the system, and

suited to the needs of the students; these media may include specially prepared correspondence texts, books, newspaper supplements, posters, radio and TV broadcasts, audio-and video-cassettes, films, computer-assisted learning, kits, local tuition and counselling, student self-help groups, lending-library facilities, and so on.

Finally, the following logistical and economic features are characteristic of distance learning systems:

- great potential flexibility compared to conventional provision in implementation, in teaching methods, and in student groups covered;
- centralised, mass production of standarised learning materials (such as texts, broadcasts, kits and so on) in an almost industrialised manner, implying clear division of labour in the creation and production procedures;
- a systematic search for, and use of, existing infrastructure and facilities as part of the system (e.g. libraries, postal and other distribution services, printers, publishers, broadcasting organisations, manufacturers, etc.);
- potentially a significant lower recurrent unit cost per student than that obtainable through conventional (classroom or equivalent) teaching arrangements and also potentially a considerably lower capital cost per student."

Distance methods, using the mass media for publicity and motivational functions as well as for some direct teaching, combined with animateurs and volunteers at local level for help, guidance, and problem-solving, can play a very important role in enhancing existing provision of basic education for adults, as the case-studies included in this book demonstrate.

Case-studies On Multi-media Provision

The seven projects described in the following chapters represent widely different approaches to using multi-media methods for various sectors of provision within the general field of adult basic education. They are all fairly wide-scale projects: three are regional (Just the Job, Télé-Promotion Rurale, Radio ECCA), the remainder provide coverage at a national level. Some are or were, pilot projects (Just the Job) or campaigns (Adult Literacy) and now, as such, no longer exist. Others are run by distance learning institutions with a guarantee of continuity (Radio ECCA, OU Community Education). Others have changed significantly over the years (e.g. Télé-Promotion Rurale, since TV transmissions of their programmes were stopped).

The variety and range of different media within each project is shown in Table 1.3 below. Note in this table the importance of personal contact (e.g. study groups, meetings, personal tuition or counselling), and the consistent use of specially prepared print materials.

Table 1.3. Use of Media in the Case Studies

	Personal Contact	Print Materials	News-papers	TV	Radio	Non-broadcast audio-visual
Télé-Promotion Rurale	†	†	†	†	†	†
Just the Job	†	†	†	†	†	
OU Community Ed'n	(†)	†	†	†	†	
UK Adult Literacy	†	†		†	†	
Danish for Adults	†	†		†		†
Open School	†	†		†		†
Radio ECCA	†	†			†	

Although Table 1.3 suggests a certain uniformity in that all the projects use personal contact, print, and broadcast materials, the ways in which the media are used, and the relative weight attached to each medium or learning method, varies enormously amongst the projects. Only two of the projects (Radio ECCA, OU Community Education) and a variant of one other (distance option of Danish for Adults) could be described as integrated distance learning 'systems' of the nature invoked in the preceding section of this chapter. The other projects are more flexible, less integrated, and less 'systematised'. For example, the UK Adult Literacy Campaign deployed a wide variety of support (TV, radio, newspaper articles, posters) to encourage and facilitate the primary learning mode of one-to-one or small group tuition. However, there was no overall systematic plan underlying the articulation of these various supports. The campaign encouraged individual learners and tutors to select what they wanted for their individual needs, and to ignore what was irrelevant.

Two general points are of particular interest concerning media use: firstly, the widespread use of broadcasting for publicity, awareness-raising, and 'enrolment', and the often hitherto hidden needs and demands which were thus revealed; secondly, the articulation, in many projects, between a central broadcast provision (say at national level) and local broadcast and press support from regional radio stations and newspapers.

Many other points come to mind in reading through the case-studies, but unfortunately space does not permit a fuller treatment in this chapter. However, a brief checklist of some important prescriptive points which have emerged from analysis of the case-studies is given below as the final section of this chapter.

A CHECKLIST OF IMPORTANT POINTS CONCERNING THE USE OF MULTI-MEDIA METHODS FOR ADULT BASIC EDUCATION

General

1. Adult basic education projects - particularly functional projects - aimed at disadvantaged groups, should help create conditions which encourage participants to help themselves, to become autonomous, and to take on responsibility for their own situations.

2. Programmes should be of immediate relevance in terms of object-ives, style, content and approach to the real problems, situations, and needs of the participants; they should provide the informa-tion, knowledge, and skills needed to bring about concrete changes in the situation of the disadvantaged individuals, comm-unities, and groups in question; aims should be clearly defined and communicated.

3. Key questions which need answering at the early stages of plann-ing a new project, the answers to which will considerably influence

the project design, including the following:

- will the primary learning mode be through self-study or through face-to-face tuition on a group/individual basis (i.e. will it be a media-based project or a media-supported project)?
- will the project encompass variants in learning methods (e.g. an independent study option, a distance learning option, a class-based option)?
- what will be the primary result or output of the project (achievement of personally set, functional, objectives, delivery of a diploma or certificate, actions at community/local level to improve or change a given situation)?
- will the project include elements designed specifically to favour the disadvantaged groups and individuals who do not spontaneously take up adult education provision?

4. New projects should extend and build on existing provision, and use the experience of those already working with members of the target groups.

Needs Analysis

5. Functional basic education programmes should where feasible be designed in terms of real-life situations and issues (e.g. finding employment, organising a tenants' association, managing a household budget) rather than in terms of basic "disciplines" such as literacy, numeracy, economics etc.

6. Educationally disadvantaged groups and individuals do not generally articulate their objective needs for educational resources; objective needs must generally be determined through an analysis of problem situations, and through discussion of subjective needs with eventual participants and with appropriate intermediaries (teachers, social workers, adult educators etc).

7. Provision of an educational resource that is relevant to subjective needs, and which is able to meet objective needs, if publicised through appropriate channels, will stimulate a demand.

Media and Methods

8. Multi-media education projects - whether functional or examin-ation-oriented - should exploit to a maximum the popular comm-unication styles of radio, television and the press, thus removing possible psychological barriers to access.

9. Participation levels in multi-media programmes will be enhanced if
   - the procedures for enquiry and enrolment are as simple as possible (e.g. telephone referral, a "drop-in" shop)
   - the provision itself is as flexible as possible in terms of timing, location, pace and methods of learning
   - there is redundancy amongst the different elements in the project i.e. a participant who misses a broadcast or a tutorial class can obtain the information needed through another channel - for example, a printed self-teaching text.
   - very close integration between the different media used, (leading to an imposition of a relatively rigid study sequence) is avoided.

10. In designing a project, clear functions should be assigned to each medium; these functions will include: publicity, awareness-raising, recruitment, instruction, resolving learning problems, providing feedback, and so on; each of these functions should be consciously assigned to one or more of the media used: face-to-face tuition/counselling, broadcasting, print materials, telephone referrals, etc.

11. In publicising a new project, and in encouraging recruitment, as wide a range as possible of information channels should be used: broadcasts, press, posters, personal and institutional contacts, leaflets, etc; specific information channels (e.g. particular radio or TV programmes and broadcast times, specialist newspapers/ magazines) should be used to get through to specific sub-groups of the target population.

12. Multi-media basic education programmes intended to reach educationally disadvantaged groups will need, for many members of such groups, to place a strong reliance on face-to-face tuition

and counselling in both group and individual situations, with the media probably playing a supporting role.

13. Recruitment and training of staff to work at local level is of major importance in any multi-media project aimed at disadvantaged groups; development of specific skills in working with adults in the following situations is required:
    - pre-enrolment counselling
    - group counselling during the course/project
    - one-to-one tuition
    - group tuition
    - group leadership and 'animation'

14. Distance learning methods based essentially on home-based, independent study, with minimal tuition and group work, will on the whole only be appropriate for individuals who are strongly motivated to study independently and have previous successful experience of learning at a distance. Educationally disadvantaged groups and individuals will in all likelihood need some form of guidance, preparation and support before embarking on a distance learning programme.

Materials Creation and Production

15. Learning materials suitable for adults in skills such as numeracy and literacy will need to be developed from scratch, as few suitable materials exist in these areas, and those used at school level are not appropriate for mature students.

16. Centrally produced materials (broadcasts, print materials) should be designed for flexible use in a variety of situations ranging from independent, home-based, learning to supported group study.

17. Learning materials for basic education progammes should be extensively piloted, both with representative members of the target group, and with adult educators familiar with their needs, before they are finalised.

18. Procedures for obtaining feedback on a regular basis from

participants and local animateurs and tutors on the quality and effectiveness of centrally produced print and broadcast materials should be built into the design of any multi-media project; likewise resources should be allocated for revision and up-dating of materials in the light of this feedback.

Working Methods

19. A team structure, with close working relationships between members with different specialist skills, is generally the most appropriate one for the creation and production of multi-media materials; where feasible, every effort should be made to involve eventual project participants (learners and tutors/animateurs) in the process of materials creation.

20. To be effective, adult basic education programmes will generally need to involve a whole range of partners and agencies, both central and local, educational and non-educational. Working methods should ensure good contacts between all such partners, and a consistent overall control of the educational process, so as to minimise dangers of over-professionalisation or even of commercialisation.

21. Projects which involve collaboration between a number of different agencies in preparing materials and in providing local publicity and support, should be based on a clear allocation of functions, responsibilities, and resources between the different partners; regular opportunities for monitoring and comparing progress need to be built into the project brief.

22. Centrally planned projects using central resources (such as broadcasting), which will create an increased demand for provision at local level (such as evening classes) should be planned from the start in close collaboration with the organisations and authorities responsible for local provision; extreme care should be given to time scheduling which will ensure the necessary meshing of local and central provision when the project starts, as the time-scales for obtaining decisions on resource allocations may vary widely

between one agency and another.

Evaluation

23. Projects which do not have automatic monitoring of learners' progress through assessment/examination procedures should include in their design, procedures for monitoring participants' progress in other ways, to enable participation and drop-out rates to be ascertained.

24. In designing new projects, every effort should be made to keep a record of the actual costs of each element and component in the project, regardless of the source of finance involved; standard procedures for describing, analysing, and projecting costs should be devised.

25. Evaluation procedures for assessing the effectiveness of the various components of the project should be incorporated into the design of any new multi-media project; particular care should be given to devising methods for evaluating the effectiveness of non-assessed, functional projects where participants have the possibility of setting their own learning objectives and levels of participation.

26. Project evaluation should be a continuing process going from the initial planning phase to the stage of implementation, and should include both qualitative and quantitative elements.

Notes and References

1. P. Demunter, L'Education Permanente en Belgique, 'Contradictions', No. 21 (1979), p. 23.
2. J. Robinson, 'The Role of Educational Broadcasting in Learning Opportunities for the Socially Deprived', paper produced for the Fourth International Conference on Higher Education, University of Lancaster, August 25th–September 1st 1978.
3. K.B. Start and B.K. Wells, 'The Trend of Reading Standards' (National Foundation for Education Research, Windsor, 1972)
4. B. Pasquier, 'Further Vocational Training in France' (EEC, Brussels, 1977)
5. Figures quoted in B. Schwartz, 'Une Autre Ecole' (Flammarion, Paris, 1977)
6. Le Monde, Supplement 'Europa', June 2nd 1981
7. A. Kaye and G. Rumble, 'Distance Teaching for Higher and Adult Education' (Croom Helm, London, 1981), pp 18-19.

Chapter 2

TELE-PROMOTION RURALE, RHONE-ALPES, AUVERGNE, FRANCE

Marc Girardin *

INTRODUCTION

The Télé-Promotion Rurale (TPR) experience dates back to 1966. At that time a ministerial working party on audio-visual methods asked Professor Malassis, at the Ecole Nationale Supérieure de l'Agriculture to mount an experiment aimed at using television to 'promote the rural world'. This became the first regional TPR project (TPR Bretagne). Later, during 1969, and the early 1970's, four more regional centres were created:
- TPR Toulouse (Midi, Pyrenées, Aquitaine)
- TPR Montpellier (Languedoc-Rousillon, Provence, Côte d'Azur)
- TPR Grenoble (Rhône-Alpes, Auvergne)
- TPR Nancy (Alsace, Lorraine, Ardennes)
Thus, although TPR developed into practically a national institution, activities were devolved to regional centres, and adapted to particular regional needs and characteristics. Five relatively autonomous projects existed, each with its own programme of activities. Of these five projects, only two continue today (TPR Grenoble and TPR Nancy).

Although originally conceived - as its name indicates - as relying primarily on television as the principal means of reaching its (mass) audience of agriculturalists, TPR has evolved constantly over the last fourteen years in response to a variety of pressures. In the early years, TPR's audience would meet in special local viewing centres with an animateur/trainer, to view the programmes collectively, discuss them, and consider possible follow-up actions they might take. These special 'TPR-days' would occur during the winter months, when time was available from farming duties - always more onerous in spring, summer, and autumn. Such group viewing was also a response to a situation at a time when individual ownership of TV receivers in poor rural areas was very limited. From 1970 onwards, following the initiative of TPR

* Translated and edited by Anthony Kaye

Grenoble, TV programmes were designed and broadcast for individual domestic viewing, at peak viewing periods - again during the winter months. The training function of the earlier viewing groups was thus lost. The role of the broadcasts was now seen as that of making people aware of opportunities for training ('sensibilisation à la formation').

Then, progressively, and to accompany the TV programmes, the use of more flexible (non-broadcast) media was introduced: 8mm films, video cassettes, and tape-slide presentations. In 1979, broadcasting of TPR programmes was halted, and a further re-orientation took place.

The gradual change and evolution of TPR's activities can be linked to a number of factors. Firstly, the project started, in 1966, at the same time as France's entry into the Common Market, and coincided with an urgent need in France for modernisation of agricultural practices. Hence the emphasis on the use of broadcast media to reach as large a number of agriculturalists as possible.

Secondly, during the last fifteen years, there have been systematic changes both in distribution of TV receivers, and in TV technology. The initial emphasis on viewing groups, meeting collectively, suited a time when private ownership of TV sets was relatively limited. Since then, domestic receivers have become commonplace, and modes of viewing and perception of messages on the small screen have radically altered. Also, during the 1970's and especially in the last few years, the technology and ease of ½inch video equipment for education and 'animation' has evolved considerably, leading to an ease and flexibility of use of the medium which would have been unthinkable ten years earlier. Finally, TPR has been both a beneficiary and, to some extent a victim of changing emphasis in France during the last decade concerning government policy on continuing education ('education permanente'). In the early 1970's, a number of important legislative measures to promote continuing education facilities were introduced. This was a key factor in the development of TPR and many other initiatives. However, the effects of the worsening economic climate at the end of the 70's led to a diminution of credits for projects which were not directly linked to maintenance and creation of employment opportunities.

Thus it is important to bear in mind the constant adjustment of TPR's activities to changing economic, technical, and social circumstances over the last fifteen years. This report examines the evolution of TPR-Grenoble's programme since 1970 in the light of these changing conditions.

THE OBJECTIVES OF TPR

The idea of using television for the promotion and development of agriculture, and for associated training needs, arose from three factors:

- as a means of accompanying and promoting the changes in agricultural practice needed with the creation of the Common Market.
- as an extension of the early experiments in rural 'animation' and training which started in France after the last war.
- as an application of new ideas concerning the integrated use of multi-media methods for training purposes.

Before describing the current work of TPR, it is worthwhile briefly reviewing each of these factors, so as to give a necessary historical perspective.

Changes in Agricultural Practices

Legislation was introduced in France in 1960 concerning the modernisation and orientation of agricultural practices, to encourage and stimulate new production methods and increase the competitiveness of French products in the Common Market. It was thus considered necessary to launch a variety of activities which would help the great mass of agriculturalists - particularly the large numbers of small-holders - in this process of modernisation. These various activities were soon followed by increasing demands for training facilities, and for information, from many agriculturalists. A variety of measures were adopted, including the mounting of specialist training courses, and the development of the existing network of agricultural technicians, advisers, and animateurs. However, these measures were not seen as adequate to meet the needs within the required time-scale, hence the idea of using television to reach a potentially unlimited rural audience.

The Extension of Earlier Experiments in Rural Animation

Early initiatives immediately after the Second World War in France were developed to bring together at a local level groups of independent agricultural small-holders, under the guidance of animateurs and technicians, to discuss and introduce more modern methods of exploitation. The methods used contrasted strongly with traditional teaching and this was particularly necessary given the limited level of basic school education of many of the people involved. This notion of the informal learning group which meets periodically with an animateur has always been one of the key foundations of TPR's activities. In the early years, in Brittany (TPR-Rennes) the 'TPR-days' brought together some 300 groups at a time, each with 20 or 30 members. In the morning, each group would watch a 50 minute TV broadcast, then launch into a discussion session with their animateur - relating the themes covered in the broadcast film to their own problems and pre-occupations. Then, in the afternoon, the groups were able to address questions directly to the TV studio in Rennes, and subsequently watch a round-table discussion of these questions, broadcast live from the studio. Later, when TPR gave up the idea of collective viewing groups (in 1970), in favour of individual domestic viewing, this did not imply the abandonment of the learning group. Such groups would still meet, in the villages and hamlets, to discuss the programmes afterwards. These discussions would often lead, eventually or directly, to individual participation in conventionally organised training courses. To summarise, it has never been the objective of TPR to dispense training programmes as such, but to help support existing training initiatives, and to help make people aware of their needs for training and information.

Integrated Multi-media Methods

The provision of training and information needs to the mass of agricultural workers can be seen as requiring two principal stages:
- a stage of raising of awareness ('sensibilisation') and expression of needs, leading to the definition of a training programme.
- a stage of training and knowledge transfer as such.

TPR has always maintained that the audio-visual media should be predominantly concerned with the first of these stages. And as the second stage - of actual training - is organised regionally in response to regional differences (climate, crops, etc.), so the first stage - of awareness - also needed to be organised regionally. Hence the five different centres for TPR.

In the future, and since the interruption of TPR broadcasts in 1979, it is probable that TPR will also produce audio-visual materials for direct use in training programmes.

TARGET POPULATION

TPR's target population has been characterised as representing a group disadvantaged along three main dimensions.

Firstly, the great majority of small-scale agriculturalists in France, certainly in the early 1960's, were clearly excluded from the process of modernisation of French agriculture. This was especially the case in Brittany, a highly agricultural region in which structures and practices had remained essentially unchanged over a long period of time. Later, when the other regional projects started up, it became clear that the 'viewing group' pattern was not reaching the majority of those excluded. In fact, many of the keenest members of such groups were precisely those people who had already started modernising and developing their small-holdings. That is, to some extent, TPR was already 'preaching to the converted' through these viewing groups. Hence the decision in 1970 to change over to broadcasts aimed at individual households at peak lunchtime winter viewing hours.

Secondly, the group is one which to a large measure was excluded from professional training opportunities - or any educational opportunities beyond the school-leaving age.

Thirdly, the small agriculturalists in France also represent a group which has been excluded from the general development of rural areas, and who had also grown to envy the relatively higher standards of living and life styles of many urban dwellers. The very fact that TPR's broadcasts dealt with the problems of poorer agriculturalists, and used agriculturalists as their principal actors (e.g. in film sequences) was of great importance in this respect, for it represented a significant counterbalance to the predominantly urban and more 'sophisticated' norms and values inherent to the majority of TV programming.

MEDIA AND MATERIALS

Four principal elements are - or were - involved: broadcast films, broadcast debates, print materials, and non-broadcast audio-visual materials.

At the present time, the main emphasis is on the production of non-broadcast and associated print materials, but we will review all four elements in the paragraphs below.

Broadcast Films

These films take the form of documentaries, interviews, or fictional situations, and their purpose is essentially to raise questions concerning typical problems and situations of concern to agriculturalists. The purpose of the films, then, is not to provide ready-made answers to real-life problems, nor to carry a direct teaching message, but to give the viewer a chance to identify with a particular problem and to start thinking about ways of resolving the problem in their own specific situation.

The organisation of the production of films started off on a purely regional basis, each Centre producing itself, for a purely regional use, a certain number of films. Later, an inter-regional production system was adopted, films produced in one region being broadcast also in the other regions. In 1975-76, the Centre in Grenoble produced all five films for that winter's campaign. Subsequently, until the final year of broadcasting in 1979, there was a return to a regional production for regional use.

Typical themes and topics covered in these films include:
- the role of agricultural co-operatives
- agricultural price mechanisms
- land speculation
- land ownership
- problems of rural schooling
- self-help and cooperation with neighbours
- financing of the purchase of new equipment
- problems of family inheritance and succession
- trades union action
- use of and access to veterinary and other services
- helping young agriculturalists to get established
- production factors
- managing money
- ordering of supplies (e.g. foodstuffs, fertilizers, etc.)
- the rural exodus

- getting married
- changing over to new crops: 'modernisation'

Broadcast Debates

These are live, round-table discussions relating to the broadcast of a particular film, and analysing the topics and themes covered previously in the film. Various formats have been used for these broadcasts, ranging from relatively structured debates in a studio, to informal and unstructured discussions in villages, with agriculturalists who had just watched the film in question. In general, and over the years, the tendency had been to reduce the proportion of 'experts' (e.g. agricultural teachers and technicians) in these debates, and to put the emphasis on the views of agriculturalists themselves.

Print Materials

TPR Grenoble started out in its early years of broadcast campaigns with the preparation of printed materials to accompany each programme, aimed at the animateurs, technicians, and trainers responsible for running group sessions based on the broadcasts. These documents served two principal functions:
- to act as guides to the animateurs for the running and organisation of group meetings.
- to provide additional information on the themes treated in the film.

The materials were distributed directly to the animateurs in the form of small booklets. However, it was soon realized that it would be useful to provide print support materials directly to the agriculturalists following the programmes, and as a result, from 1973 onwards, TPR Grenoble used rural newspapers and the regional agricultural press to do this. Special series of articles and technical notes were prepared and printed in these newspapers, at the same time as the dates and times of the broadcasts were announced.

Non-broadcast Audio-Visual Material

These include a variety of flexible - and low-cost - audio-visual materials:
- tape slide presentations

- ½inch video-cassettes (as opposed to the 2inch broadcast standard programmes)
- 8mm films (as opposed to the 16mm film for broadcast transmission)

TPR Grenoble started experimenting with the production of such materials in 1972/73, as a complement and support to the broadcast programmes, for use in meetings and discussion groups by agricultural animateurs and technicians. These materials gradually took on increasing importance, and currently, as TPR no longer makes TV programmes, they form the totality of their audio-visual production.

USE OF MULTI-MEDIA METHODS

The plan developed by TPR Grenoble for combining the use of broadcasts and group meetings - and for integrating their activities with those of the various regional organisations responsible for training, is particularly interesting. This plan - which in practice was not always realized because of delays in finance and production schedules - was made up essentially of four phases, spanning the winter months:

1. November/December/January: weekly broadcasts of the winter series of TPR films; broadcasts which, according to a number of surveys, were viewed by around 55% of agriculturalists in the region, in the years when they were transmitted on the most popular channel ('première chaine');

2. December/January/February: organisation of group meetings, in the evenings, at which a particular film - on 8mm cassette - would be viewed and discussed in the presence of an animateur/ trainer. This is an occasion for the agriculturalists who had seen the broadcast film to exchange views and ideas related to the film's theme. The animateurs used the printed support materials provided by TPR to guide the meetings.

3. January/February: the running of training courses and programmes by the staff of the organisations responsible for training and advisory activities for agriculturalists, covering, in part, themes related to TPR films.

4. February/March: broadcasts of the televised or filmed debates,

the debates themselves being based on the results of phases 2 and 3.

Of these four phases, TPR's responsibility was to organise the first and last - the second and third phases were the responsibility of the various agricultural organisations concerned with provision of training and technical advice to the agriculturalists. In reality, as mentioned above, it did not prove possible to follow this model every winter during the period 1971-1979, when TV broadcasts were used, because of a variety of financial and practical difficulties. Furthermore, the broadcasts themselves were moved to successively unfavourable transmission slots, which undoubtedly reduced their impact. Nevertheless, the rationale for the particular schedule of activities, and the way they were intended to relate to each other, is of particular interest, and deserves further development.

The broadcast films were quite clearly not intended as direct training or teaching material, but had three specific functions, of a different kind:

–   to contact the agriculturalists in the target group; this function may sound self-evident, but it must be remembered that, in the Rhône-Alpes Auvergne region, there are over 160,000[1] agricultural 'units', the great majority being family-run small-holdings. Many of them are isolated geographically, culturally, and socially, and only about 5% are reached by, or make use of, the training/ animation facilities provided by the various agricultural organisations. They represent a group largely ignored by the mass media and rarely contacted by any channel in respect of any sort of adult or continuing education activity.

–   to encourage thought and reflection concerning the issues covered in the film, and to make people aware that there are others who have the same or similar pre-occupations; this can provide the motivation and encouragement to go on to consider the possibility of the need for various forms of training and information.

–   to provide, as a counter to the predominantly urban values underlying most television programming, something which would, on the contrary, show and promote the values, interests, and lifestyles of the large numbers of agricultural families in the region. This is the main reason why TPR has always made strong efforts to involve agriculturalists in the planning, creation, and actual filming of their audio-visual materials. The fact that there were

38

many requests - not satisfied by broadcast authorities - to repeat the TPR broadcasts in the evenings, when more people could have seen them, gives some indication of the interest aroused by TPR's films in this respect.

The group meetings - stage 2 above - where one or other of the broadcast films (or an audio-visual document produced by TPR on a related theme) is viewed and discussed in the presence of an animateur, were, and still are, intended to:

– follow on from the broadcasts, which had already contacted and motivated the group members, to provide a chance for group discussion to take place.

– from this group discussion, to lead on to the identification of training and information needs.

– thirdly, to provide a basis for planning training programmes and information activities designed to meet these needs.

Despite a variety of practical difficulties inherent to the organisation of such meetings, and the provision of the necessary projection equipment, the numbers of people reached in this way built up quite rapidly in the early years of TPR Grenoble's activities, as shown by the data below[2] :

winter 72/73 : 168 meetings   3944 participants
winter 73/74 : 215 meetings   5970 participants
winter 74/75 : 389 meetings   9154 participants

Note that these meetings were not organised by TPR, but all used TPR films to pick up and elaborate on the themes covered in the broadcasts.

In the 1978/79 winter, the last year of TPR's broadcasts, about 11,000 people took part in viewing meetings/discussion groups. However, by the following winter, numbers had fallen by about 50%, which suggests that the broadcasts had a strong influence in motivating attendance at the meetings.

However, a number of problems arose in practice in passing from the stage of raising of awareness/discussion of needs, to a phase of training/information as such:

– very often, the animateurs and trainers involved in organising and participating in group meetings did not have the necessary experience or skill in identifying the needs of group members and translating these needs into training and education programmes.

39

—   the fact that the films used as a basis for group discussions (and broadcasts) were made at a regional level (and also used on an inter-regional basis) meant that identification with the pre-occupations of individual agriculturalists was not always possible.

As a result of these two problems, TPR has developed training programmes for animateurs and trainers in the use of audio-visual aids, and has also put more effort into production of flexible, low-cost, audio-visual materials such as tape-slide materials and video-cassettes.

THE CREATION AND PRODUCTION OF AUDIO-VISUAL MATERIALS

At the beginning of TPR's activities, no clear ideas were held concerning the most appropriate ways of preparing the television and other audio-visual materials. There were few relevant experiences in France on which to draw, and the project staff started off very pragmatically, evolving their working methods as they went along. From the progress that was made, two particularly important aspects can be identified.

—   an increasing level of participation by agriculturalists in the planning and creation of the materials, in order to achieve some measure of collective expression by the target group.

—   a gradual change in the format of the programmes, from a 'documentary' style to a 'fiction' style.

Participation/Collective Production

The aim of the films - as has already been stressed - has always been to portray situations, events, circumstances, and attitudes as close as possible to TPR's concerns. The films are not intended to provide solutions to specific problems, but to show how these problems materialise and how people react to, or deal with, them, so that the viewers - themselves agriculturalists - might identify with these problem situations.

To achieve this objective, two important principles have been followed in preparing the programmes:

—   the planning and creation of the programme is the responsibility

40

of a group of agriculturalists from a specific region.
- the production team is a small one, composed of a TPR staff member, a producer, and an animateur/trainer with a good knowledge of the region; this team takes responsibility for all production matters, but under the direction of the group of agriculturalists.

The production schedule involves four principal stages:

1. *Survey/Reconnaissance Stage:* This is the starting point for the development of a script. Interviews are conducted with a sample of agriculturalists to identify their principal pre-occupations and problems, as far as the planned topic of the programme is concerned. This stage also represents an opportunity to collect relevant anecdotes and incidents which might be included in the script, as well as to identify potential 'actors', 'actresses', and interviewees.

2. *Preparation of Script and Filming Schedule:* This is a process which essentially involves a series of meetings between the group of agriculturalists and the production team, at which the details of the script for the film are progressively refined. By the end of this stage, the meetings will have arrived at decisions on:
   - the principal themes (never more than two or three) which will make up the film's message
   - the principal objectives of the film
   - a set of 'typical' attitudes, situations, events relevant to the film's main theme, encountered at the survey stage, which will be included.

3. *Filming:* Filming itself is preceded by a day of 'familiarisation' with the agriculturalists who will appear in the film. They are given a chance to be filmed with a video camera and then to see the resulting recording on a monitor. Using these facilities, the agriculturalists very quickly lost any initial feelings of shyness or awkwardness, and could relax and act naturally when the actual filming started.

In general, the details of dialogue and decor are improvised at the moment of filming, and not pre-ordained beforehand.

4. Piloting: A first 'draft' of the film, after initial editing, is projected to selected groups of agriculturalists at specially arranged meetings in the villages or village where the filming was carried out. As a result of comments and reactions obtained at these sessions, the final edited version of the film is made.

The technical staff (cameramen, soundmen, etc.) needed for filming and editing are brought in as needed from outside - neither they nor the producer are full-time members of TPR's staff.

Changes in the Format of TPR's Productions

TPR's early television films adopted a 'documentary' style close to that used in news and current affairs reporting, making a lot of use of interviews, for example. However, as the project developed, this style was gradually dropped, to be replaced by a 'fiction' style, in which agriculturalists acted out scenes relevant to the theme of the film. For example, in 1978/79, the main theme of the five TPR films broadcast was concerned with ownership of agricultural land. Each of the five films made depicted an agricultural family and its reactions to specific problems concerned with land ownership, in the form of a short 'story' about how the particular family experienced and resolved the problems involved. Although the situation acted out in the film was constructed (i.e. imaginary) the actors, of course, were real agricultural workers who had direct experience of a similar situation. This format has proved to be far more effective in stimulating identification and discussion amongst viewers than the more conventional documentary format in which groups of agriculturalists would, say, be interviewed about their own personal experiences by a reporter.

This fiction format has two distinct advantages:
- it allows for a clear selection of a few important themes, in the preparation of the script for the film, and elimination of secondary themes considered not to be essential for comprehension of the subject.
- it provides for a much better grasp of the production procedures by the agriculturalists involved, and a greater degree of participation by them in the preparation of the film. This is especially evident, as pointed out above, when the script is being prepared

and the agriculturalists present at the script planning meetings can comment on successive drafts and help choose the scenes to be filmed. Furthermore, the fiction format, when it is successfully acted, can give a heightened dramatic flavour to the whole film, thus enhancing the feelings of identification amongst the viewers with the situation depicted.

This fiction format, by the way, is in many ways similar to a form of popular education very common in rural areas in France in the twenties and thirties: 'living theatre'. Theatre groups would go from village to village acting out scenes and problems of daily rural life, and promoting discussion amongst the audience. A few such groups still exist in some regions of France.

CONTACTING THE PUBLIC

Broadcasting: TPR Films

Television broadcasts were always planned by TPR Grenoble for the beginning of the winter, when the work in the fields was over. The general plan was for these early broadcasts to alert and interest the public, and to prepare the ground for the group meetings - later in the winter - when the films and other specially prepared audio-visual materials could be viewed collectively, and discussed with an animateur. However, delays in obtaining finance for the broadcasts, and associated delays in production schedules, often meant that it was not always possible to start broadcasts at the beginning of the winter.

The television broadcasts have always occurred between 12.00-14.00, with one programme being broadcast each week. This timing was a relatively good one, as during the winter it is the custom for agricultural workers to have lunch at home, at a regular time, and - certainly until recently - with the television set in the dining room.

At the beginning, each programme was repeated once, during the same week, and this was a very valuable facility, as it gave a chance to those who had missed the first broadcast to see the programme. Unfortunately, however, as a result of increases in transmission charges, repeats were withdrawn in 1975.

During the first four years, broadcasts were transmitted on the first channel, then subsequently were transferred to the second and then the third (regional) channel. These successive changes, which corresponded to some extent with general changes in broadcasting structures in France, and with the development of a third channel, meant a fall-off in viewing figures for TPR's programmes. This was partly due to the competing influence of news and entertainment programmes at the same time on other channels, as well as the fact that during this transition period many people did not have sets which received the third channel.

Finally, as a direct result of increases in transmission costs, the length of TPR's programmes was progressively shortened: from one hour in 1970 to thirty minutes in 1979, and from ten programmes each winter to five.

(This gradual diminution in access to broadcasting, with its cessation altogether in 1979, can only be seen as regrettable, given the relative lack of TV programming in France aimed specifically at disadvantaged rural communities, and the general paucity of programmes concerned with adult education in general: Editor's note).

Broadcasting: General Information/Publicity

The regional television and radio stations, during the 1970-79 period, promoted TPR's programmes and activities via short information items at peak viewing and listening times. From time to time, thirty-minute radio programmes publicising TPR's activities were also broadcast.

TPR staff are currently hoping to be able to start using the radio more often in the future. The advantages - in flexibility and cost - over television are self-evident, particularly in terms of complementing TPR's work with viewing groups. Furthermore, the habit of listening to the radio whilst at work (in the fields, stables, etc.) has developed significantly amongst the rural population in recent years.

Distribution of Print Materials

Various procedures have been used for providing print support and information materials to accompany TPR's broadcast films and non-broadcast audio-visual materials:

1. booklets/guides for animateurs, summarising the main points of a given film or film series, providing additional relevant information, and giving hints for discussion and follow-up activities.

2. information and support materials aimed directly at agriculturalists, disseminated as special supplements in the regional agricultural press, which is read by around 90% of the TPR's target population. These supplements, which appeared in each case a few days before the relevant broadcasts, formed an extremely successful support. They were often accompanied by short articles, prepared by TPR, in the body of the newspaper, both before and after the broadcasts. The articles which followed the broadcasts analysed reactions to the programmes, and provided follow-up information on appropriate training facilities and programmes provided by the regional organisations (trades unions, 'Chambres d'Agriculture' etc.) responsible for professional training. TPR continues to use the local agricultural press to publicise and accompany its current programmes (even though broadcasting is now no longer used).

3. posters and tracts were distributed each year to the various agricultural organisations to publicise TPR's broadcasts. About 1500-2000 posters and 70-100,000 tracts were printed for each year's television campaign. This widescale distribution has now stopped - for financial reasons, and related to the cessation of broadcasting. However, TPR publishes and distributes each year a catalogue of films and other audio-visual products for use by agricultural technicians and animateurs.

Films and other Audio-Visual Materials for Group Viewing

TPR's films are all available for use by regional agricultural animateurs and technicians who will telephone or write in for copies as and when required. Copies are sent through the post, accompanied by a short evaluation checklist which the users are asked to complete after showing the film. The other audio-visual materials (video-tapes and tape-slide presentations) are available through the same mechanism. Users are advised to view the materials before showing them, and receive guidance notes for their use in a discussion group situation.

TPR's current catalogue lists:
-   26 'super 8' film cassettes
-   6 16mm films
-   7 tape-slide presentations
-   3 ½inch video-tapes

Most of these documents seem to be in relatively constant demand by regional animateurs and technicians for use at group meetings.

SUPPORT ELEMENTS IN TPR's PROGRAMME

TPR undertakes a number of activities to support its principal current role as a regional audio-visual resource centre for the agricultural/rural sector. These supporting activities are aimed at helping the technicians and animateurs to accomplish their training activities, and to define and discover specific training needs. TPR's support activities can be grouped under four main headings:

1. Provision of films, video-tapes, and other audio-visual materials, but on a wider basis than TPR's own productions alone. TPR is currently involved with other organisations in cataloguing a wide range of audio-visual documents relevant to rural agricultural problems and issues. Requests are dealt with by provision of brief information notes on appropriate materials, which can then be viewed and selected by interested technicians and anima- teurs at TPR's headquarters in Grenoble. In the future, TPR hopes to develop a computer-based information bank on the whole range of materials available regionally and nationally.

2. Training of animateurs, technicians and trainers in the use of audio-visual materials is also undertaken. The short training courses run by TPR have two principal functions:
    -   to demonstrate the effectiveness of the use of audio-visual materials in the training and education of agriculturalists: this is achieved by practical courses in which the technicians and animateurs involved produce a document (e.g. a tape- slide presentation or video-tape) of their own, which can

subsequently be used by them in the field
- to introduce more general ideas about improvement of the effectiveness of the teaching methods used by the animateurs and technicians, many of whom have little formal training in this area.

Current TPR courses cover: photography, sound recording and interviewing, graphics, and the production of tape-slide presentations and video-tapes.

3. Consultancy and advice on teaching/training methods and on use of audio-visual materials and equipment is also provided by TPR, covering a number of principal areas:
   - the planning of new audio-visual materials, or adaptation of existing ones
   - the choice of specific items of hardware for use in training programmes, meetings, etc.

This type of advice and consultancy has developed considerably in the last few years, as TPR has put more and more emphasis on production of non-broadcast materials.

4. The lending out of audio-visual equipment is the last of TPR's current support functions:
   - a number of 'sub-regional' centres have been provided with projection equipment by TPR, which can be borrowed by animateurs and technicians. The equipment includes overhead projectors, slide projectors, video-tape equipment, and cassette film projectors.
   - TPR's own production equipment can also be made available to agricultural trainers and technicians who wish to make their own productions.

EVALUATION OF TPR's ACTIVITIES

Since the early days of TPR (in Brittany, 1966) a large number of evaluation studies and reports have been prepared on the activities of each of the regional centres. References to some of these can be found in the bibliography in Chapter 9 of this book.

Although the number and variety of these studies clearly demonstrate the interest that has been aroused by TPR's work, it is difficult to draw definite conclusions about the results obtained, and efficacy of, the various actions undertaken. This is practically inevitable, because:

– the originality of the methods used, and the fact that the objectives of most of TPR's broadcasts and films are specifically concerned with raising awareness, provoking questions and identifying needs, makes any clear measure in terms of learning gains impossible.

– the methods used by TPR link in to other activities organised by the local and regional training and education organisations, and it is not possible, in reality, to differentiate the specific effects of TPR's inputs from the inputs provided by these organisations. For example, it has never been possible to clearly state that a given number of agriculturalists, in a given year, joined training courses or programmes solely as a result of TPR's actions in this direction. In the real-life situation, TPR's programmes, meetings, press articles, tracts, and posters formed only one set of influences or elements within an overall framework of determining factors.

The evaluation work that has been carried out can be classified as either of a quantitative or a qualitative nature. Most of the former studies were carried out at the request of the various organisations that have contributed to TPR's finances, whilst many of the qualitative studies were inspired by the interests of TPR's staff in gaining information for correcting and improving their actions (formative evaluation).

Quantitative Studies

As far as TPR Grenoble is concerned, most of these were carried out in the early years of the project, and were concerned with three main themes:

– the viewing figures for the broadcasts, and the principal characteristics of the viewers; these studies were very important in that they clearly demonstrated that the viewing figures were respectably high (a typical campaign reached about 55% of the total rural public) and, that the specific target group arrived at - the excluded rural population - was being reached

–   the level and mode of use of the printed support materials: data
    from these studies led TPR to change over from a distribution to
    the animateurs/technicians for group meetings, to an individual
    direct distribution to the target audience via the agricultural press
–   the participation rates at group viewing sessions and meetings,
    and identification of the problems involved in arranging and
    running these meetings, as well as providing follow-up to them.

Qualitative Studies

These fortunately, are the most numerous, and were mainly concerned
either with identifying particular features of importance in specific
components of TPR's programmes, or in identifying specific gaps or
problems in the overall programme. From this work, two really important features can be noted:
–   a clearer idea of the relative roles and limitations of the different
    media in raising awareness ('sensibilisation'), and of the ways in
    which the various media complement, or interfere with, each
    other in this process. Specifically, TPR has tried to use the
    insights gained by experience, in refining the methods used for
    identifying and helping to express the needs of their target group.
–   a development and improvement in the methods of planning and
    producing films and other audio-visual documents, involving both
    a change in format and a much enhanced level of participation by
    agriculturalists themselves in the process.

ORGANISATION, CONTROL, AND RESOURCES

As will be evident from the history of TPR which has been traced in
this study, there have been many changes and developments, both at a
regional and national level, since TPR Rennes started up in 1966. We
shall briefly describe here the structure of the TPR Rhône-Alpes/
Auvergne and show how it fits into the national and regional framework.

TPR Rhône-Alpes/Auvergne

This centre developed from links between the University of Social
Sciences of Grenoble and the various professional bodies in the region

concerned with training of agriculturalists. These links have given rise to two associations:

- APRO-TELE[3] : this association groups together all the professional agricultural organisations in the Rhône-Alpes region, and part of those in Auvergne. Its functions are to decide on TPR's programme, to control its content, and to ensure coordination with training activities organised in the field.

- The Centre-TPR: this is, legally, a second association which brings together, on an equal basis, teachers and researchers from the University of Grenoble and INRA[4] on the one hand, and the executives of the regional agricultural organisations, mandated by APRO-TELE, on the other hand. The Centre has the formal responsibility for producing audio-visual and associated materials, and for managing the budget allocated to it for this purpose.

Working Mechanisms

In the early years, TPR Grenoble operated through a working group structure, each group having a separate, functional, responsibility:
- working groups for planning and production of films
- working groups for planning and organising viewing meetings, in coordination with the various networks of animateurs and technicians in the field
- working groups responsible for preparation of supporting print materials.

Gradually, over the years, this structure was superseded by a more integrated one, in which a team comprised of TPR staff, field workers, and agriculturalists took joint responsibility for an entire programme or campaign, including preparation of all relevant materials, and the organisation of meetings at local level.

Coordination Mechanisms

These have developed and changed significantly over the years, corresponding to the evolution of TPR's activities and programme. However, there has always been both a national and a regional framework:

–   at the national level, and during the period of activity of all five centres, a national federation was created, with its headquarters in Paris (the 'Federation Nationale de Télé-Promotion Rurale' - FNTPR); this Federation is meant to coordinate the activities of each of the regional TPR centres, but its role is much diminished at the moment as only two centres are currently functioning. However, it is possible that in the next year or so, one or two more of the currently defunct centres may start up again.

–   at the regional level, coordination with the regional professional and training organisations is organised mainly through the FAFEA[5] and through various regionally based Government training and agricultural bodies (L'Inspection Régionale de l'Agronomie' and 'La Délégation Permanente à la Formation Professionnelle Régionale').

Overall Control and Planning

Planning and control of TPR's broadcast programmes involved essentially three main stages:

1. decisions on the themes of the programmes involved suggestions being proposed regionally and then coordinated centrally by the FNTPR, to ensure some degree of coherence between each of the regional centres. Once a theme had been established for a particular winter's campaign, each centre then organised its own production on a regional basis.

2. approval of the content of each planned film or programme was the responsibility of APRO-TELE: this was done on the basis of written notes on each film, approved before actual production began at a meeting which also included the agriculturalists involved in the programme.

3. the final versions of the films were viewed at a second meeting with representatives from APRO-TELE before they were broadcast.

Nowadays, for the non-broadcast audio-visual productions, as we have seen earlier, the planning, control, and approval of each production is the responsibility of the working group which prepares it.

Financial control of TPR's budget is exercised through annual bids and accounts to the main funding body (the 'Secrétariat Général de la Formation Professionelle et de la Promotion Sociale').

TPR's Resources

TPR Grenoble's budget contains two main elements:
- a recurrent budget for salaries, travel costs, and secretarial support
- a production budget geared to the specific costs of the audio-visual materials planned and prepared each year.

There are four full time staff at TPR Grenoble: three based in Grenoble, and one in Clermont Ferrand. For particular productions, of course, additional staff resources are available in terms of:
- agriculturalists involved in specific programmes
- regional animateurs and technicians
- technical support staff brought in from outside.

TPR's equipment includes cameras, tape-recorders, editing facilities, video-recording and play-back facilities, and film recording and projection equipment. TPR does not have its own production studios, but uses facilities available in Grenoble when needed. TPR's offices are based in the buildings of the University of Social Sciences at Grenoble, as also are their viewing/projection facilities.

Notes and References

1. The precise number for 1979/80 was 167,760 (Source: 'Recensement Général Agriculture).
2. P. Boisseau, M. Girardin and P. Augagneur, 'Télé-Promotion Rurale, Rhône-Alpes-Auvergne: Rapport d'Evaluation' (Centre TPR, Grenoble, 1975).
3. Association Professionelle Régionale pour l'Organisation d'Emissions de Television en vue de la Promotion des Agriculteurs.
4. Institut National de la Recherche Agronomique
5. Fonds National d'Assurance Formation des Exploitants Agricoles

Chapter 3

JUST THE JOB
WESTWARD TV/NEC, UNITED KINGDOM

Barry Reeves

INTRODUCTION

Just the Job was originally a pilot project in South West England, which aimed to investigate the contribution which television, printed materials, and a voluntary counselling network could make in assisting unemployed school leavers to make decisions about their futures. The project at first consisted of seven half-hour Westward TV programmes, a Just the Job office which provided follow-up materials (Jobhunter Kit), and advice and help to young people who Freefone in after the television programmes by putting them in contact with a local volunteer Counsellor (part of a counselling network).

Eventually the project ran for three years from June 1977 to June 1980, with a new series of TV programmes each year, a Just the Job series being developed on independent local radio, and a series of linked features in local and regional newspapers. In January 1979 the Capital Jobmate scheme in London began as a direct result of the Just the Job experience in the South West of England. In the three year period to May 1980 just under 10,000 young people had contacted the Just the Job project.

The three television series were primarily aimed at arousing interest and as a springboard for further activity by the viewer. The series presented information about the employment situation, the services and agencies which exist for young unemployed people, opportunities on the Manpower Services Commission (MSC) Youth Opportunities Programme, openings and requirements for training and what to expect in the world of work, as well as constructive survival in unemployment (leisure/informal employment). Thus the television series could arouse in young people hope and determination where these had waned and could show them how they could help themselves.

The Jobhunter Kits attempted to develop some of the themes of the television series and were available to young people who contacted the Project by Freefone. The Kits were presented in an informal style,

with a low literacy content, they were in a magazine format with comic strips and illustrations. They involved the user in a series of activities designed to:
− increase his or her awareness of services and facilities available in the area and
− develop the skills necessary for job-seeking and coping with unemployment.

Like the television programmes, they covered such topics as using the telephone, writing letters, handling job interviews, claiming benefit, voluntary work, leisure activities, the Youth Opportunities Programme and self-employment, plus specialised information on housing, legal advice, leaving home and health topics etc.

The network of volunteer counsellors supported the young person in his or her use of the materials, so as to help in making better use of existing services. The young person was offered the opportunity of joining a small local group with other unemployed youngsters who together worked towards solutions to their situation.

The Just the Job project has been significant in the area of social action broadcasting for two reasons: firstly, because of its impact upon the youth unemployment situation in the South West of England and secondly, because of its practical relevance in showing how the broadcasting media can cooperate with other agencies in trying to alleviate an identified social problem.

ORIGINS OF THE PROJECT

One of the areas of increasing social concern throughout the 1970's has been the rise in the level of unemployment, especially youth unemployment. As the Holland Report[1] stated "During the course of 1976 over 800,000 young people between 16 and 18 registered as unemployed and perhaps as many as 80,000 more experienced a spell of unemployment but did not register. In several parts of Great Britain including the centres of our major cities, as many as one in four young people are now unemployed". In order to try and alleviate this problem the Government encouraged several new approaches.

Thus Just the Job was created in this context of deteriorating employment oportunities and owes its origin to initiatives originally conceived independently by Westward Television[2] and the National Extension College. Media interest in programming for the young unemployed coincided with the developing trend towards community service broadcasting encouraged by the BBC and the IBA, the latter focussing on the social responsibility requirement of the fourth channel in the 1980's. Interest in the young as a special group also enabled the media to concentrate on a section of the national audience traditionally held to be the 'lost generation' to the mainstream products of television.

During 1975/1976 Westward TV was looking at the possibility of producing a series of programmes aimed at the young, produced as an integral part of the Company's normal educational output. The impetus for this initiative was the growing problem of youth unemployment (as referred to in the 1976 Holland Report) in Westward Television's mainly rural transmission area.

At about the same time, the National Extension College (NEC) was looking at the potential development of distance teaching techniques, and one of the areas of interest was in relation to the problems of youth unemployment. Before stating the more clearly defined aims and objectives (in 1976/7) of the Project it is important to briefly outline some of the previous thinking on the use of the multi-dimensional approach and some of the more significant influences that determined the concepts of the original Project aims.

The Rural Family Development (RFD) Project (Wisconsin, USA) and the TEVEC Project (Quebec, Canada) were both multi-media approaches to target audiences in rural areas. They both had the components of broadcast media (in both cases primarily television), specially prepared printed materials and local support systems (spontaneously organised family friendship groups and home visitors).

The RFD Project is described as 'a highly flexible multi-media information delivery system' aimed at assisting the participant to develop life-coping skills as he feels relevant to his particular situation. The potential appropriateness of this approach in the context of the unemployed young person seems obvious. The 'coping skills' were the core around which all the programmes and materials were built. The home visitors provided the all important personal contact, they assisted in identifying learning needs and providing feedback and problem solving mechanisms. In addition, the RFD Project employed a 'distance teaching' element - an 'action line' Freefone arrangement.

The TEVEC Project used a somewhat similar approach (but more specifically aimed at upgrading adult students), using home visitors who encouraged participation of those with little previous education. Local committees organised 'teleclubs' (group discussions). One of the key functions of the system identified by the Project was to provide feedback to the organisers, so adaptation could take place as the Project developed. They also stressed that the feedback and participation need building into a project the whole way through (viz action research). Lessons learned in the first phase were used to change the approach of the second phase (this also occurred with Just the Job). The communication process was constructed to meet the people where they were - socially, psychologically and culturally.

A conclusion drawn by Paulo Freire in a different context was that an approach built around the socio-economic situation will interest and attract the target audience.

A follow up study of the Springboard Project (for unemployed young people in Sunderland) revealed an important change in the opinions of workers (young people) about employment services. It seems that attitudes to Careers Offices and Job Centres are moulded by previous contacts, which if unsuccessful, lead to a withdrawal from the administrative structure for finding jobs. Support brought the young workers back to a more effective use of the system.

Finally, the British Adult Literacy Scheme (see Chapter 5), provides another model of a multi-media approach to tackle a specific problem. Some of the background thinking and the operation of that scheme influenced the setting up of the Project.

The evidence and experience from the RFD, TEVEC and other schemes led the NEC to the conclusion that a useful contribution to the plight of the young unemployed particularly in rural areas might be alleviated by these 'distance teaching' methods. When Westward TV's interests were discovered discussions took place. The outcome was an application by the NEC to the newly created Special Programmes Division of the MSC for funding to provide support services in order to develop a 'multi-media' pilot project in the Westward TV region. The television series was to be produced entirely at the expense of Westward TV. This application was accepted and it was originally envisaged that the Project would be funded from April 1st 1977. In reality, however, the project was not officially commissioned until 29th June 1977.

56

TARGET POPULATION AND OBJECTIVES

From the background and previous thinking summarised in the last section, the following more clearly defined aims and objectives were arrived at. It is important to emphasise that these were viewed by the Project staff as 'guides', so as to allow flexibility in an action research context. The later sections of this report show how the Project evolved and developed in years 2 and 3, in terms of the needs of the young unemployed and of the support and training requirements of the volunteer counsellors from the community. The outline of the Project as stated below from the MSC commissioning letter of the 29th June 1977, does not determine a more definitive approach:-

"The Project will last twelve months and will consist of a television Series (by Westward TV) linked to a package of printed correspondence - based information pamphlets, both to be supported and followed up by local counselling and careers advice. The purpose of the Project is to assess employment problems of school-leavers in a predominately rural area with limited and scattered job opportunities where young people may be out of touch with the statutory agencies (the Careers Service, the Youth Service, the Employment Service Agency, the Training Service Agency, etc.) and to identify the ways in which these problems may be overcome. The Project is intended to arouse the interest of unemployed young people, to inform them of the services available and of the range of employment and training opportunities open to them, and to advise them on how to seek out and select these opportunities".

At the start of the Project we had these general aims:-

1. The Project aimed to equip young people with the skills to increase their chances of finding a job through improved social and communication skills, job-search skills (including interview skills) and skills needed to survive constructively if unemployed (unemployment allowances, support services in the community and the use of leisure time). It also aimed to arouse the interest, hope and purpose of young people in relation to unemployment.

2. To evaluate the use of a multi-media approach in reaching out to

the unemployed young person, with particular reference to the interaction between the three media components of the approach.

3. To evaluate whether the volunteer counsellors approach increased the number of job and training opportunities for young people.

4. To test whether the initiative created by the Project generated any new forms of activity.

5. The development of methods that can be used elsewhere, particularly in rural areas.

These general aims led to the definition of some more specific objectives, namely:

1. To define more specifically who the young unemployed people are (i.e. the target audience).

2. To find out how young people set about getting jobs and why they are unsuccessful in their efforts.

3. To determine what type of television broadcasting and printed materials engages the young peoples' interest.

4. To understand the specific problems young unemployed people face in looking for work (particularly in rural areas).

5. To look for ways in which young unemployed people can be helped to use the agencies more effectively.

6. To investigate how individuals and organisations can collaborate to mobilise help for the young unemployed.

7. To establish whether lay volunteers effectively aid young unemployed people with this approach and what community resources can be used to support their need.

Finally, the Project aimed to determine what positive contribution could be made to overcome the predicament described in the British

Youth Council's 'Youth Unemployment: Cause and Cures' :

"that long stretches of unemployment are bound to severely damage the morale of young people and make them far less confident and satisfactory employees if employment is eventually found."

To summarise then, the Project was set up as an alternative source of information, advice and support to the young unemployed. The criteria of its effective operation could not solely be that of the number of young people who entered employment or a training opportunity as a result of its intervention.

The Project's client group was the unemployed school leaver probably disadvantaged by personal, social and educational difficulties resulting in uncompetitiveness in the job market, rural isolation and some degree of alienation from the statutory job finding agencies.

Table 3. 1 Age and Status of Young People Contacting Just the Job
(Summary for 1977/8, 1978/9, 1979/80)

	1977/8	1978/9	1979/80
School children and those in Further Education	892(35%)	574(27%)	N/A
Unemployed aged 16-20 years	845(33%)	869(41%)	N/A
Unemployed over 21 years	146(6%)	189(9%)	N/A
Not known/other	678(26%)	514(23%)	N/A
TOTALS	2561	2142	5100

Although total numbers decreased by 16% in 1978/9, the target group of unemployed 16-20 year olds increased proportionally from 33% to 41% (869 in 1978/9) an improvement of 8% over the level of the previous year. In 1978/9 the Project had a further 380 contacts after Exeter University's data collection.

Evidence from research undertaken by Exeter University[3] (1978/9) concludes that:

"Just the Job was particularly effective in attracting younger unemployed, both the seasonally unemployed and school leavers who have never worked. In addition, in a sample of 404 unemployed who responded to the Project, 36% had been unemployed over 5 months at the time of contact including a substantial proportion of 18, 19 and 20 year olds, indicating that Just the Job did succeed in reaching those young adults who are more disadvantaged in terms of employment."

This pattern was even more strongly followed in the 1979/80 Project phase but a detailed break down of response is not available.

Over the 3 year period 1977-1980 the characteristics of the employment market in Devon/Cornwall/Somerset and Dorset for the under 20's have remained fundamentally the same. There has been a steady decline in the job opportunities on the open labour market. This decline has been partially disguised by the smokescreen of the MSC's Youth Opportunities Programme which has dramatically increased in size during the 3 year period and has effectively resulted in the unemployed school leaver now being the unemployed 18/19 year old, who has perhaps had up to a year on the Youth Opportunities Programme but is still unable to find permanent employment. This was reflected in the higher proportion of 18 and 19 year olds who responded in 1978/9 and 1979/80. In this respect the Project never exclusively catered for the unemployed school leaver but for all young people under 20 who wished to use the services available to them from Just the Job.

The situation of the 19+ unemployed person is in many ways as serious as any since there is very little in the way of training or job creation programmes available to them and the more disadvantaged in this group have had little open employment experience since leaving school.

There are two more signficant factors in the employment environment of the young unemployed in the South West. Firstly, there is the seasonal influence of the tourist industry, which is quite significant in many parts. Secondly, because of the importance of agriculture and its associated services, there are many opportunities for part-time seasonal work both formal and informal in the rural areas.

Other factors that affect the young unemployed directly include poor communications and transport, employment legislation relating to small businesses (the South West has an above average number of small firms) and the general 'risk' many employers feel is involved in taking on young untrained and inexperienced workers. In December 1977 the over-all percentage of unemployed in Devon was 40% higher than the national average (6.5%) and nearly twice the national average in Cornwall.

During December 1977 in the middle of Westward TV's first Just the Job series there were 10,089 young people under 20 registered as unemployed.

PROJECT COMPONENTS

We were aiming at young people who felt a deep sense of frustration at having been through a system which geared them to the world of work, only to find that when they left school they were instantly and in some cases permanently unemployed. They felt that the system had let them down and many expressed dissatisfaction with the Careers Service both in and out of schools. As indicated earlier these are young people with few or no qualifications, low drive, little motivation - in fact those who are at the opposite end of the scale to the Open University student.

Before the role of television and the printed materials (Jobhunter Kits) can be fully described it might be useful to remind the reader briefly how the three main components of Just the Job were linked together (see Figure 3. 2)

The Westward TV Series

In 1977 at the start of the Project the TV series consisted of seven weekly 26 minute programmes. The programmes covered such topics as: 'Who says you have failed?', 'It's your time - use it', 'Be your own Boss', and were transmitted in the South West region at 5.15 p.m. from November 1977. In 1978 the six programmes were each 20 minutes long and in 1979/80 there were fourteen programmes of 6 minutes

Figure 3.2 Schematic Presentation of the Basic Components of
'Just the Job'

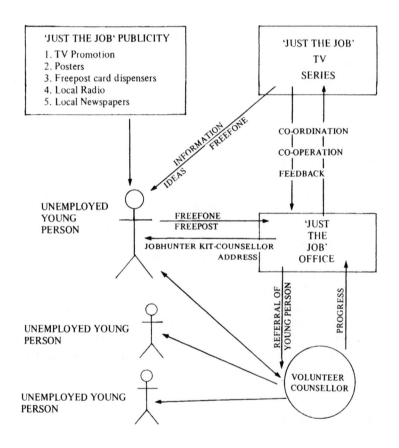

each (6.50 p.m. Friday evenings).

The Just the Job series was classified by Westward TV as 'adult education' output. This classification means programmes are destined for the less popular transmission times e.g. Sunday mornings. It was therefore some measure of the importance of Just the Job that all three series had 'peak' viewing times, particularly the 1979/80 series on Friday evenings.

The programmes were intended to perform the following functions:

1. to dispel the feeling of isolation amongst the young unemployed

2. to provide facts and information on employment and unemployment

3. to motivate those young unemployed who were no longer in touch with the existing agencies, to use the Project's facilities.

In addition the second series, by developing as a theme the Government's Youth Opportunities Programme, gave greater emphasis to:

4. encouraging the young unemployed to maintain, or re-establish contacts with the statutory agencies, thereby creating a balance between the innovatory resources of Just the Job and the new opportunities available with the permanent agencies.

Westward TV wanted to reach the 16-20 year age group, especially those with few or no educational qualifications, since it is this group which often seems to bear the brunt of the unemployment situation. But this age group is often called the 'lost generation' in terms of television viewing, since it displays the lowest viewing figures of any age group. It was necessary therefore to produce a style of programming to which this age group generally would be attracted, and to pitch the programme content at a level which would take into account the low educational ability of some of the target audience. In other words the information content had to be introduced simply and in such a way as to maintain interest.

The programming style developed was informal and included several local case histories which, it was hoped, would maintain some level of intimacy with the target audience as well as teenage presenters, teenage language, competitions and modern music. The programmes regularly featured the Just the Job back-up service - Freefone, free Jobhunter kits and friendly advice and information as well as a 'local friendly adult who knows about your local job scene'. Westward TV realised that television has its limitations and detailed information, particularly to the kind of audience they were addressing themselves to, tends to go in one ear and out the other - hence the Jobhunter Kits with detailed information.

In the light of the fact ('Broadcasting and Youth' - Gulbenkian Foundation) that the 16-20 age group are a lost generation to television, in the second and third years we developed the mass media component further by working with local radio (Plymouth area) and a local and regional newspaper chain. The Project staff were, in both cases, involved in the production and presentation of Just the Job weekly features. In the case of local radio there was a regular weekly half-hour Just the Job slot complementing the television series and offering the Just the Job back-up service. These programmes were researched and written and recorded with the help of a small team of unemployed local people on a local Youth Opportunities Programme scheme. Similarly we wrote and sub-edited a full page Just the Job feature in three local newspapers. Here we attempted follow up information and ideas covered on television - a job the written medium can do much better - assuming a literate target audience!

The Jobhunter Kit

These kits were intended to function in three situations:
- to act as a bridge between the television series and the young unemployed people who were not in contact with a volunteer counsellor
- to act as a starting point for discussions for young people who did have a counsellor
- to act as an independent aid to young unemployed people who had neither seen one/all of the television series, nor had a counsellor.

Within the specialised area of each section of each Jobhunter Kit the following general functions were identified:
- situations portrayed by cartoon strip and photographs with which young unemployed people might identify

    —   motivation to positively alter such situations where required
    —   explanations of agencies and programmes intended to help
    —   initial contact procedures and data related to appropriate agencies and programmes
    —   self-assessment exercises
    —   technique trainers (e.g. letter writing)
    —   ideas related to constructive use of time during unemployment
    —   concrete evidence that 'somebody' cared enough to produce a specialist kit and it was available free with offers of help and advice. At the time of production of the first 5,000 Jobhunter Kits (Mk 1) there was virtually nothing similar available to young people; consequently a great deal of interest was shown by professionals and workers in the field.

Design and Authorship. The delay in starting the Project (June 1977) meant that we were in something of a race to catch up with the intended starting date for the television series. As a result we did not feel we were able to reach optimum levels of authorship, design or editing. More importantly we were not able to make the kits correspond very closely to the television series, over which we had a small and belated influence (with the exception of programme 7). This situation was greatly improved in years 2 and 3 where the co-operation over design of kits and content and style of the television programmes was much closer.

    Of the six Jobhunter Kit sections, four were commissioned from people with a specialist knowledge of the subject matter and the particular target audience. Two (as well as a supplement) were written by Project staff. The series was rough drafted by National Extension College staff in Cambridge[4] and returned for piloting. We were only able to pilot three of the sections. Five people from the area were selected and after initial briefing sessions to discuss methods and purpose, the five agreed to find a group of six young people, currently unemployed, with as full a range in terms of ability, sex and background as possible, who would agree to meet three times to respond to and criticise the drafts. Comments were also requested and received from the statutory services mentioned in the packs.

Results of Piloting. Piloting did not produce any universal comments suggesting that the format of the Jobhunters was substantially wrong as it stood. There were many detailed comments that reflected the degree of satisfaction, or otherwise, with particular items.

The major area of disagreement among the piloting groups was in appreciation of language and the use of cartoons. The majority found that they enjoyed the language and use of cartoons, or found it acceptable (thus possibly identifying themselves as an appropriate target audience). Other individuals thought the cartoons a bit childish or patronising. The comments received asked for better presentation, clearer instructions, better linkage of materials within each pack, less miserable faces and welcoming the intended use of colour. These comments provided sufficient pointers to enable us to identify the following criteria to be used in determining a 'good' Jobhunter:

1. The material should be easily understood by young people (16-20) with generally low level of literacy and academic achievement.

2. That the target audience should identify with the characteristics and situations portrayed.

3. That the target audience should find the information relevant and appropriate to the situation in which they find themselves.

4. That the materials should provoke both dicussions and action.

5. That the general style of presentation should be seen as attractive and desirable by the target audience.

In addition there were comments of fact from professional sources covering points of accuracy and omission. The Project staff and the NEC editor then re-drafted the sections of the Kit, which were then passed to a professional designer for final design, art-work and photography, before they were returned to the NEC for printing. Final editing and proof reading should have taken place at this stage but was not possible in the time allocated. Piloting was made difficult by the shortage of time, the small sample group, and the fact that the piloting drafts were only in monochrome.

Distribution of Jobhunter Kits. The Kits were despatched to every young person who requested them through the Freefone or return of the Freepost cards. Included with their Jobhunter Kit was the name and address of their local counsellor and a letter of introduction from the Just the Job office. We initially despatched the Kit folder with two sections only so as to encourage the young person to contact the Project again or obtain other sections from their local counsellor.

The Volunteer Counselling Network

Introduction. A face to face counselling network already exists to help young people with their employment problems. This is primarily the Careers Service of the Local Education Authorities for the school/ college leaver and the Employment Services Division of the MSC for the older, unemployed person. There is also the Youth Service. The picture, however, is consistently one of overstretched facilities, limited resources and personnel, and difficulty in reaching out to the significant number of people not effectively using the services which are available.

To help overcome this problem of contacting and assisting the young unemployed, especially in the more remote areas of the South West, it was decided that the Project should develop a Counselling Network of its own to supplement the work of the statutory agencies. By definition, the isolated unemployed are out of touch and often have formed a very unrealistic impression of their abilities and prospects. It was hoped that in establishing a counselling service for the young unemployed we could raise morale and encourage more positive thinking in their efforts to find suitable opportunities.

The counselling undertaken by the Project would not normally be of the conventional one-to-one model, but would operate through small groups (probably about six young unemployed people with one adult as Counsellor). It was considered that group formation would be appropriate as an efficient method of helping young people with job searching skills, identification of common problems, social interaction, as well as providing the isolated unemployed with the opportunity of making contact with similar people from different locations whom they might not otherwise meet.

This latter point was conceived with the hope that unemployment problems internalised by young people because of their isolation could be externalised by contact with others in a similar position, so helping overcome the feeling of so many of these young people that they have something intrinsically wrong with themselves which accounts for their predicament, rather than the overall shortage of employment opportunities.

The role of the Counsellor was described to interested enquirers in the following way:

"The Counsellor will help a small group of local unemployed to work through the activities contained within each of the packs. The Counsellor should be in a position to expand upon the information and to illustrate with examples he or she is familiar with. Several of the packs contain quizzes which should provide a stimulus to further discussion and analysis. The packs provide a starting point for assessing interests and abilities, as well as providing basic information about existing agencies and opportunities for young people. Each pack should lead the group towards thinking about a positive initiative of self-help in either a traditional or novel direction. The role of Counsellor will be to help the group, or its individual components, find a direction into which they can channel their efforts. The idea is that the Counsellor should provide the mature lead that will stimulate and motivate the individuals to action. It is here that the Counsellor's local contacts and knowledge will be of utmost importance. The Counsellor will also be used in evaluating at a local level the impact of the Project."

The concept of forming a personal support system to supplement a multi-media problem-solving exercise is not entirely new. The Rural Family Development (RFD) Project had developed the concept of the home visitor as one element in a multi-media information system. They felt that the under-educated were unlikely to publicise their lack of education by being seen to attend classes, and it would therefore be necessary to reach into these peoples' homes. Television could reach into the domestic environment, but the value of face-to-face personal communication was also recognised. A system of home visiting was developed, with trained 'home-visitors' calling participants to advise them on their problems and to help them make use of the television programmes and follow-up materials. The RFD experience was a major influence in our decision to incorporate a network of Counsellor-Advisors to supplement the Just the Job programmes and Jobhunter Kits. Our materials were designed 'inter alia' to prepare the young person to make more effective use of existing services. We felt this aim was unlikely to be effective unless the young person was supported in his use of these media. The idea was reinforced in the knowledge of a Youthaid Study showing that nearly 50% of first year school-leavers reach their decision about their future job with advice from personal contacts, especially parents, and only 25% from careers advisors.

Remuneration and Expenses. We felt the volunteer ethos had much to offer in helping the young unemployed. In making a wage or session payment there was the inherent danger that we would be creating, in the eyes of the unemployed, another paid official, another agency. Making session payments also presented problems of administration in terms of supervision and accountability and other complications relating to the employment of staff. To overcome the need for a complex administrative claim system each counsellor was allocated a lump sum to cover all their expenses (transport, telephone, refreshments, photocopying etc.).

Recruitment. It was decided (1977) that fifty volunteer Counsellors should be recruited to cover the Westward TV transmission area. We realised that fifty Counsellors would not provide full coverage, but the Project was an experiment and was qualitively testing the whole multi-media approach and not trying necessarily to satisfy the quantitative demand. Essentially the selection of areas in which Counsellors would be based was a combination of factors such as the distribution of unemployed young people, the availability of suitable volunteers, and the Project's rural bias. In the second and third year, demand for the services of the Project, particularly in Plymouth (the South West's largest urban area) was catered for by an increase in the number of volunteers to one hundred, and an additional field worker.

Personnel Specification. The use of volunteers in this field of work is novel and as such we could not be resolute in determining which characteristics would be absolutely necessary to fulfil the tasks envisaged. The following loose pointers were used in attracting 'suitable' applicants:
- a desire to help unemployed young people
- the resource of a few hours spare a week
- availability to the Project for about four months from October 1977

— the ability to relate to young people and their problems (perhaps instanced by experience in working in voluntary or other roles with young people)
— being well enough known in a local community to be able to facilitate action response by the group
— a self-starter approach indicating the ability to 'get things moving'.

We stressed that it was not necessary to have any previous experience of 'counselling'. In the context of the rural community the trained professional is often not a local person nor acceptable in the role of advisor/friend.

The Counsellors were recruited through television (six one minute promotions on WTV and later on BBC TV as well), press coverage and information leaflets. The 155 applicants were interviewed in their own homes against a set of practical criteria as well as the above mentioned characteristics. Fifty people were selected, and of these thirty were male and twenty-five female. Their age breakdown was as follows: 25-39 years (41%); 40-54 years (44%); 55 years + (14%). Concerning qualifications: 11% had no qualifications; 32% had teaching qualifications; 6% had a qualification in careers guidance; 14% had a youth/community work qualification.

We recognised that there would be a demand where there was no Just the Job provision and so twenty-one additional 'ad hoc' Counsellors were linked with the Project from various Youth and Community services and Government sponsored Job Creation workers.

Counsellor Support Systems. It was anticipated that lay Counsellors would be unable to cope with all the demands made upon them without support. This support was provided in three main ways:
— a Counsellor's Handbook
— a system of regular personal support by Project staff
— a newsletter to keep Counsellors in touch with Project developments.

The Project Office provided personal support by acting as the central resource for handling Counsellors' queries/problems and in providing a ready response to those Counsellors wishing to promote some form of group action following on from a group session.

It was also considered that Counsellors could learn as much from each other as they could from the Project Staff. It was planned that groups of about six Counsellors should meet together with their

Counselling Service Co-ordinator about every three weeks. The intention was partly to provide a forum for exchanging ideas, experience and contacts and partly a mutual support session.

Counsellor Training. Here we were presented with a complex problem. Having selected our Counsellors, how should we prepare them for what lay ahead when we had an unclear idea of what that was ourselves?

Our Counsellors were geographically spread from Weymouth (Dorset) to Lands End (Cornwall). To reduce the expense of using outside speakers more than once, to simplify arrangements, and because of time constraints, we decided that 'training' should take place on one weekend, centrally and residentially.

Because of the wide range of background, age and experience of our Counsellors the one thing that was clearly inappropriate was a formal training approach. We hoped to be able to support and develop their motivation, to broaden perceptions of what the work might involve, to loosen, though probably not to alter, some of the attitudes to young people and their unemployment problems.

We could certainly provide information, we could discuss strategy and procedure, and identify support systems. Perhaps most importantly, we could provide an opportunity for all of us who would be involved to talk together and allay anxieties.

We invited outside speakers to describe the general background to the unemployment situation, the work of the MSC, the Careers Service, the Employment Service Division and the Work Experience Unit at Bristol. We used Project staff from Bristol Youth Workshop and from Dartington Work Experience Programme (WEP) scheme to talk about the attitudes of young people to their situation and some methods that were being used to assist them.

Our own Project staff presented the general aims of the Project, showed the possibilities and practicalities of work with groups of young people, discussed the evaluation and recording methods that would be used, and explored possible theoretical solutions to the unemployment problem. Counsellors also had their first opportunity to examine the Project materials and see several of the television programmes.

Throughout the weekend we worked from plenary into groups of about eight Counsellors plus a group leader.

By the end of the weekend, we felt reasonably confident that most of the Counsellors knew where to go for most of the information they would need, that support systems had been identified and a wide range of attitudes and perceptions had been exposed. Most of the Counsellors' motivation still seemed very high. Although people were looking forward to referrals arriving, there were still apprehensions and anxieties that confirmed the need for regular support from Project staff, and the importance of them establishing good relationships with the statutory services in their own areas. Many of the anxieties were personal - "Will the young people get on with me?", "Will the young people come back each week?", "Will my attitudes be flexible enough?". There were also Counsellors who expressed an extraordinary degree of self-confidence.

A rough head count by Project staff at 5.00 p.m. on Sunday expressed about 85-90% confidence in the Counsellors who had been selected. We expected, realistically, to 'lose' one or two people during the weekend or by letter on Monday, but in fact did not.

The group leaders were virtually unanimous in identifying the 10-15% of Counsellors about whom we felt some anxiety and it was agreed that we should offer them extra support in the early stages.

Finally, perhaps one of the most instructive sessions of the weekend came towards the end, when each group of Counsellors was given a typed 'case history' of a young person to consider, with a view to identifying the sorts of support and advice they might be able to offer. After a period of time, the actual young person was introduced to the group (from the WEP scheme at Dartington). In most cases, their aspirations had undergone drastic change from those suggested in their case histories, as a result of their experience on a Work Experience Programme.

We felt that the training weekend was more appropriately about orientation than hard training, that Counsellors should feel confident in their own networks, personalities, access to information and support, rather than in para-professional counselling or group-work skills, and that they were clear about their potential roles in relation to the other agencies in the field.

The Telephone Referral Service - Freefone System

At the commencement of Just the Job activity in 1977 it was considered essential to develop an efficient system to allow the television viewer easy access to the printed materials accompanying the series and to provide personal information to individual enquirers both at the point of contact and over time in local counselling groups.

The characteristics of the client group (young unemployed people under the age of 20) were analysed and it was concluded that response could be assured only if the method of contact was as simple and as cheap as possible. Any complication would lose us the very group we were aiming to help.

Our initial contact with the client group was to be primarily through the medium of television. The impact of television is immediate but short-lived. Any message within a programme, e.g. a specific request to contact Just the Job, has to be acted on immediately. By the following day interest and memory will have waned (at least until a reputation exists). The only communication system that can currently offer an immediate response is the telephone. This would be our main link with viewers.

By establishing a Freefone number (the Project bearing the total cost of each call), we could meet both our criteria - simple and cheap - for the client group.

The Post Office installed five exchange lines and five key and lamp units, thus providing a simple means of connecting any one of five telephones to any one of five circuits. Additionally, an answerphone was installed, which subsequently proved useful for taking calls at night and weekends.

The peak loading period was expected to be immediately following transmission, i.e. 5.45 p.m. onwards. We engaged volunteers to assist the Project staff in manning the system for each of the seven Monday evenings of transmission in 1977. Two people were allocated to each telephone, with alternate answering of calls, thus permitting a slight break for completion of the necessary documentation. 417 Freefone calls were taken on the first evening alone - the staff and volunteers were faced with a continuity of calls for over four hours. Our personnel survived - just!

An answering procedure was designed to speed the flow of calls and ensure all young people were given the same information. As Westward TV did not give any mention of the Counselling in the early programmes of the first series, all information about the form- ation of groups had to be transmitted within the space of a few seconds of telephone time. It was important that all those answering calls provided similar information about groups to prevent our volunteers having to face misconceptions and contradictions at their first meeting with the young person.

For each client making contact a pre-printed index card was completed recording the minimum of information necessary to identify callers' needs, despatch of materials and, where appropriate, transfer to local Counsellors.

The system described above and established in 1977 has developed to the point where in Autumn 1979 the telephone service - Freefone 9206 - was utilised by three different television series and one local radio programme per week, namely:

Just the Job	WTV	Fridays 6.50 p.m.
Just the Job	Plymouth Sound ILR	Tuesdays 7.00 p.m.
Roadshow	BBC TV	Sundays 10.40 a.m. and 6.30 p.m. Mondays 11.30 p.m.
Your Own Business	BBC TV	Sundays 10.00 a.m.

THE RESULTS AND LESSONS OF THE PROJECT

Evaluation and Monitoring

In the original grant application from the NEC to the MSC a research officer was included in the staffing. This position was commuted to another counselling services co-ordinator and so the evaluation and monitoring in 1977/8 was undertaken by all the Project staff with the temporary assistance of a research assistant. The results of this appear in the Just the Job Interim Report of March 1978. During the 1979/80 phase the Project was independently evaluated by a team from the Department of Sociology at the University of Exeter and is available in a report produced from the MSC (October 1979). This report was the subject of considerable criticism. The Project evaluation results appearing in this report are drawn from the whole three years of the Project's work and some of these are at odds with some of the conclusions drawn by the University of Exeter. Table 3.3 summarises the principal features of the Project during its three years of operation.

The Role of the Media

The role of the media was extensively researched (1978/9) by the University of Exeter team and some of their conclusions are presented below.

Television. The major thrust of Just the Job publicity was contained in the TV series, but there was a considerable back-up operation using leaflets and posters to advertise the series and all the major Just the Job services.

Both the informal (family, neighbours and peer group) and the formal structure (the statutory agencies) play a major influencing and supportive role in client response to Just the Job. It has been concluded that the family network reinforces the impact of the television to encourage telephone contact by the client, while the statutory agencies contributed with support and publicity to the high postal response and to those who are referred directly to Just the Job.

The researchers concluded that on the basis of the JICTAR (TV audience research) survey, the Just the Job television series improved its position strongly over the last two years as an alternative to Blue Peter (BBC). In both years (1977/8 and 1978/9) it maintained a constant level of audience percentage - a successful result for an innovative programme of this type. Their results show that television is less successful in reaching less motivated young people and it suggested that television gains support by its association with Just the Job counselling in general, and by its power as a referral mechanism in particular. They concluded that its informative/educational value is limited to its function as an animateur. They went on to say that Just the Job would not be as accessible as it is to the target group without a very strong emphasis on the written publicity and postal channels of referral.

The researchers generally concluded that for the young people the television series achieved its aim most clearly for those in counselling groups who were initially referred to Just the Job via the television.

Table 3.3: Comparisons between years 1, 2 & 3 in the development of the Just the Job project

		1977/78	1978/79	1979/80	
TV PROGRAMMES	number	7 (WTV)	6 (WTV)	12 (BBC TV)	14 (WTV)
	length	26 min	20 min	10 & 30 min	6 - 7 min
	start date	5.11.77	9.11.78 & Rep. 14.11.78	30.9.79	30.11.79
	frequency	weekly	twice weekly	2 weekly	weekly
	transmission	5.15 pm	5.20 pm	6.20/11 pm	6.50 pm
INDEPENDENT LOCAL RADIO	number	-	29	26	
	length	-	26 min	26	
	start date	-	24/10/78	9/10/79	
	frequency	-	weekly	weekly	
	time	-	7.00 pm	7.00 pm	
NEWSPAPER FEATURE		-	Cornish Papers 3	Sunday (Regional) Independent	
MATERIALS	jobhunter	√	√ New edition	√ New edition	
	special handouts	-	√	√	
	roadshow guide	-	-	√	
	badges	-	-	√	
VOLUNTEER COUNSELLORS	applications	155	131	180	
	method of recruitment	poster, leaflet, press,WTV	poster, leaflet, press,ILR,WTV	poster, leaflet LOC radio, (ILR, BBC) WTV, BBC TV, press	
	no. active	78	84	95	
	training weekend	√	√	√	
	counsellors handbook	√	√ New edition	√ New edition	
YOUNG PEOPLE RESPONSE	total	2,572	2,142 + 300	5,044	
	% of total under 20 unemployed	13.64%	11.26%	N.A.	
	numbers in effective counselling	413	424	925	
RESEARCH AND EVALUATION		internally	Univ. Exeter	-	
STAFFING	project director	1	1	1	
	C.S.C.'s *	2	3	3	
	office manager	1	1	1	
	clerical	-	1	1	
BUDGET		£54,000	£68,000	£76,000	

* Counselling Service Co-ordinators

These young people felt that the television had been of more value to them (in terms of support, ideas etc.) than it had to the young people who had been referred to Just the Job by other means.

As one 19 year old girl put it:

"It (the TV series) works, it has helped me to know that I can get into college without qualifications and that there are Government projects going on. I didn't think there were any down here."

Another favourable comment was:

"Just the Job cheered me up, showed me I wasn't alone in my situation, but I gained no definite ideas from it."

The researchers argued that the two principles emerging most strongly out of the series for the young people are 'caring' and 'self-help' underpinned by a layer of practical advice and information. These effectively combine to form the means by which the majority of the audience acknowledge and accept the aims set by the programmes and ultimately the principles of counselling itself. There was a close correspondence between the defined aims of the programmes as set by the programmers and the Just the Job team and the perceptions of those aims by the sample of young people who received counselling.

In summary the television component of the Project performed well within its accepted limitations and was well complemented by the closely linked Just the Job back-up service. Television brought an instant credibility to and awareness of the whole scheme and was invaluable for publicity and counsellor recruitment.

Local Radio. In the sub-area for Plymouth (one of three sub-areas chosen by Exeter researchers for close study and control group comparisons) although none of the respondents had been referred via the radio, 20% had listened to Plymouth Sound, and in the control group as many as 40% had listened to the programme. It is interesting that the control group were interviewed at a time when the programme had been running for at least two months, while the Just the Job group were interviewed one month after the start of the programmes. The listening percentage had increased for the control group as a result of the increased opportunity for exposure and publicity. On the basis of the small sample in the sub-area, it was concluded that the radio initiative has succeeded in reaching more than one quarter of the potential target audience, despite its low initial impact on referrals.

Local Newspaper Supplements. In 1978/9, 10% of contacts to Just the Job in Cornwall were made via the newspaper based Jobhunter Series. Although this was a small proportion of the total it was found that target group readership built up slowly for the newspaper and there was evidence of a much larger response at the end of the series, to the extent that 250 of the 300 post-March (1979) contacts were found to belong to this category. 50% of these were unemployed and 50% pre-school leavers. One would expect newspapers to be accessible to this kind of audience in the long run and indeed as the authors of 'Broadcasting and Youth'[5] point out: "relative to the adult population as a whole young adults are more likely to see (if not read) a newspaper than their elders".

Counsellors' Evaluation of the Just the Job TV Series. The findings show nearly 50% of Counsellors had a favourable comment to make about the transmissions, a similar percentage to the young people in the counselling groups. However, Counsellors were far less convinced of the intrinsic value of the programmes to the young people, the majority response being that the programmes only had value as a trigger to make contact with Just the Job. In this respect the Counsellors were more critical than the young people. In addition, the Counsellors tend to interpret the response of the young people in their groups to be somewhat more negative than was found in the researchers' interviews in the sub-areas.

The researchers were of the opinion that their findings were not wholly conclusive since it should be pointed out that a substantial proportion of the young people did gain something from the programmes other then the simple impulse to make contact. The final comment about a client by one of the Devon volunteers should not be necessarily taken as an isolated example:

> "It is interesting that in the case of X the television acted as the only catalyst necessary. By the time we were in contact she had already contacted Careers and got information about training schemes. The TV had acted as the spur to personal motivation on several fronts".

The Counselling Relationship

Putting unemployed young people into contact with a voluntary Counsellor in their local area was a very important feature of Just the Job. The main conclusions drawn from the analysis of the counselling relationship were:

1. Just the Job counselling was effective in providing personal support, knowledge and skills and in lessening the isolation of the young unemployed. This was in spite of the expectation among Counsellors that the majority of young people could be highly motivated and job-orientated.

2. Counselling style (whether in groups or with individuals) was strongly influenced by accessibility of clients. There was evidence of transport problems in rural areas and social isolation and difficulties of contact in urban areas.

3. Training and support for Counsellors was in general sufficiently effective for Counsellors with motivated younger school leaver clients. It was less so however for the disadvantaged, unmotivated older and long term unemployed.

4. Counsellors who either started out with or moved towards a client-orientated approach to counselling were more successful in dealing with 'problem' clients and more likely to carry out group counselling.

5. Counsellors' relationships with the statutory agencies were improved in 1978/9. Direct contact however did not substantially increase, most Counsellors preferring to act as a catalyst to encourage their clients to use the agencies. When problems did arise between volunteers and the statutory agencies they tended to be the result of a lack of clear demarcation between the sphere of competence of the more active volunteer and that of the professional.

Counsellors' definitions of the aim of their role varied broadly into three main areas of responsibility. First, the job-orientated approach in which the Counsellor was prepared to take on the responsibility of job finding for the young person. Second, the practical helper (job-search helper orientation) who stayed closely to the Just the Job remit of practical advice and help for the young person in job finding and skill acquirement. Third, the client-orientated approach in which Counsellors aimed to remotivate the young unemployed to the extent that they would act independently and effectively in job search.

One of the early aims of Just the Job was to encourage the formation of small groups of unemployed young people to meet with their local Counsellor. Only a quarter of the Counsellors succeeded in forming a group, even though the proportion may well have been higher if there had not been problems of accessibility to young people in rural areas. The sub-area studies revealed the extent to which young people can be motivated towards groups given the right circumstances.

Counsellors' Handbook. It can be concluded that the Handbook was useful to volunteers as a reference point and source of practical information. Few Counsellors relied on the Handbook to provide the basis for meetings and a proportion did not use it at all. The Handbook performed the function of codifying the introductory information acquired at the training weekend and provided the written link between the basic training and the counselling process. By comparison the Job-hunter Kits had a more immediate function in group work. As such the two sets of resources were complementary.

Jobhunter Kits. 78.5% of the Counsellors made use of the Jobhunter Kits in the counselling process. The particular use made of the kits by Counsellors, however, was not systematic. Only one Counsellor read all the kits with the young people in his group. Instead some Counsellors used the kits to structure the initial contact with the young people: "I use them as an ice-breaker with the young people". The majority used items and features of the kits as bases for discussion and reference sources in group work.

From the evaluation of the use of the Jobhunter Kits it seems that they were too simple for some and too difficult for others. Effectively the problem seemed to be that the kits were attempting to be of use to a broad spectrum of young people with a wide range of requirements and could not be right for all of them. The major suggestion coming from the evaluation was the production of additional and separate information sheets. This approach proved effective during the 1979/80 Project phase.

A major part of the counselling role was taken up with contacts and communications with the informal and formal networks surrounding the clients.

The researchers' findings conclude that Counsellors' contacts with statutory and voluntary agencies and educational institutions were maintained and improved in 1978/9. An increase in support and co-operation for Just the Job counselling was very marked in the Careers Service in all three areas.

The majority of Counsellors made contact with between six and a dozen employers during their main counselling period. There is evidence that at least one third of these employers learnt about Government Schemes and the problems of the young unemployed through this contact and were willing to help where possible.

The researchers found that the Just the Job back-up system worked very well for the majority of Counsellors. Where the role of the Counsellor involved the routine contact with the more motivated client this support was entirely adequate. For Counsellors with long term and specialised cases to deal with, the co-ordinators in the areas tended to take on the extra burden as part of the normal duties. This resulted in a degree of dependence by certain Counsellors on the team member for their area, which, coupled with the demand for professional advice and skills that emerged throughout the period, revealed the extent of extra responsibility taken on by the co-ordinators.

The findings show that over half the Counsellors defined an instrumental job-seeking expectation from young people. Subsequent experience plus substantiating evidence from the sub-area studies however show, in general, young people approached counselling with the expectation of help in terms of personal support and social skills as well as information about the system of job search. Short-term problems arose chiefly out of difficulties on making initial contact. The major long-term problems facing Counsellors, however, were those clients who lacked motivation and who were defined as unrealistic in their expectations and who resisted advice. The 'difficulties' were almost always associated with personal problems, psychiatric or physical handicap, educational and social problems, long-term unemployment and a history of frequent job change.

Project Control

The Just the Job Project was managed and controlled by the NEC's project team based at Dartington in Devon. The Project Director was directly responsible to the NEC's Executive Director based in Cambridge. In addition to this internal management, a Project steering group was constituted and consisted of representatives from the Manpower Services Commission and the NEC. Over the three years of the Project this body met rather infrequently and did not really fulfil its role as a 'steering' group. Meetings were not arranged at regular intervals, but often at the request of the Project team. Minutes were not always kept and the steering group had very little influence on the decision making process relating to the future continuation of the Project.

There was considerable confusion over which member of the MSC's staff had day to day responsibility to liaise with the NEC, and the MSC's decision making was almost entirely reactive.

The Project was grant aided by the MSC (London) and therefore related to MSC London staff. However, the MSC have evolved an Area management board structure. This meant that the Just the Job Project was 'controlled' by MSC centrally which was rather at odds with the MSC declared policy that Area Boards had responsibility for all measures to assist the young unemployed. This situation created a number of difficulties for the Project, particularly when applications were being made for further funding. Just the Job was initially set up as a pilot project with a one year life and that meant the last three months of that period were spent negotiating with the MSC for a continuation of the Project based on the first year's results. This process happened three times and demanded significant time and resources and prevented coherent future planning. Thus the development of the Project was on a 'stop-go' basis, which the NEC felt prevented it from adopting a more long term and developmental role. It also handicapped relationships with statutory agencies and generally the credibility of the whole scheme.

Conclusion

This case study has attempted to describe the Just the Job Project which was aimed at helping young unemployed people. It has shown that over the three years of the Project's life the overall approach appears to have been successful in the South West of England. Using mass media (especially TV) the Project has demonstrated how outreach activities supported by volunteer Counsellors from the local community can assist the more disadvantaged unemployed young person. This help has been provided in the form of direct assistance with job searching and indirectly through improving the young person's 'basic competencies', providing moral support and creative survival in unemployment.

The Project has shown that there are a significant number of young people who do not make effective use of the statutory agencies and that there is a requirement for an 'alternative' channel or system based on the 'unofficial' network of volunteer Counsellors linked to the power of the mass media.

Already the basic principles of the Just the Job Project are being used very effectively in London (Capital Jobmate using local radio) to contact and help the ethnic minorities. In Somerset the Local Education Authority has adopted the basic principles developed by Just the Job, and the Somerset Careers Service are now using volunteers from the community as extension workers co-ordinated by them and linked with the Jobline series transmitted by the Bristol based HTV. In Exeter volunteers are continuing in operation (independently of the statutory agencies), have raised supporting funds from industry and now function on a self-management basis. Regular newspaper features have been produced by the local volunteers for inclusion in the Exeter Weekly News as a means of attracting young unemployed people to their counselling scheme.

Notes and References

1. Manpower Services Commission, 'Young People and Work: Report on the Feasibility of a New Programme of Opportunities for Unemployed Young People' (Manpower Services Commission, London, 1977) (The Holland Report)
2. Westward TV is an independent commercially operated regional TV station working under the franchise of the Independent Broadcasting Authority to provide programmes in the South West of England.
3. D. Gladstone, J. Etheridge and C. True, 'Just the Job: an Evaluation. A Report submitted to the Manpower Services Commission' (Department of Sociology, University of Exeter, Exeter, 1979).
4. The main editing, design, production and printing facilities of the NEC are based at Cambridge.
5. 'Broadcasting and Youth: a Study Commissioned by the British Broadcasting Corporation' (Calouste Gulbenkian Foundation, London, 1979), p. 46.

Chapter 4

THE OPEN UNIVERSITY
COMMUNITY EDUCATION PROGRAMME
UNITED KINGDOM

Judith Calder and Nick Farnes

ORIGINS AND OBJECTIVES

The community education programme which is the subject of this case study is based at the Open University (OU) of Great Britain. Since the programme started in 1977, it has had over 60,000 formally enrolled students, with about 20,000 people registering each year for community education courses. The reason for the use of distance learning methods in this programme must be seen in the context of the University's earlier success with its undergraduate programme.

The Undergraduate Programme

The Open University was created on the initiative of the Government of the day and was granted its Royal Charter in 1969. One of its main aims was to offer adults the opportunity to study for a degree at home in their spare time. It was intended primarily for those who had missed out on educational opportunities in the past and might not possess the normal university entrance qualifications. Therefore there are no entry qualifications and admission is on a 'first come first served' basis. The first 25,000 undergraduate students began their studies in January 1971. Since then a total of 180,000 undergraduates have been admitted and 30,000 degrees awarded. Around 20,000 new undergraduate students are admitted each year, while there are 60,000 undergraduate students currently studying at any one time.

The University created a complex multi-media distance learning system with the bulk of students' learning centred on print materials - correspondence texts, set books etc. This is supported by TV and radio programmes, tutorials and summer schools, home experimental kits, computer and tutor marked assignments, and so on. Students can select from over 120 courses covering Arts, Science, Technology,

Maths, Social Science and Educational Studies to build up to the award of a degree after 4-8 years part-time study.

While the undergraduate programme was radical in its methods of teaching, it is relatively conventional in the subject disciplines taught. The teaching methods were designed for students studying at home in their own time and not dependent on attendance at an institution at fixed times. But the content of the courses is largely determined by the requirements of the subject disciplines and the need to provide students with coherent programmes of study. The courses are subject centred rather than need based.

Community Education Provision

The objects of the Open University, stated in its Charter[1], are as follows:

> "The objects of the University shall be the advancement and dissemination of learning and knowledge by teaching and research, by a diversity of means such as broadcasting and technological devices appropriate to higher education, by correspondence tuition, residential courses and seminars and in other relevant ways and shall be to provide education of University and professional standards for its students, and to promote the educational well-being of the community generally."

Given the obligation imposed by the Charter, and given that the original founders quite clearly intended that the University should become involved in non-degree areas of educational need, a high level committee was set up in 1974 with Sir Peter Venables as its chairman. Its aim was to report on how the University should proceed with meeting its full obligations under the Charter. A total of around 400 submissions were received from outside bodies. From these it was clear that a substantial body of opinion felt that the University should commit itself to the development of adult concern courses and packages of learning materials in collaboration with others.

The contribution the University was to make was seen as being quite different from the offerings of the traditional providers of adult education in Great Britain, who have, in the main, a long and honourable tradition in organising cultural and recreational courses, using face-to-face tuition methods. As Venables pointed out . . . "more of the same is not enough - to increase access we must have different forms of provision in wider areas". This provision was seen as being mainly in areas where needs could "best be assisted by independent learning and distance teaching methods".[2] At the same time it was felt that the University had the potential to act as a catalyst in drawing together local and national agencies who could provide expertise, knowledge of needs, resources, delivery and support networks and publicity. Members and clients of those agencies could then take advantage of educational opportunities appropriately delivered.

What is Community Education?

Community education is concerned with the learning of adults in their roles of parent, consumer, employee and citizen in the context of their family, workplace and community. It helps people to reflect on their experience through a process of dialogue, become aware of alternatives, decide what they want and take appropriate action to achieve this. It is also concerned with community development in that it can facilitate, inform and enable participation and help people take action to influence the direction of social, cultural, environmental or economic changes that affect individuals and their communities. Similarly it is concerned with social networks in that community education must build on the resources within the community; the development of 'local' materials and the provision of local support to encourage individual learners to draw on and value their experience can lead to a renewal of the local networks and agencies who are involved in the programme. There are many local agencies who, although not primarily educational providers, are concerned with the well-being of their members or clients and who have an educational component to their activities. They are part of the social infrastructure of local communities.

Collaboration between the OU and these local agencies can lead to a strengthening of their educational role and, for the OU, provides access to learning opportunities for people who would never attend traditional classes. There are also responsible national governmental and quasi governmental bodies who seek ways to deliver education to the general public. For example, the bodies responsible for health and consumer education use a variey of means of public education and have welcomed the opportunity to collaborate with the University in developing a more substantial educational provision in these areas.

Aims and Objectives

The Community Education programme is concerned with promoting 'the educational well being of the community generally' and is part of the University's Continuing Education programme which also includes professional education.

The objectives of the University's programme of Community Education may be described as follows:

1. to meet the learning needs of individuals at various stages in their lives: in their roles as parents, consumers, employees and citizens, in the context of their family, workplace and community by:
   - encouraging learners to value their own experience and the experience of others and to facilitate dialogue between learners and others.
   - providing information to assist personal and collective decision making.
   - helping learners make personal and collective decisions based on their own experience, values, resources and on information provided; and to implement changes.
   - enabling learners to take action individually and collectively to improve the services and facilities in their communities and workplaces.

2. to reach as wide a range of learners as possible regardless of prior educational achievement, through appropriate learning materials and support for their learning.

3. to collaborate with national and local organisations in defining needs, developing learning materials, sharing resources, publicising and promoting learning opportunities, organising support for learners and in evaluating the provision.

4. to finance this work, within the rules laid down by the University, from student fees, external grants and other sources of income.

TARGET POPULATION

As the overall aim of the programme indicates, the target audience could be said to be the whole community. Even being a little more specific, the target group is somewhat broad ranging encompassing as it does, all adults aged 16 or more.

The Problem

The primary objective of the Community Education programme is 'to meet the learning needs of individuals at various stages in their lives: in their roles as parents, consumers, employees and citizens, in the context of their family, workplace and community'. In order to meet these relatively specific needs, courses and learning packages have to be designed and developed with well-defined target groups (i.e. sub-groups within the community) in mind. These target groups are not, however, comprised of a homogeneous group of individuals. Even if a group of adults at a similar stage with similar roles (e.g. new parents) is identified as having a particular learning need, the degree of learning experience and educational attainment, the level of motivation to learn will differ substantially between individuals. Thus the problem of defining the many different target groups is relatively complex.

The Solution within the OU Programme

The solution within the OU programme has been to identify target groups along two main dimensions: materials and support needs and learning needs.

The materials and support needs of the target audiences are similarly complex. Learners are handicapped by problems such as lack of motivation to study, access to appropriate provision, lack of confidence and non-ability to 'study', variation in familiarity with learning skills, and external commitments and pressures including lack of money to pay for learning materials or courses. Thus any given learning materials and student support system may be ideal for one group of learners with a particular learning need, and entirely inappropriate for another group with the same learning need.

Learning needs within the Community Education programme are dichotomised into a) stages and b) roles e.g. . . . .

a) Illustrative stages of adult life:		b) Illustrative concerns for each role:	
Being single		Parent Role: Child Development	
		Happy Families	
Getting married		Adoption and Fostering	
		Schools	
Planning Families			
		Employee Role:	
Pregnancy and Birth	*	Starting work	
		Women returning to work †	
Babies		Job Change	
		Unemployment	
Preschool child	*	Retirement	
Childhood 5-10	*	Consumer Role:	
		Consumer Decisions	*
Adolescence	†	Energy in the Home	*
		Health Choices	*
Marriage Problems		Food	
		Money	
Middle Age		Housing	
		Transport	
Planning Retirement	†		
		Citizen/Community Role:	
Retirement		Governing Schools	*
		Magistrates	
Old Age		Community Advisers	
		Local Councillors	
		Race Relations	†

* Courses in these areas are currently available within the OU Community Education Programme

† Projects for developing materials in these areas are either approved or are actually underway.

The strategy adopted by the Community Education programme at the Open University has therefore been to initially determine the target audience as a whole by the age and stage the learning materials relate to, in other words, the learning needs, e.g. 'all those about to retire or who have retired'. The formal course is then designed with the aim of reaching as wide a range as possible of learners within the target group. 'Rare' groups or groups of particular types of learners which are then found to be missing from the formal student body then become 'target groups' themselves for both formal and non-formal provision. Learning materials from the course are further developed or adapted to meet special needs, while further support services, or special forms of support are organised where possible. In this way learning materials can, with varying degrees of adaptation, successfully reach audiences ranging from semi-literates to university graduates.

LEARNING MATERIALS

The Nature of the Materials

The nature of community education materials as produced at the Open University can be defined as follows:

1. the materials are multi-media, with each medium used to exploit its particular characteristics.

2. the materials are designed to lend themselves to multiple uses and adaptations.

3. they are accessible and attractive to a wide ability range.

4. they contain devices to engage learners in examining their own experiences, values and resources and to organise these to make decisions and to take appropriate action.

In general terms, the materials are designed so that the learners are able to examine issues and make decisions over a range of situations.

The material is developed in such a way that individual issues can stand alone, and can be studied in isolation (e.g. as leaflets), and the same material can be put together with other material on interrelated issues (e.g. as a booklet). Because this type of development is planned from the conception of a course, the cumulative impact of a highly structured and interrelated series of materials (i.e. the course) on the learner is greater than the sum of the individual and independent parts.

Formats

Materials are developed in a variety of formats, adapted to particular delivery and support systems and to the needs of different subgroups within the target population. Examples of various formats which have been used include:

1. *Multi-media Course Materials:* consisting of eight 32 page full colour structured learning booklets, a resource pack containing leaflets, posters and cardboard cut outs, computer marked assignment booklet, Study Guide, Information booklet; 4x25 min. TV programmes, 4x20 min. radio programmes, 3x20 min. gramophone discs.

2. *Book of the Course:* 256 page full colour version of the 8 booklets reprinted for sale in retail bookshops.

3. *Part Works:* 20x16 page partworks sold by newsagents bi-weekly.[3]

4. *Booklet:* 64 page booklet based on course materials adapted for distribution in clinics.

5. *Booklet:* 16 page booklet adapted from course materials for use in conjunction with 6 local radio broadcasts.

6. *Leaflet:* 2-4 page leaflets reprinted from course materials for use by Health Visitors in clinics and home visiting.

7. *Extracts:* half-page adapted extracts from the course material published in 8 issues of a mass circulation magazine.

91

Materials Development versus Course Development

Course production was initially the main vehicle through which learning materials were developed, with the course materials being designed so that they would lend themselves to multiple uses and adaptations. Historically then, the courses were offered first and the other formats came afterwards as 'spin-offs' and adaptations.

While course production will continue to be an important means of building up a resource of learning materials, materials development projects are in existence which take a more developmental approach which involves discussing, transcribing, editing, testing and adapting. This process of dialogue leads to the production of items of material (e.g. 2-4 page leaflets) which may then be linked with other leaflets into packages or booklets and eventually courses. Also the adaptations from the early courses can be fed back into updated and revised versions of the course.

The Process of Materials Development and Redevelopment

Thus the development of materials is a cyclical process involving a variety of formats and a range of learners. The diagram in Figure 4.1. shows the main print formats, learners and inputs. A similar process can apply to audio visual materials.

The materials development process is in two main phases:

The dissemination phase (the first half of the cycle) where course material is adapted for various delivery and support systems and for different target audiences.

The assimilation phase (the second half of the cycle) starting with dialogue with local people which is captured in some form which is then transformed into leaflets. These can be grouped and used by other learners. The common core of a group of leaflets can be extracted and produced as a booklet which can be made available and tested widely. These booklets can form the basis for a new or revised multi-media course.

Currently there are two major grants funding materials development. The first, from the Health Education Council, is funding course development for parent and health education. These courses are then exploited to produce booklets and leaflets for use by non-registered students.

ASSIMILATION   DISSEMINATION

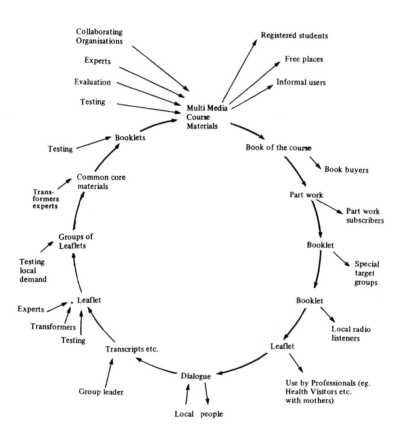

Figure 4.1 : Materials Development Cycle

Thus this activity is in the dissemination phase of the materials development cycle. The second major grant is from the Bernard van Leer Foundation which is funding collaboration between the University and four local community education projects in disadvantaged areas of the UK. This work involves local dialogue which provides the source material for the development of leaflets and booklets based on the experience of local people. Materials developed through this process will feed into the creation of new courses and are in the assimilation phase of the cycle.

Funding Materials Development

The Community Education programme, as part of the Centre for Continuing Education of the Open University, has to be run on a self-financing basis. The two main sources of income for the programme are, in consequence, grants from external agencies and student or user fees.

The resources necessary to develop multi-media course materials which have to compete in quality with mass circulation publications are substantial. The size of funding needed for the development of new materials (as opposed to adaptations) restricts sources of funding to national agencies. One obvious danger with this sort of funding base is that a funding body might seek to influence unduly both the subject matter of learning materials and the type of learning materials which are produced. It is therefore particularly important that the objectives of both the University and the funding body are seen to coincide.

The Community Education programme at the Open University has been particularly fortunate to date with its collaborating partners. Those without funds have contributed access to volunteer networks built up over many years. Those with funds have either awarded grants for very specific projects, such as a grant from the Department of Education and Science (DES) for a course for School Governors, or for a whole programme, as the Health Education Council (HEC) has done. Whenever a grant of any size is received, a joint management committee is set up to oversee the project or programme. In all instances of collaborative effort, however, the Community Education programme has been free to select, innovate and experiment with the most appropriate materials, media and message within minimal mutually and publicly agreed constraints (usually of cost, target audience and overall subject area e.g. 'health').

MEDIA AND METHODS

The Community Education programme at the Open University is as much concerned with informal users and the extension of access to its learning materials to 'non-registered' users as it is with is formally registered students. Thus the media and methods used both to deliver the learning materials and to support users' learning are diverse, with different combinations of media, delivery and support systems being used in the attempt to create effective learning opportunities for learners with different needs.

Media Used

There are three major media used in the teaching/learning process:
- audio-visual (both broadcast and non-broadcast)
- print-based materials
- face-to-face support

The core component or medium is the printed text. The size (in terms of number of pages), layout, amount of colour, balance between student activities, pictorial content and straight text can all vary, depending on the target user and the amount of finance available for developing the material and meeting printing costs. The 'typical' text for a whole course however is designed to provide, with the other components, around 40 hours of study over an 8-10 week period.

Audio-visual components play an important role in the learning materials, packages, and courses produced for users. While the major audio-visual components for the courses are broadcast on national TV and radio networks, non-broadcast material such as sound cassettes and record discs are included in the learning packages for registered students. At the same time regional TV and local radio are used in 'localised' provision for 'informal' users, as are locally made video films for replay to groups of learners.

The face-to-face support varies a great deal. No formal face-to-face teaching is provided by the University within the Community Education programme. While other bodies can and do provide formal face-to-face tuition based on our distance-learning packages, the University itself can only advise, encourage and facilitate face-to-face provision at the local level for both the formally registered students and the informal users. Thus face-to-face provision can involve professional subject 'experts' (such as health professionals), para-professionals (e.g. activists in voluntary organisations), and other learners/users in groupings ranging from 1 to 1 to quite large groups (50+).

In addition to the three main media, phones have been used for counselling (with limited success); local newspapers and national magazines have carried series of extracts from the correspondence text, thus extending the reach of the learning materials, and computers are used for student assessment.

Methods of Delivery

The methods of delivery used reflect the major media which are used, i.e.

1. Mail: e.g. from the full course to 'follow-up' booklets after local radio programmes

2. Retail distribution: e.g. the book of the course

3. Broadcast networks: programmes can be followed on their own or in combination with materials delivered by other means

4. People.

The fourth method of delivery, people, is a particularly flexible method as the amount and content of the material delivered can be individually tailored to the learner's needs. This applies whether the intermediary is a professional in the content area, a para-professional or a fellow learner. Intermediaries can deliver learning materials in such ways as:
- word of mouth transformation
- working together with the learner on some (or all) of the material
- directly handing over the learning package to the learner
- acting as an animateur to encourage participation and open up access to the materials for the learner.

The other forms of delivery used at present are newsprint and magazines. This method has played a relatively small part in the delivery system to date.

Methods of Support

With the wide range of both media and methods used within the programme, support for learners needs to be very flexible and will depend
on the extent to which the learner is already engaged in the material.
First, there are various kinds of support that affect whether or not a
learner will come into contact with and take up the provision. If the
opportunity is mediated by someone who is trusted or if barriers such
as the fee are removed the provision becomes more accessible to the
individual. Once the learner has made the decision to become 'active',
the support given to them can range from continuous one to one
tutoring within various local initiatives, through group learning which
may or may not include a 'professional', to the distance support from
TV or radio given to all learners. It is difficult to rank order these
kinds of support, but clearly more support can be provided by direct
contact, on an individual basis, where it is adapted to the needs of the
learner. Less support can be given where contact is limited to groups
of learners through a distance medium, where it cannot be adapted
to individual needs.

The main forms of support for learners within the OU Community
Education programme are:
-   national networks of local voluntary co-ordinators to set up
    student self-help groups.
-   content professionals associated with collaborating agencies.
-   voluntary intermediaries
-   other learners
-   computer marked assignments
-   a central enquiry service (phone or mail enquiries)

The needs which the different forms of support attempt to meet are,
again, varied. Support at the local level is provided right from the
outset with volunteer 'enthusers' or 'animateurs' assisting the University to extend and widen access to the learning materials by placing and
delivering publicity and promotional materials. Barriers to access are
often more complex than simply lack of awareness. Special schemes
have been set up whereby professionals and para-professionals can
allocate free places on certain courses, organise group discounts, or
arrange for learning materials to be shared, thus bypassing economic barriers. Where lack of confidence is a major disincentive to participate, individual personal support for study within a group can often be organised.

Just as important as the support provided by professionals and para-professionals however, is the support provided by other learners. The self-help groups, set up by volunteer co-ordinators, can provide 'moral support' for anxious learners and boost their self-confidence in a way which would be impossible 'at a distance'. Again, the contact between these groups and the local professionals or para-professionals can vary: some groups operate totally independently while others have a professional in attendance who can provide additional local resources, organise viewing or replaying sessions for audio-visual aids, and who may also help guide and advise the group.

CREATION, PRODUCTION, AND DISTRIBUTION OF MATERIALS

Course Creation: Procedures Currently Used

The learning materials are developed by a central production team which can include a chairman, lecturers, educational technologists, BBC producers, and seconded employees of a collaborating agency. Also extensive use is made of outside consultants and of pilot work with typical members of the target audience.

The production time depends on the nature of the project and may be up to two years. Materials usually go through distinct stages of development, during which detailed objectives are defined, content is structured and teaching approaches are developed. The materials are tested out and further developed before production is begun. After the materials have been in actual use by formally registered students, further evaluation of student interaction with the materials takes place.

This is a relatively conventional (for the Open University) way of developing structured learning materials and clearly has limitations in that radical changes to the materials are unlikely to occur even at the re-development stage because the framework for the materials has already been established for the learner by the course team. A far more radical approach to materials creation and development is how-ever now under way.

The Van Leer Project

The Van Leer Foundation is currently funding a national project on materials development based at the OU. A Project Officer in each of four community education projects located in disadvantaged areas of the UK has been appointed (3 Urban, 1 Island rural). The project officers are linked to staff at the University who are working on this project.

The local project officers are working with groups and individuals and using the discussions as the basis for developing learning materials. In practice this usually involves tape recording the discussion of a topic of particular concern to the individuals in the group. This recording is transcribed and then analysed and structured to produce draft learning material. The draft material is presented back to the original group so that they can validate it and develop the issues further. Versions can be introduced to other groups who may develop the issues in other directions. The learning materials become a vehicle for capturing the experience of the group and individuals, for reflecting this back to them and for enabling them to take appropriate action.

The staff at the University assist in transforming the materials while the work with individuals and groups is carried out by the local project officers. This process is leading to a collection of materials based on the experiences and needs of local people. It will be possible to draw out common core material from that developed in each local project. This core will contribute to materials and courses that will be made available nationally.

Thus intensive work of this kind can link local dialogue to materials development and these materials can be fed into course development. However it is both labour intensive and expensive. It requires bridging between what are often quite separate sets of skills. Face-to-face contact skills, transcript analysis, materials development and presentation skills are rarely possessed by a single individual. Individuals carrying out face-to-face work in disadvantaged areas and University employees developing learning materials must create a common language and understand each other's aims and constraints.

It is hoped that this project will enable these methods to be made explicit so that they can be used by many other community education groups and involvement in materials development can become an important means of community learning. It might then become easier for Community Education at the OU to draw on locally produced materials and make them available on a wider scale and develop them for nationally offered formal courses.

Materials Production

The major proportion of course materials are produced in the same way and to the same sort of timetable as are courses in the undergraduate area, with most of the course materials being produced internally or being co-produced. The 'Project Control' office first agrees a production timetable with the course team, all other departments involved in the production of the materials are informed and their time is booked. Thus the Design Studio and Publishing Department deal with the print materials, audio cassettes are produced by the Audio-Visual Department, while programmes for broadcasting on the national BBC networks are produced by BBC/OU Productions (a department of the BBC).

With a new and innovative programme such as Community Education, however, flexibility in the area of course production is as essential as in the other areas. Therefore for experimental approaches, material is produced directly by members of the project team with the assistance of the materials development officer and, if necessary, outside printing contractors to meet the often very tight deadlines.

Distribution of Materials

The need for flexibility also occurs with the distribution of materials. Certainly for the routine assembly, storage and despatch of course materials for large number of students, the main Open University Correspondence Service provides a good reliable service. However, this service is designed for the control and despatch of undergraduate course material, and with over 60,000 course packages per week to despatch, only routine systems can be handled. For experimental approaches, alternative materials development, and non-formal users of materials therefore, the assembly and despatch of materials is handled by clerks working on the programme.

Despatch of materials is normally directly to the user by post; however, where the collaborating agency is particularly involved (i.e.

with a network of volunteers), materials are sometimes sent via the regional representative of the network as a way of personalising and encouraging communication between the relatively isolated volunteers and the regional organisers.

Broadcast transmission via the national BBC network is agreed after annual negotiations between the OU and the BBC. At present, the provision of air-time for the undergraduate area takes precedence, with programmes being broadcast between the end of January through to October each year. This has traditionally left a 'gap' in the calendar between October and January. When the first Community Education courses were first presented three years ago, agreement was reached between the OU and the BBC that air-time would be provided for these courses during this period. The day, and the time of day during which Community Education programmes are transmitted, are the subject of discussion between the two bodies, but the final decision is that of the BBC.

Clearly, although there are many benefits in having air-time on national radio and TV networks, there are some important drawbacks to the provision available at present. Primary among these is the limitation of the air-time for Community Education programmes to a particular time of year: people's learning needs, particularly for functional education, can be immediate and urgent and it is a nonsense to have to tell them to wait six months until the next course is offered. The problem has been met to some extent by mailing out the printed course materials at whatever point in the year the students register, but the learners still have to wait for the broadcast period of the year before they can formally study the course as a course.

STUDENT ENROLMENT

Publicity

An annual publicity campaign begins in May each year. The two main components of this drive are:
- press advertising in national mass circulation and special interest periodicals
- leaflet and poster distribution through collaborating networks.

In addition to the national publicity drive, locally based publicity work takes place via 'enthusers', local radio, and the local press and sponsored place organisers. An OU community education newspaper is also circulated to students and former students twice per year.

Enrolment Procedures

Applicants wishing to formally register for a course must complete a simple application slip (in the form of a 'cut-out coupon') and send it, together with their fee, to the central office at the University. Anyone wishing to register for more than one course must register for each course separately. There are no entry requirements at all except that the applicant must be over 16 years of age and resident in the United Kingdom. Applications can be made at any time during the year.

There are three variations to the basic enrolment procedure to deal with special circumstances.

1. Sponsored place students are given special vouchers by the local sponsored place organiser which they then enclose with the application form instead of their fee.

2. Group discounts - a special application form is used which five applicants must jointly complete, then return to the central office together with the fees for four places. Thus either one place is free or they all get the course at a reduced price.

3. Partial registration - to accommodate demand from 'informal users' of course material who wish to either share one set or who have already bought the 'book of the course', it is now possible to register at reduced cost for the supplementary materials and assessment part of the course only - no course materials are sent.

Although there can be no enrolment procedures for informal users, clerical records are kept of those who contact the University in order to buy or borrow sets of course materials. Similarly a form of 'snowball sampling' is used to identify intermediaries using the materials informally with learners and the OU initiates contact wherever possible.

Records System

Students records are computerised and held on course-based files. If a student has registered for more than one course, then he or she is registered separately for each course. No historic data is held on file. Data for individual students can be accessed from terminals both at the centre and in the regional offices of the University, although data can only be entered from the centre. All students have the right to request a print-out of their file on payment of a small fee.

STUDENT SUPPORT

As indicated earlier, there are two distinct phases in the support provided for learners. During the first phase, support takes the form of 'enthusing', persuasion, to encourage the learner to participate, thereby opening up access to the provision. The second phase comprises support while the learner is actually engaged in his or her studies.

The First Phase of Support

No professional admission advice, tutoring or counselling is provided with the Community Education courses. Clearly other agencies and individuals who use OU Community Education materials provide a whole variety of different types of support for learners. However the support provided by the OU is based totally on the concept of self-help. Four different types of approach are currently used during the first support phase:

1. Enthusers: the role of volunteer co-ordinators, originally limited to a 'post-box' role, has now been extended at the request of the co-ordinators themselves. Those who wish to are now encouraged to actively seek out and talk to prospective students, both in groups and as individuals. A special co-ordinator's pack which includes guidance notes, samples of course materials, posters and leaflets is now provided for all co-ordinators to encourage and help them to take on an active enthusing role.

2. Sponsored place organisers: volunteer organisers take on an active 'animateur' role, seeking out, contacting and encouraging individuals whom they consider suitable to participate in the sponsored places scheme.

3. Local radio: local radio disc jockeys and other professionals known in the area encourage and support their listeners to become 'informal' learners, not only by listening to the local radio programmes related to the learning materials, but also in encouraging them to write in for associated print material which is provided free of charge.

4. Community Education newspaper: 'Routes' is an 'in-house' newspaper sent two or three times a year to all students and former students. Former students are now recognised as providing an extremely valuable service in supporting prospective students (data suggests that around a quarter of the students first heard of their course from a friend or colleague at work). The newspaper keeps past students up-to-date with new developments and courses and seeks to introduce prospective students to the aims and ethos of community education provision at the OU.

Support for Formally Registered Students: the Self-help Group Network

The second phase of support is organised at the local level by volunteers. Separate networks of volunteer 'co-ordinators' are set up for each course. These volunteer co-ordinators may be professionals in the content area, e.g. health education officers for the course 'The First Years of Life', or committed activists e.g. women involved in the running of local pre-school playgroups for the course 'The Pre-school Child'.

The co-ordinators are recruited at the local level after agreement with the appropriate agency has been reached at the national level. For example, for 'The Pre-school Child', the local branches of the Pre-school Playgroups Association (PPA), were asked to nominate PPA members to act as co-ordinators. This network differs a little from that for 'The First Years of Life' in that there was an additional tier of volunteer co-ordinators at regional level (13 regional co-ordinators for England and Wales). These volunteer regional co-ordinators helped both with the recruiting of local volunteer co-ordinators and, where there were gaps in the co-ordinator network, by covering the area themselves.

The self-help group system was set up to enable students to share their experiences and resources and to enable them to help each other. Those who wish to study alone or with a friend or neighbour are perfectly free to do so. Those who wish to participate in a self-help group (about half the students) normally have to take the initiative by contacting the local co-ordinator for their course, using an annually updated list of co-ordinators sent to all students. If there are any other students in the area studying that course who have also signified an interest in joining a self-help group, the co-ordinator will then put them in touch with each other. This activity is called the 'post-box' role and is the minimum role for a co-ordinator.

There are however many problems in setting up groups in this way, and the proportion of students who want to join a group who actually do so (about a third), is, unfortunately, smaller than we would wish. Problems in actually making contact with a co-ordinator, problems in contacting other students, distances between students, or sometimes the total absence of other students in the same geographical area all contribute to the problems of the students and co-ordinators in trying to set up groups. Many of these problems do not apply of course to sponsored students, who consequently have a much higher participation rate (1 in 4) than do fee paying students (1 in 8).

Even given these problems, students appear to receive such great benefits from self-help groups that considerable efforts are being made to overcome the problems identified. The typical self-help group has about five or six members and meets at the house of one of its members about once every two weeks. The role the group appears to play is that of a forum for airing problems, the giving and receiving of advice between members and, in effect, acting as a 'counterbalance' to the course 'proper'. The group provides the participants with a secure non-threatening environment in which their own attitudes and behaviour can be challenged and either modified or reinforced. The reassurance that each participant provides for the other students in terms of shared problems is essential within this process.

Recruitment and Training of Volunteer Co-ordinators

Volunteer co-ordinators are not selected by the University. Rather the collaborating network provides volunteers who may vary considerably in degree of motivation and extent of commitment. Given that overall there are now almost five hundred volunteer co-ordinators spread over the whole country, face-to-face training would be far too expensive, even if it were operationally feasible. Instead, distance methods are used. A special co-ordinator's 'pack' has been developed, and an up-dated pack is sent annually to each co-ordinator.

Some face-to face contact does exist however. The regional co-ordinators are given an annual briefing and training conference which is seen as essential in motivational terms. They themselves may well hold briefing conferences for local co-ordinators, but this is usually run in parallel with some other event organised by the external agency to which they belong, as no finance is available to fund this type of training.

ASSESSMENT AND EVALUATION

Assessment

The course designers felt from the start that 'failure' had no meaning within the context of courses which were designed to be facilitative, to help learners make and implement decisions relating to their roles as members of the community. While a 'letter of course completion' is awarded to students who have submitted the requisite number of assignments, the award signifies participation rather than level of achievement.

Evaluation

Evaluation plays an integral role within the cycle of provision, dissemination and assimilation (see Figure 4.1.). It contributes both to course specific/learning materials concerns and to policy decisions. In addition it is expected to carry out a self-assessment of the effectiveness of evaluation in affecting decision making and to identify and contribute to the solution of methodological problems associated with evaluating community education 'at a distance'.

106

Both formative and summative evaluation are carried out on the three major areas:

1. The dissemination and support system

2. The learning materials/components

3. The outcomes for participants

Thus, for example, evaluation investigates such questions as the level and type of demand for community education courses; differences and conflicts in aims between the learning materials providers and the users; the actual use made of the learning materials by different groups of learners and any associated problems; outcomes of study; the type and range of structures of support networks and their effectiveness; the development of selection criteria for off-prints of course materials and appropriate methods of distribution.

The evaluation work is carried out primarily by two full-time, core institutional research staff with other academic and research staff carrying out work associated with the programme on a part-time basis. Other staff are called on for help during 'labour-intensive' phases of research such as observation, personal interviews and group interviewing. Other methods used include group diaries, self completion questionnaires and phone interviews.

The timing of the various studies within the evaluation programme is determined to a large extent by the decision-making time-table. The base line data collection which is always needed for management decisions has almost all been routinised, which leaves the evaluators free to design special 'one-off' studies or series of studies to investigate particular problems. However, given the speed and scale of many of the new developments within Community Education, priorities have to be revised regularly so that the evaluation input remains responsive to the concerns of the moment, as well as to the longer term or more entrenched problem areas.

As already noted, the speed and scale of the new developments in the Community Education area has been considerable and so the formal evaluation programme has, to date, concerned itself almost exclusively with provision from the Centre. It would be misleading however to say that there had been no evaluation activity within local communities.

A number of external local agencies have devised and carried out small locally based evaluation studies.

Finally, insofar as the dissemination of evaluation findings is concerned, a range of approaches and devices are used in order to ensure, as far as possible, that the findings play their role in the decision-making process. Where an issue of general concern arises, working papers are prepared, and workshops are set up by the evaluators. While full reports are prepared on the completion of various substudies, far more important is the formal feeding in of findings and recommendations to the various decision-making bodies. Formal and informal membership of key committees and groups by the evaluators greatly facilitates this process.

ORGANISATIONAL AND COLLABORATIVE FRAMEWORKS

Collaboration is a vital part of the Community Education programme at the OU. We have already indicated the reliance of the programme on outside agencies for funding. However there are two other aspects to collaboration which are just as important, albeit in different ways, namely in the identification of learners' needs, and in providing or facilitating access to national networks.

Identification of Learning Needs

Except for the partnership with the BBC, collaboration is not necessary in the undergraduate programme because the contents of courses are determined largely by the requirements of the subject disciplines and the need to provide students with coherent programmes of study. In Community Education courses our materials must be based on the needs of the learners and on the problems they face in their everyday lives. The staff at the University do not know what the needs are, what problems should be tackled, nor do they possess expertise in all the possible areas of knowledge that might be brought to bear on an everyday problem. They do however have expertise in designing integrated multi media learning materials.

It is in the area of needs identification and problems identification

108

that national agencies, particularly those which have been built up from the grass roots, are particularly well qualified to help answer. They can also provide access to or at least facilitate access to a wide range of national and international subject experts whose knowledge relates to the 'everyday' problems a course may try to grapple with.

Support Networks

The undergraduate programme established its own network of regional offices, study centres, tutors, counsellors and so on. Community Education works through existing community networks and resources and these links must be established and developed.

Organisational Structure

Community Education is one of four Sections which together make up the Centre for Continuing Education. The Centre is a part of the Open University, but has to be self-financing. There are a small core of full-time tenured Community Education staff (3 academic, 3 support staff, plus secretaries and clerks), the remainder of the staff being recruited for specific projects or courses, either as consultants or on short-term contracts.

The policies of the Centre for Continuing Education are formulated by a Delegacy for Continuing Education to which the Senate of the University has delegated certain powers. This Delegacy provides one form of collaboration in that a third of its membership comes from external bodies, these members being deliberately selected so as to represent a wide range of interests relevant to the development of continuing education.

Before a specific collaborative project is begun however, extensive position papers and proposals are discussed by the University and by potential collaborators. A detailed proposal is then considered by committees of the University before being approved by the Delegacy. During these discussions an assessment is made of the need and the objectives for the provision proposed and the likely take up, how materials will be produced, how they will be delivered and how learners will be supported.

On each major collaborative project a management committee is created to oversee all aspects of collaboration between the OU and one or more agencies. For a bilateral collaboration this committee might have joint chairmen. The production teams report to the management committee which in turn reports to the Delegacy.

CONTROL

Forward planning of specific projects within the Community Education programme is carried out by project teams and supervised by project management committees. Agreement is reached on an overall writing and production timetable for specific courses or learning packages with the University's Project Control office.

Quality Control

There are two major components of the 'quality' of learning materials: the academic quality and the quality of the material as a teaching tool. Control, or more accurately, responsibility for the safeguarding of the academic quality of the material, is based on the procedures set up for the undergraduate courses. These safeguards involve a range of academics inside the University, including not only the Project Team Chairman but also the University's Academic Board and Senate. In addition, for major projects, academics from outside the University are appointed as external assessors, and may also serve on the project management committee.

The quality of the material as a teaching tool is primarily the responsibility of the Project Team Chairman. While a variety of expertise is available to the project from the University (e.g. editors, designers, photographers, etc.) the responsibility for the final product is very much that of the Chairman.

Financial control differs somewhat from the quality control system. Initially, resource allocation is controlled by the Centre for Continuing Education within the constraints of the self-financing principle subject only to approval by the University's Planning Board. Responsibility for and approval of spending and control of spending is then exercised within the managerial hierarchy, with the Project Team Chairman being answerable to the management committee but responsible to the Head of Section and subsequently to the Head of Centre.

Evaluation is the responsibility of committed staff from the Institutional Research Division of the University's Institute of Educational Technology. Resources for evaluation are normally built into any programme or project funding, so the cost of the evaluation is borne, in the main, by the programme. However, administratively and operationally, evalution work is designed and carried out by staff outside the Community Education programme. In practice, priorities are agreed jointly between project staff and evaluators, and close liaison is maintained.

RESOURCES

Staff Levels

There are currently twenty-seven staff committed to the Community Education programme (including seven secretarial and clerical staff). Less than half of these are full-time permanent 'core' staff, the remainder being on short-term contracts, on appointment to specific projects. However the programme does have access to the wide range of academic research and technical staff working in the main University campus, although any substantial input by staff not employed by the Centre for Continuing Education does have to be paid for.

Physical Plant and Equipment

Office space is provided by the University; other physical resources (including computer facilities) and services are funded from a grant in aid from the Department of Education and Science. Access to reprographic, printing and design and editing facilities within the University is relatively easy, although for experimental work, the Community Education programme has its own IBM word processor, and darkroom and silkscreen printing facilities for the use of the materials development officer. In addition the programme is building up its own specialist library which includes portable displays of materials for use at exhibitions and conferences.

Expenditure

Clearly there has been a very rapid growth of the programme over the past three years. This growth may well continue for some time, although in the present economic climate any such forecast must necessarily be tentative. It is, therefore, difficult to give any sort of 'average' expenditure or income figures. What can be given are the figures for 1981 which are now pretty well settled, with the comment that these figures indicate the sort of scale of our financial operations.

Expenditure 1981 (Estimated)		Income 1981 (Estimated)	
Staff costs	£200,000	Fees	£280,000
Direct student costs	£160,000	Grants	£150,000
Production Budgets	£ 70,000		
Total	£430,000	Total	£430,000

Other Resources

The outline of the resources of the programme would be seriously deficient if the non-financial inputs from the external collaborating agencies were omitted. The chief 'resource' which they provide or create access to is committed manpower 'on the ground'. This volunteer unpaid manpower provides us and hence the learners with volunteer co-ordinators for organising local self-help groups, animateurs and enthusers to reach out to those in need and to publicise our provision, organisers for sponsored places schemes, and intermediaries with extensive local contacts who can participate in experimental schemes. In addition, collaborating agencies can provide meeting rooms and premises for learners to meet together when home conditions are too cramped or unsuitable for learners themselves to provide a venue.

112

Postscript: Transferability and Adaptation of Methods and Materials

The case study has described how the adaptation of course materials for a variety of delivery and learner support systems is planned into the way the materials are designed. One particular aspect of this that has surprised the staff involved in Community Education has been the success of the materials overseas. Considerable effort is made to develop materials that are relevant to the lives of people living in the UK. However, the materials have been used in other English speaking countries and have been translated into four other languages. These uses include adult and community education, as well as commercial publishing ventures. While these ventures have been particularly successful for middle class learners the association with the Van Leer network of world projects has led to the translations of the materials being used in disadvantaged areas in Brazil, France and Israel. It appears that the important finding that attractively designed activity based learning materials can be used by a wide range of learners given appropriate support, also applies elsewhere in the world - even with materials that have not been developed for the various countries and cultures. This probably highlights the dearth of appropriate materials world wide - another surprising finding given the volume of magazines, baby care literature, books and so on. Distance learning materials must fill an important gap not met by traditional publishing. It is hoped that studies such as the one for the EEC on which this book is based will lead to greater international collaboration in sharing, translating and adapting materials.

Notes and References

1. Open University Charter, para. 3.
2. 'Report of the Committee on Continuing Education' (The Open University, Milton Keynes, 1976) (The Venables Report), p. 14, para. 1.
3. The part works are sold in Brazil.

Chapter 5

THE ADULT LITERACY INITIATIVE 1974-79 UNITED KINGDOM

Arthur Jones and Alan Charnley

ORIGINS

The adult literacy initiative emerged in 1974 for a variety of reasons, which, taken together, produced a uniquely favourable climate for innovation in the adult education service.[1]

The Russell Committee (1973) recommended 'the planned exploration of new areas of work especially with the disadvantaged, and an experimental stage in the application of educational technology to multi-media learning'. The Alexander Committee (1975), the Russell Committee's equivalent in Scotland, included illiterate adults in a list of priorities in their report. But the influence of these committees of enquiry pre-dated the publication of their final reports, the very activity of collecting evidence led to research and evaluation by many field providers and out of these discussions adult literacy appeared as a priority.

Adult illiteracy in England and Wales had attracted the attention of researchers in the early 1970s. Peter Clyne mentioned the adult illiterate in assessment of the needs of the disadvantaged adult published in 1972, and R.M. Haviland completed a survey of provision for adult illiteracy in England in 1973.

As Haviland demonstrated, local education authorities and voluntary organisations had increased their provision for illiterate adults from less than ten 'programmes' in 1950 to more than 230 in 1973. The most rapid growth in numbers of students occurred from 1967. According to Haviland, some two million adults could be classified as either 'illiterate', that is, having a reading age of seven years or less, or as 'semi-literate', that is, having a reading age of between seven and nine years of age, yet he estimated that only about 5000 adults in England were receiving tuition.

In 1972, the BBC's Further Education Officers reported on this mounting evidence of need for a service for illiterate adults and argued that as non-readers obviously could not be contacted through the medium of print, broadcasting could make a unique contribution by reaching people in their homes. In 1973, the BBC Further Education Advisory Council approved a proposal to consult local education authorities and voluntary organisations with a view to a major broadcast series in this field. The BBC's intentions were announced during a conference organised by the British Association of Settlements in November 1973.

The British Association of Settlements included voluntary organisations such as Cambridge House and the Liverpool University Settlement - which was already providing literacy tuition for adults, using volunteers for one-to-one teaching. In 1974 they combined with certain other educational agencies to form a National Committee for Adult Literacy which was chaired by Lady Plowden, an educationalist of international repute, and announced a public campaign under the title 'A Right to Read'. Provision was also being made by the Army education service and in penal establishments by the Prison Education Service.

However, laudable educational plans are not always translated into action; to answer why adult literacy initiatives succeeded in 1974, we must consider the politics of the situation. Though central government was already attempting to limit educational expenditure, a good deal of political support was secured for the 'Right to Read' campaign and hence Gerry Fowler, then Minister of State for Education and Science, was able to announce a special grant of £1 million to provide the resources for a rapid expansion of literacy teaching.

Through the services of the National Institute of Adult Education (NIAE), an Adult Literacy Resource Agency (ALRA) was created to administer the grant. Some local education authorities, fearful of yet further demands on their restricted budgets, were less than enthusiastic about venturing into this field and there is no doubt that their compliance and the government's action in making the grant were precipitated by the BBC's determination to proceed. That in itself, however, had a political aspect, for the prospect of a fourth television channel was beginning to emerge and in the discussion about its allocation the concept of public-service, or 'social action' broadcasting became prominent. Hence the broadcasting authorities, and not just their education staff, were favourably disposed. In this way a combination of educational vision, social purpose and political realism released an enterprise which again proved in the words of the Alexander Report that 'supply may well stimulate demand and acts of faith must increasingly be a feature of pioneering adult education'.

In other words, what the British experience shows is the way in which dedicated educators could engage the media, not only as a prime contributor of educational resources (and the BBC's contribution in this kind is set out in a later section), but also as a major means of extending public consciousness about the problem to be tackled and of reinforcing the political will to release the funds.

It would however be simplistic to speak of a decision at this stage to adopt a multi-media solution. The three major participants - the BBC, the government, and the local educational agencies - shared the same objective (the eradication of illiteracy) but they held different views about the means. The BBC's initial concern was for an independent initiative by television and radio, with no more print materials than would normally accompany a substantial educational series; the government's intention in setting up the Adult Literacy Resource Agency was to provide resources (which in the first instance were thought to include much audio-visual and other equipment) for teaching; and the education authorities' emphasis was on schemes of local face-to-face tuition using volunteers.

Early on, however, two general problems emerged that changed the base-line for planning. The first was the recognition that individual learning from a broadcast was not likely and that therefore the main aim of the broadcasts must be to stimulate the target population to come out and seek help; and the second was that virtually no teaching materials suitable for adults existed. Out of the first grew the referral service; and out of the second grew the BBC's publications in support of the broadcasts, and ALRA's switch of emphasis from equipment to publication, and to training for the production of teaching materials.

The referral service was set up, after great difficulty over finance, by the creation of the Adult Literacy Support Services Fund, with a major grant from the Ford Foundation and smaller amounts from other major sources.[2] This was necessary because BBC licence revenue could not be used for this non-broadcast activity. Telephone referral points were established in London and Glasgow, and for a short time in one or two provincial centres, and the numbers were prominently displayed on the TV screen. Those who rang were asked to give their name and address and this was passed to the appropriate local education officer for follow-up. Hence the link between the broadcasts as a recruiting medium and face-to-face tuition became much closer. Moreover, as many of the local schemes in the early days turned to the BBC workbooks when they found children's reading material inadequate, the relationships became even closer and a multi-media project evolved almost by accident.

The NIAE research team found little perception of this interdependence among the students and volunteer tutors. The main impact of the broadcasts was in recruitment of both students and volunteers. But it was also found that the popularity of the 'On the Move' television programmes had a considerable influence on the general public's awareness of adult illiteracy and their attitudes towards it, and there can be little doubt that this change of public attitude in turn affected the frame of mind in which people sought or offered help. There was therefore more mutual support among the media and agencies involved in the work than was generally recognised by the participants.

Indeed it may be said that, without the BBC's initial decision to move into this field, little of the provision made by either central or local authorities would have happened and adult literacy could well have remained a tiny minority concern of a handful of voluntary bodies.

TARGET POPULATION

In the original plans the target population was visualised as illiterate adults, barely able to read or write beyond a few words. The BBC envisaged a double role, to give such people enough of a start at home to enable them to join a class if they so wished and to help in attracting adults into tuition by removing the social stigma attached to illiteracy. But the general experience in the first year - as the NIAE research team found - was that the severely illiterate adult was either not common or was reluctant to come forward, for the constituency embraced quite a varied range of the semi-literate. Despite the much publicised claims of the 'Right to Read' campaign, which fastened on the figure of two millions, both the extent of adult illiteracy and its nature were guessed at rather than known.

The received wisdom at the time was that individual tuition was the only effective method, chiefly because the students would be so shy and shame-faced about their deficiencies that they would shun any kind of public appearance, even in a small class. This notion could be translated into action only if sufficient volunteers came forward to help, all over the country. Thus, the BBC also produced programmes and materials designed to attract and inform volunteer tutors, and training programmes for them were broadcast on radio.

The numbers involved year by year are given in the annual reports of ALRA and its successors. Certain general features may be noted:

1. Although the proportion of the putative two millions that has so far been recruited is small (not more than ten per cent overall), all the students have by definition never been involved in adult education previously and this must count as evidence of successful outreach.

2. In the early stages four-fifths of the students were men and four-fifths of the volunteer tutors were women. More recently these ratios have become less extreme, but the majorities remain as they were.

3. A graph of the age distribution would show a very flat arc, with roughly equal proportions in the 25-35, 35-45 and 45-55 ranges and considerably fewer in the younger and older groups; though collaboration with the Manpower Services Commission in the last two years has brought rather more young students into tuition.

4. As already indicated, the proportion of the totally illiterate has not been large (the NIAE research team estimated it at less than 30 per cent in the first three years), and over a quarter of the students have been 'spellers' (that is, with reasonably adequate reading skill but poor writing and spelling). There is some evidence that the number of virtual beginners has increased in recent years.

5. Although the concept of disadvantage has been at the heart of this whole initiative, the students have not all shown the features of social disadvantage. Many are holding jobs of some intricacy and even of responsibility; many have come forward because they have been offered advancement at work that would require greater literacy than they possessed; many show astonishing ingenuity in evading discovery of their deficiency and in evolving

strategies of their own to cope with their daily lives. Although there is an appreciable minority of slow learners, and some mentally sub-normal, the majority are of average ability and intelligence and their lack of literacy cannot be ascribed to dullness.

6. As far as is known, there are no major discrepancies of social class, intellectual ability or motivation as between urban and rural literacy schemes. But in a few inner-city areas there is a preponderance of the socially deprived.

7. Finally, it is of interest to note that, especially during the first two years of the telephone referral service, an identifiable number of callers seeking help with their reading were schoolchildren.

The characteristics of those joining the scheme cannot be defined with any precision. The standards of literacy skills of those seeking help vary so much, as do the other indicators of social or occupational status, motivation, and so on, that the NIAE research team concluded that the only workable definition of an adult illiterate was, 'one who thinks he is'. That is, the perception by the individual of his need for improved literacy skills is the criterion for his inclusion in the target population. This finding, of course, raises very extensive questions about the demand for literacy - and other forms of basic education - in our society.

LITERACY MATERIALS

Introduction

As indicated above, the lack of adult materials for learning came out at an early stage as a major problem. Many of the earliest volunteers had been primary-school teachers who brought to the task both the methods and the books they had used with 6-10 year olds, and the inappropriateness of these soon became apparent. What then could be used?

When the BBC project team came to consider what print materials should accompany their television programmes (as they would for any substantial educational broadcasts) this question had to be faced. In the extensive consultations they undertook about the content and format of the programmes they were able also to gather experiences and expectations about the learning materials needed and their Students' Workbook and Tutors' Handbook were the result. These were sold in large numbers, but the evidence for their actual use is unclear. There was much criticism of their level of approach, but that may reflect more upon the variations of expectation in the field than upon the material itself. One of the most important elements in the raising of public consciousness, however, was the copyright-free material made available by the BBC and distributed mainly through the Tesco Supermarket chain during October-November 1975 (as the first broadcasts began): 1,200,000 units of this material were issued. Another was the well-known literacy symbol which was first displayed on posters in supermarkets and bookshops at this time.

The care with which the BBC approached the design of their print materials is indicated by the following extract from a report prepared for the Adult Literacy Support Services Fund:

"Our first two books On The Move (1975) and Your Move (1976) accompanied the television programmes for adult non-readers of the same name. They were built around an instructional progression devised by Catherine Moorhouse, Central Director of Literacy Schemes for the Inner London Education Authority. This progression was basically phonic - letters and sounds were introduced more or less in the order of their frequency in written English. In each unit we also tried to teach one social sight word on a whole word 'look and say' basis. Thus in the weeks when we were teaching the recognition and writing of the letter 'T', we also taught the recognition of useful words beginning with that letter which were often seen on signs in the environment: 'Tickets', 'Toilets', 'Telephones'.

This element in our aims was crucial to the design of our first book, On The Move. Each unit depended heavily on illustrations cueing the non-reader to an intelligent guess at what a group of written symbols probably said. For example, if a non-reader did not see our television programme which taught recognition of the word 'Accident', then our book unit must contain illustrations so unambiguous that he would be almost certain to deduce from them the likely meaning of the cluster of eight letters beginning with 'A' on the signs in the picture. In order to eliminate misleading detail from the picture (and to make copyright free reproduction at the local level easier) we decided to use line drawings, in which the cueing of a sensible guess at a word could be aided by extreme simplicity of image.

Besides its function in teaching the recognition of social sight words, each unit of the book had to instruct how to write a particular letter of the alphabet, both capital and lower case, and had to cue the practice of this writing. It also had to develop the easy steps of reading made possible by the blending of each new letter and sound with those previously acquired. And all this without written instructions, because the learner couldn't read such instructions, and wouldn't wish to ask for help. This placed a great burden upon the design staff of BBC Publications, and made the book a particularly challenging design task. It had to be self-explanatory to an isolated non-reader, and also adult, both in its look, style and content. We proceeded by preparing batches of units and testing them with groups of non-readers already in literacy classes all over the country. Their responses led us to realize many errors of design. Planned sequences of ideas frequently didn't work because the non-reader didn't look first at the top left-hand corner of the page, but looked randomly within it at whatever caught his eye first. Our illustrations frequently cued the wrong word in the student's mind. We redesigned each page and tested it a second time."

Equal care was shown in piloting the television programmes, and the stages of planning and re-planning have been fully recounted by David Hargreaves, head of the BBC project. The difficulty at first was that there were relatively few literacy schemes to consult and their participants were not the isolated non-readers that the programme sought to reach. These early consultants were often highly critical and even hostile to the proposed programmes and their reactions, as described by Hargreaves, were very different from those found later by the NIAE research team among students who had seen the programmes and been influenced by them. In part this is due to the sensitivity with which the BBC team reacted to the field comments they received.

Materials Provided by the BBC

For Students. Television, radio, print, and audio-cassette materials were prepared:

1. 'On The Move' (50 TV programmes, each of 10 minutes); transmitted at peak viewing time attractive to general family audiences designed to encourage the non-reader to seek local help; accompanied by a student workbook.

2. 'Your Move' (20 TV programmes, each of 25 minutes); addressed unambiguously at the non-reader and including more instructional material than 'On The Move'; accompanied by a Student Workbook.

3. 'Next Move' and 'Move On' (radio programmes), which were readings by, and about, well-known figures in the entertainment world. Printed texts were supplied for students to follow the readings; cassettes of the readings were available for further practice.

For Tutors. Radio and print materials were provided:

1. Two radio programmes: 'Helping Adults to Read' and 'Helping with Spelling'.

2. Print materials:
   - Copyright-free material - the first ten units of the Students' Workbook arranged as ten weekly sheets and available for local copying and distribution.
   - Adult Literacy Handbook, for tutors, produced first in May 1975 to accompany the radio series for tutors.
     Students' Workbook, called 'On The Move'.
   - 'Your Move', 'Next Move', workbooks to accompany the later series.
   - 'Using Current Broadcasting', and 'Uses of Current Broadcasting II', leaflets for tutors, were commissioned by the Adult Literacy Support Services Fund and distributed by both BBC and ALRA.
   - BBC Adult Literacy Newsletter, an information sheet for organisers and tutors (distinct from ALRA Newsletter: see below).

Adult Literacy Resource Agency (ALRA) and its Successors

The government grant of £1 million, originally for one year (1975-76), established, through NIAE, the Adult Literacy Resource Agency. Its terms of reference were severely limited because, under English law, education is not provided by central government but by the local authorities and the financial boundaries are complex but strict.

It was evident that the work of the Agency in creating resources could not be completed in one year and its life was extended for a further two years (1976-78). When it came to an end, it was replaced, following heavy pressure from the field, by the Adult Literacy Unit (ALU), with a much reduced budget, for two further years (1978-80). That in turn has now been succeeded by the Adult Literacy and Basic Skills Unit (ALBSU) with a wider remit than just literacy and a somewhat larger budget (approximately £½ million). There has been some continuity of staff between the three bodies and a serious attempt to maintain continuity of policy.

These agencies have had certain important effects:

1. They have been the major influence on the materials and methods used in teaching and learning.

2. They have stimulated and often directed the training of local organisers and tutors and have thus established some comparability of standards across the country.

3. By their ability to fund special projects they have stimulated innovation and experiment and have directed the attention of the local education authorities towards unrecognised areas of work: for instance, basic education courses for the young unemployed.

Materials provided by ALRA. In the following account, reference will be made only to ALRA: it should be read as meaning ALRA, ALU or ALBSU as the case may be. ALRA provided the following materials and resources:

1. Resource materials for tutors and students.

2. Advisory services.

3. Financial resources for training and the appointment (in conjunction with the local education authorities) of organisers who themselves have often used ALRA as a clearing house for resources, ideas or experimental schemes.

4. Publications for student use:
   - The Bookplace Series - a set of simple readers, produced by Peckham Bookplace in London, sponsored by ALRA
   - 'Write First Time' - a national newspaper largely written by adult literacy students - funded, then grant aided by ALRA

   The ALBSU Newsletter No 1 lists a number of Literacy Schemes which have produced publications for students which include student contributions.3

5. Publications for tutors:
   - Lesson Sheet for Trainers of Adult Literacy Tutors 1975
   - Resource Pack for Volunteer Tutors 1975
   - Newsletter, first issued May 1975, thereafter bi-monthly
   - 'Teaching Adults to Read' 1976
   - 'Training in Adult Literacy Schemes' 1977
   - 'An Approach to Functional Literacy' 1977
   - 'Helping Adults to Spell' 1977
   - 'Adult Literacy: Progress in 1975/76', HMSO 1976
   - 'Adult Literacy: Development in 1976/77', HMSO 1977
   - 'Adult Literacy: 1978/79', HMSO 1979
   - 'How's It Going: an alternative to testing students in adult literacy', by Goode M. and Holmes J. 1978
   - 'From Wages to Windscale - Worksheets and how we have used them', ALBSU 1980
   - Newsletter ALBSU from May 1980

ALRA/BBC Resources. Mention might also be made here of certain audio-visual resources produced by ALRA and BBC: for example, the cassettes to accompany the BBC 'Next Move' series on radio, the cassettes with ALRA's Trainers' Kit and Volunteer Resource Pack, and the 16mm sound colour films, also available on video-tape, produced or distributed by ALRA - 'Training Adults to Read', 'Group Tuition', 'It's No Longer A Secret' (which traces a student's successful experience) and 'A Well-Kept Secret'.

The Local Education Agencies

These are of two kinds: the 104 statutory local education authorities (LEAs) in England and Wales and the 12 in Scotland are responsible for ensuring the provision of all educational services in their areas, and most of the schemes for adult literacy are provided by the LEAs. There are however independent voluntary bodies in a number of places which provide their own schemes of literacy tuition: generally they receive financial aid from the LEA and some of them have been funded by ALRA as well.

What the LEAs have had to provide includes:

1. a referral officer to whom telephone referrals from ALSSF or elsewhere can be passed

2. a local organisation for the recruitment and disposition of volunteer tutors and the placing of students

3. accommodation for this organisation and for tuition where required

4. resource centres from which materials may be distributed and sometimes produced

5. training schemes for volunteer tutors. These have changed considerably since 1975 as knowledge of the student has accumulated, and different LEAs have developed their own styles of training. The following outline of an early scheme, however, indicates the kind of topics usually covered; this course lasts for 6-8 weeks, 2 hours per week, but other formats (e.g. a series of weekends) are common:
   - Film: 'The Well-Kept Secret', background to adult illiteracy and the problems it may cause; approaches to students; materials a volunteer tutor may wish to start collecting.
   - Mechanics of reading; pre-reading skills; display of materials; methods of teaching.
   - Diagnostic testing; a structured approach to phonetics; planning a sample lesson.
   - Practical methods for teaching adults; introduction to and display of home-made material, characteristics of the adult learner.

125

- Why people fail to learn to read; spelling; development beyond functional literacy; talk on working with slow learners.
- Structure of scheme - referring to group advisers, progress reports, help in planning a programme for a student; matching student and tutor; bringing in material to be assessed; the tutors' evaluation of the course.

Library Resources

Most schemes also involved their local library, where simple readers were provided, special sections containing series of such books were mounted and special measures to welcome students were arranged. The public libraries also acted as referral centres and it may be that the number of 'spellers' in the local schemes came largely from this source.

Conclusions

The element of distance teaching came, thus, from two main sources, the BBC and ALRA. In contrast to the Open University, which has specific student groups following a course determined by the course team, those organising literacy tuition were faced by a student body which required individual tuition, the need to proceed at an individual pace and above all, the right to specify individual objectives. This is the crux of dealing with the educationally disadvantaged. Thus both the BBC and ALRA provided examples of materials, types of materials which would lead to the development and use of further materials as chosen by a student in consultation with a tutor, or by the student alone in the light of his or her own needs.

In general adoption of one-to-one tuition by volunteer tutors increased the pressure towards this flexibility of teaching styles and materials, for the crucial element in the student's progress was the personal relationship that was created. Unless the tutor could see that the student was making progress, frustration and disappointment soon broke up the partnership; but similarly, unless the student could see the relevance of what was being attempted, motivation flagged. Everything depended on the tutor's ability to sense the student's need and to

126

respond to it by the sensitive and ingenious selection of learning materials. The repertoire from which the selection could be made was indicated by the materials produced centrally. In this way an unusual and sophisticated form of distance teaching was developed by ALRA and BBC together, with the major responsibility placed on the student and tutor; and the local training courses, stimulated by both bodies, have come to concentrate very much on the production of home-made materials, using the central materials as starting-points.

A corollary of this is that notions of standard diagnostics, testing, progress schedules and specified objectives, generally inseparable from courses of further or higher education, are quite inappropriate for students who are sharply aware of their individual needs but equally sharply aware that 8-10 years of compulsory and conventional education have failed them. This point is central to the descriptive approach and commentary in the following sections of this chapter and to the concept of distance teaching that we employ here.

MEDIA AND METHODS

Broadcasts were used primarily as means of recruitment to tuition and of enlarging public awareness. These objectives were pursued not only through the specific educational series such as the radio programmes for tutors or the TV 'Your Move', but also through incidental mention on current affairs programmes such as 'Panorama' (BBC-TV), on popular disc-jockey shows on BBC Radio 1, through short informational films in the commercial breaks on independent television, and through very many and varied kinds of output on local radio stations.

The print materials have been described and their relationship to the broadcasts indicated. Here we would simply repeat that the diverse nature of the students' needs and the sensitivity of their attitudes towards formal education make impossible the customary multi-media package, pre-determined in content, sequence, pace and goal, that is usually thought of as distance learning. Herein, perhaps, as we shall show later, lies one of the most useful lessons of the literacy project.

Something has also been said about the methods used. Generally, there were three types of tuition on offer:

−   on a one-to-one basis, in either the student's or tutor's home

－   on a one-to-one basis in a group environment
－   in a small class at an adult education centre or similar locale.

In the home-based situations it was difficult for organisers to know what methods and progress were present, and there has been a strong tendency to bring as much as possible of the teaching into a group environment. Here the opportunity for student to learn from student, even when still accompanied by a personal tutor, and for tutors to learn from one another about the use of materials or different approaches, has been found of great value.

Much of the early teaching was undertaken by school-teachers (or ex-teachers) and there was a tendency to apply school-based concepts of a 'reading scheme' in which all aspects of literacy are successively covered. More recently these concepts have given way to the kind of individual planning already described. With the move towards group tuition, however, and with the increasing trend towards courses of basic education (as distinct from simple literacy) these notions of a consistent scheme are being reinforced. The experience of success in individual tuition, however, is so strong that a large element of flexibility is retained even in groups or formal courses, and it is clearly important for this disadvantaged clientele that that should be so.

CREATION, PRODUCTION, AND DISTRIBUTION OF MATERIALS

It will already be clear that the 'system' operating in this project is much less defined than in other distance-learning schemes, partly because of the variety of agencies involved. However, some of the more interesting features of the creation/production/distribution 'system' are outlined below.

Materials Creation: Piloting and Pre-testing

The BBC undertook a substantial programme of consultation and piloting in the creation of 'On The Move'. This proved initially difficult. When the initiative started in 1974, there were a number of schemes with experience of teaching semi-literate adults. As adults in these schemes had already taken the decision to reveal themselves and come

128

forward for help and had already experienced certain forms of tuition, they were not the most suitable candidates for testing materials or piloting. But members of the true target population could not be reached and therefore current students had to be used for piloting and the experienced organisers or tutors were consulted for their ability to hazard a guess about the reactions of an uncertain future student body.

In November 1974, BBC Education held 30 consultative meetings with groups of literacy students and their tutors. Pre-testing proposed programmes revealed that students strongly rejected comedy sketches: for them the problem was a serious one. Many tutors doubted the value of programmes designed on the assumption of complete illiteracy. In April 1975, a second pilot programme based on a serial story was produced, and this too was rejected. In June 1975, a new model was produced and some two hundred adult non-readers consulted about it. By September 1975 the beginnings of a format were clear: a sketch (with two actors) dealing with a letter of the alphabet, writing to music, participation film to practise discrimination of words commencing with the letter in question, an interview with a student describing his or her experience, and, finally, the referral telephone number. The effectiveness of this process of consultation is in part attested by the popularity of 'On The Move' when transmitted and by the later Original Programme Award by the Royal Television Society. But of course the major credit must go to the producers of the programme, though again part of that credit must lie in the sensitiveness of their responses to the piloting process.

The procedures adopted by ALRA in their creation of materials were very similar. ALRA had on its staff specialists with experience of adult literacy and could through its management committee and its link to the National Institute of Adult Education call upon expertise from very many organisations concerned with adult education. ALRA materials were tested, were often produced by sub-committees of literacy specialists and often had as advisers the same people who contributed advice to the BBC series on television or radio. The creation of materials was, therefore, informally linked through personnel rather than by formal agreement between institutions, and the high degree of cross-fertilisation cannot be traced through formal team structures as is often the case in some other distance-teaching exercises.

Throughout the project there was also regular feed-back, both to BBC through the Education Liaison staff and to ALRA through the field consultants and the advisory committees, and these reactions were incorporated into the succession of materials produced by the two agents.

Materials Production

The production of the television and radio programmes followed usual BBC procedures, the production of written materials was in the hands of BBC Publications but with close links to the project team who were producing the broadcasts.

ALRA engaged an audio-visual consultant who tapped part-time assistance from the Advisory Panel, or from a group of members of the Advisory Panel who agreed to specialise. ALRA certainly used the expertise available to it through its link with NIAE. Actual production of materials was allocated to various specialist printers or audio-visual bodies .

Home-made production of materials often relied on equipment provided by teachers' resource centres in local education authority areas and on audio-visual experts in institutions concerned with teacher training. But, by definition, much was produced 'ad hoc' by amateurs using their own domestic resources, such as periodicals or newspapers from which to cull stories, pictures, diagrams or other examples.

Nothing that could be called 'course production' however occurred at any stage. Such uniformity of content or method as was achieved came from the centrally produced examples of material and from the training directed or provided by ALRA.

Distribution of Materials

The broadcasts were on the national BBC radio and television networks and on BBC local radio. Printed material was available through bookshops, retail outlets, or by post on request, apart from the initial issue of copyright-free material (see above).

ALRA's materials were distributed through local education authority networks, voluntary organisations and by post on request. In 1975 ALRA distributed 2,000 copies of the Trainer's Kit free to local education staff and 10,000 sets of the 'Resource Pack for Volunteer Tutors' on the same terms. The demand for further supplies of the latter led to about a further 22,000 being sold at cost price by 1979. As ALRA was closely concerned in training programmes, much of their materials, films, video-tapes and publications were used for training and as a consequence, further local demand was stimulated. ALRA, particularly, and the BBC to nearly an equal degree, established links with other government bodies, notably the Training Services Division (formerly Agency) of the Manpower Services Commission (MSC). These activities further augmented the network of communication and distribution.

Conclusions

In retrospect, there is little one would wish to criticise in the materials creation/production/distribution 'system'. Too much faith was placed on audio-visual aids in 1975/76; by 1978/79 more attention was being paid to producing readers of appropriate levels. It had been assumed that commercial publishers would fill that gap, but difficulties in identifying a market and in distributing to such a widely spread population made the commercial publishers hesitate. By 1979/80 publishing costs resulted in sale prices thought to be unattractive to participants, whether students or tutors. From 1975/76 onwards local schemes increasingly published in duplicated or photocopied form simple texts written by students (usually edited). 'Write First Time', a quarterly national newspaper of such writing, first emerged in 1975, and Centreprise, a community bookshops and publishing project, has added material. Further instances could be cited. The purpose of these publications was primarily to boost confidence, not only for the writers but also for other students; but it is known that some of this printed material has been used for direct teaching.

THE STUDENT OPERATING SYSTEM

Student Enrolment

Here it is much easier to describe what took place as a system, for there was a conscious effort to unify the various elements and to ensure that they operated together in the most effective way possible for the individual student. The system can be seen as a series of stages.

The first stage is the enquiry, which might result from a variety of sources. By mid-August 1978, some 49,000 would-be students had contacted the ALSSF referral points in London, Glasgow, Cardiff and Belfast. A close study of the figures week by week reveals how influential was any mention of the literacy scheme on a popular TV or radio programme, especially disc-jockey shows on radio, for the number of enquiries shot up after every such occurrence. Clearly the target group is to be found in the listening audience for such programmes.

Enquiry could also be stimulated in other ways. In some areas local radio had great influence; the literacy symbol or 'logo' displayed in the window of a shop or house brought many enquiries; social services, probation officers, clergy, district nurses and health visitors all encouraged people to approach their local schemes for help. In some parts more than two thirds of the enquiries came from sources other than the BBC referral number, but there was no clear geographical distribution. The expectation that, with only a London number to ring, the enquiries would diminish with the distance from London proved not to be the case.

The second stage was the transmission of name and address of enquirer to the local scheme. Local organisers spent much time in following up an enquirer, sometimes with no success, and many of them came to face a stark choice between contacting only those who were easily found, and spending inordinate time in pursuit of the rest, to the detriment of the area tuition that was their primary charge.

It is therefore necessary to distinguish between enquiry and enrolment. Whilst the media - broadcasting and press - were most effective in stimulating enquiry, some other influence was often necessary for that enquiry to proceed to active enrolment. The influence was most commonly personal contact, either from the area organiser, from a friend, from some other student, or frequently from a member of the family.

The third stage was placement in tuition. In the early days, when the tender susceptibilities of students were much talked about and absolute confidentiality was thought to be essential, there was great concern about 'matching' - that is, the selection of a volunteer whose personality would fit with the student's. Some schemes had elaborate selection and vetting procedures for this purpose. In the event it was found that most tutors and students were much more adaptable than that attitude suggested, and pairings are now effected by what one organiser has called 'common sense and geography'.

The fourth stage is in the progress of the tuition. Most organisers attempt to keep in regular contact with their pairs, even the home-based ones, but monitoring and support are much easier when there is a common meeting-place. Progress is usually self-assessed, and in recent times attention has been given on tutor-training courses to techniques whereby the student can make his own week-by-week assessment of his learning.

Record-keeping is therefore sometimes a problem. Records of both volunteer tutors and of adults with literacy difficulties are usually held at local levels, by the local voluntary schemes and adult centres. Calls for detailed records have often met resistance from volunteer tutors; though many are conscientious in maintaining records, most volunteer tutors are equally concerned to keep such records confidential to protect their students. Here again the problem is best met where the student is actively involved in the maintenance of the record.

A further problem that arises at this stage is that of drop-out, an extremely difficult matter to define. Home-based pairs in particular may lapse into a pattern of sporadic meeting where it is not possible to say that the student has dropped out but yet little progress is being made, and because of the isolation of such pairs and the tutor's under-standable reluctance to 'inform' on the student, the organiser may be unaware of the situation. Great efforts however are made by most organisers to encourage lapsed students to return, generally by means of an offer of a change of locale or of tutor. Recently there has been some evidence that more students who had dropped out of tuition have been returning; and there is also evidence that drop-out is less likely among students who have settled into a group environment.

Not all students who cease from tuition are drop-outs. The fifth stage of the student's progress is graduation, and instances are on record in which a student's self-set objective - it might be the passing of a driving test - has been achieved and he has retired satisfied. Unfortunately, not much is known about this stage with the majority of students, for there has been little opportunity of following up their progress after leaving literacy tuition. Subjective impressions among tutors and organisers are that the access of confidence known to have been experienced by the great majority of students will have led to more satisfactory relationships at home and at work and to a greater ability to order their daily lives. But hard evidence is scanty.

Some ex-literacy students however have gone on to other forms of study. Many of the classes in basic numeracy are comprised of such students; a number have been able to take vocational training courses; and some have progressed into examination classes for O-Level GCE or other qualifications.

What is clear from the successful students' experience is that progress is nearly always slow and the period of attendance envisaged by the system must be measured in years rather than months. Expectations of over-rapid progress in the mind of either student or tutor lead only to frustration.

STUDENT SUPPORT

This may be given by the paid professional staff, by the volunteer tutors, by other students, and often also by the student's family and friends, but the crucial link is that between the professional organiser and the volunteer tutor.

The ALRA report for 1978/79 notes the gradual increase of trained paid staff to 1,603 by that year but draws attention to the wide variation in practice between local education authorities and remarks that this is a 'cause for concern'. Where there are few trained professional staff the support systems for volunteer tutors cannot be adequate and it is then the students who are likely to suffer. Even in the best staffed areas, the numbers of volunteers to be supervised by one organiser, and their geographical spread, mean that there cannot be fully adequate support for volunteer-tutors teaching in one-to-one home schemes.

A measure of this problem can be seen by examining the volunteer force involved and comparing it with that slow growth to 1,603 professional staff.

Recruitment of volunteer tutors in most schemes was initially through the established adult education networks, through voluntary bodies and through school notice boards. However, volunteer tutors came to learn of literacy schemes from many sources - broadcasts, the Workers' Educational Association, church groups, the local press are all mentioned - or from friends who were already tutors. Sometimes, more than one source of information is quoted but the local press has seemed to be the most influential, especially in articles about the BBC's plans in the early stages. The exact influence of broadcasting in recruiting volunteers cannot be identified, for it appears often to have acted at second or third hand, or as reinforcement of an interest originating elsewhere.

The volunteers are given training (as in the example quoted above) and often the training course was used as a screening process: not a few volunteers found that the commitment demanded of them was more than they had expected and withdrew at that point.

By February 1977, some 45,000 volunteer tutors were engaged in various schemes, about 41,000 of them under local education authorities. By 1978/79, the number of volunteer tutors in post had fallen to about 37,000. In part this reflects the growing tendency to organise the teaching in groups with a trained teacher, rather than one-to-one with a volunteer. But over the period more than 75,000 volunteers had been trained and engaged. Therein lies the measure of the problem of adequate support.

A common pattern now is for volunteers to act as ancillary helpers to a group tutor. They are still engaged in one-to-one teaching and can still adapt to the individual purposes and needs of the student, but they have the benefit of continual advice and support. Moreover they have regular contact with other volunteers and can discuss their discoveries and their difficulties with their peers.

The nature of adult basic education requires that such support be readily available, for individualised tuition requires constant adaptation. As problems arise they must be solved, otherwise momentum and motivation are lost. This is again why conventional distance-learning methods are inapplicable: a package or a broadcast can give only generalised advice.

In some schemes, especially in rural areas, regular telephone contact between tutors and organiser is required. In this way a measure of continuing support can be given. But, as we have said, organisers are under heavy pressure and cannot be always at the end of a telephone. There is no doubt that the education service as a whole has seriously under-estimated the resources needed to maintain and support a volunteer scheme.

This description of the machinery for tutor-support is of course based on the premise that the link between organiser and volunteer is the essential ingredient of effective student-support, though this is

135

more evident for home-based pairs, where the tutor may be the only means of contact with the whole scheme that the student ever has.

Where a good group exists, the benefits already described for the volunteers apply even more to the students. The supervision and support of the professional teacher, the opportunities to see other students and their tutors at work, and especially the stimulus of mixing with other literacy students, all conduce to greater regularity of attendance, more awareness of progress, and above all the confidence that comes from a feeling of belonging to a purposive group activity. This confidence was identified in one of our research enquiries as the most important achievement of the students ('Concept of Success', pp 174-178) and as affording the psychological release that made skill-learning possible.

There is also evidence that where active support is given by the student's family, or by friends or workmates, this can be of great value in sustaining motivation. The desire to keep up with the family is often stated by students as a reason for joining: for instance, to read to the children, to help with their homework, to be able to write a note to school, or simply not to appear foolish before the children as they reach reading age. Moreover, it was often the wife of the student who telephoned the referral service or made the first enquiry, and the student's subsequent progress is seen as a shared achievement. Here again is evident the highly individual nature of the learning objectives and the need for the operational system to allow for this.

ASSESSMENT AND EVALUATION

The problem already identified with the keeping of records applies equally to assessment. The individual nature of the learning makes any external or standardised assessment very dubious. In some schemes opportunities are given to students, if they will, to undertake the assessments that have been introduced experimentally by the Royal Society of Arts or the City and Guilds Certificate in Communication. Relatively few candidates have emerged for these examinations and there is little prospect of their coming into general use.

Rather more students wish to prepare for other forms of assessment. Trade and occupational tests are often quoted, usually as set by an employer; some students wish to enter TOPS or other vocational training courses and require basic general education to do so; and an appreciable number need to be able to read the Highway Code and other such material in preparing for a driving test or heavy goods vehicle licence.

The problems are revealed in some of the evaluative research that has been published. The chief such study is 'The Concept of Success in Adult Literacy' (Huntington Publishers, Cambridge, 1979). In brief, this study demonstrates that skills of literacy are acquired only slowly by these adults who have already experienced many years of failure. How far they use their skills depends on the building up of their self-confidence. 'Confidence', a word often used in literacy education and in adult basic education schemes, is shown to be a complex notion; the role of the volunteer tutor is interactive and the success with which confidence is built up largely determines progress in literacy skills. Perhaps the major lessons to emerge from this study are the need to appreciate the time taken by adults with literacy difficulties to make any secure progress, and the realisation that progress can be defined only in terms of the student's individual abilities, potential and objectives.

An unpublished M Ed Thesis of the University of Liverpool - ('A Study of Adults Applying for Literacy Tuition in Liverpool', G.C. Allen, 1977) - has confirmed our view that at least two thirds of the adults with literacy difficulties who come forward were of average or above average intelligence. For such a population the explanation of their failure to learn cannot be sought in the conventional formulae of education, and the application of standardised literacy tests or intelligence tests is of very questionable utility. We have argued in 'The Concept of Success' that the whole concept of normative reading ages is inapplicable to adults whose linguistic age may be close to their chronological age, whatever their lack of skill in reading and writing. The kinds of assessment suggested by Goode and Holmes or that demonstrated in 'The Concept of Success' are much closer to the needs of the schemes as they actually operate.

So far as literacy provision in general is concerned, it is clear that the existence of ALRA as a central agency prompted local education authorities to find matching resources of their own. ALRA was not a centralising body removing local responsibility: it was a focus of resources pushing out to local areas and receiving from localities ideas and information. Its financial subventions were often necessary to start local initiatives but these moneys were always given after full consultation with and often after the request from local areas. Moreover, the fact that applications for funds in later years would be viewed in the light of ALRA's assessment of what had already been done made possible a kind of running evaluation that had widespread effect.

An evaluation of the impact of the broadcasts in the first three years is contained in 'Adult Literacy - a Study of its Impact', (NIAE, 1978). Briefly, as already shown, the main impact was upon recruitment and upon public awareness, two crucial areas for the success of the whole enterprise. Moreover, the light and entertaining style of 'On The Move', and its association in the public mind with popular entertainment personalities, helped to avoid those associations of dreary rectitude that commonly accompany educative efforts. There can be no doubt that any initiative towards general basic education for adults must be able to count on a major and positive contribution from the media especially television and radio. This is equally true at the level of local transmission as at the national.

Finally, an evaluation must be made of the quantitative success of the literacy project. As already shown, if the target population is indeed two million, less than one in ten has been reached. But the absolute numbers are impressive and they show that 'submerged minorities' can be reached by multi-media collaboration. Nevertheless, the demand for basic skills in a complex and changing modern society becomes more insistent and not less. Research in North America as well as here shows that continuing learning is becoming increasingly necessary throughout life if full participation in society is to be available, and the threshold of basic skills for embarking on that learning may also be rising. Those below the threshold cannot catch up without special help. There remains therefore much still to be done in the provision of basic learning skills, among which literacy is the most essential. And there is no ground for believing that this is a problem of the UK alone.

ORGANISATION, ADMINISTRATION

The BBC broadcasting organisation consisted of national and local broadcasts. Mrs. Jenny Stevens acted as a focal point for national enquiries, as a spokesman at conferences, as liaison officer, and as the responsible person for producing newsletters and information sheets. She was supported by the BBC's production staff whose project leader was David Hargreaves and by the BBC Further Education Officers. By having an identifiable figure at Broadcasting House, the BBC received comments from the field more effectively and quickly and had someone responsible for action. The flexibility of response by the BBC was quite impressive. At the same time, the BBC was closely linked to the National Referral Service, which was financed by the Adult Literacy Support Services Fund. The national referral service passed on enquiries to 'referral officers' in local education authorities and voluntary organisations. In turn, the Adult Literacy Support Service Fund had representatives of the National Institute of Adult Education on its board of management and the National Institute was itself responsible managerially for the Adult Literacy Resource Agency, through a Management Committee representing various interests. There were further links. The Department of Education and Science was represented on the Council of NIAE, the Management Committee of ALRA and advisory committees to the BBC. Local education authorities were similarly represented, as were the major voluntary bodies. At working levels, 'ad hoc' committees contained representatives of field workers and various types of expertise. It should be noted that by 1980 the BBC's broadcasting contribution has diminished considerably, but the Referral Service is still in being and ALRA has developed into new units.

From 1975 to October 1978 ALRA provided financial help, liaison and advisory services.

In October 1978 ALRA was replaced by the Adult Literacy Unit concerned with liaison and advisory services.

In May 1980, ALU was replaced by the Adult Literacy and Basic Skills Unit, responsible for liaison and advisory services in literacy, numeracy, and other appropriate basic skills. The evolution of ALRA to ALBSU reflects changed educational intention rather than new administrative patterns.

The national institutions - the BBC, the Referral Service (Adult Literacy Support Services Fund), and ALRA - did not exercise any legal controls over local education authorities. LEAs are free to operate as they wish. But usually, local education authorities had a referral officer who listed enquiries, and at least one area organiser (either an existing member of staff allocated extra responsibility, a full-time member of staff appointed for a short period with ALRA financial support, or a part-time officer.) The organisers (or advisers, as some LEAs preferred), recruited, interviewed, and introduced students to schemes; they recruited, trained and placed volunteer tutors, undertook various administrative duties and were responsible for the educational well being of the schemes in their area. Much of their work has devolved to the Principals of Adult Education Centres or to leaders in voluntary schemes, but the pressures on them often proved to be unreasonable and organisers in rural areas found it very difficult to carry out their duties to their satisfaction. The report 'Adult Literacy, a Study of its Impact' notes that 'it was not uncommon to find full-time organisers working up to 80 hours a week simply in coping with the influx of new students and tutors' (p 36).

The administrative structure is completed when we add the tutors. Their duty was, of course, educational to learn with the students and to teach, but there were other requirements such as maintaining progress reports and remaining in contact with organisers. Much depended on the individual tutors, but, judged administratively, there were great advantages where volunteer tutors operated in groups under the control of a professional organiser/tutor. As we have already explained the pressures on organisers, it will be readily understood that the organisers' knowledge of what was happening in home teaching was understandably sketchy, and this must be regarded as an unsatisfactory feature of the administrative structure in many schemes.

At local education authority levels there were a variety of linkages which were of some importance. Some local education authority staff established close working relationships with, among other bodies:

- local broadcasters, both BBC and Independent
- librarians, as resource providers
- social service departments, as recruiters
- psychological services of local education authorities for specialist help
- local Trade Unions
- local Employers' Associations
- personnel officers of local factories
- religious organisations and groups.

With hindsight, two features emerge for comment; first, the remarkable goodwill shown to the idea of helping adults who were lacking literacy skills, and second, the complete under-estimate of the role of the local authority organiser as the lynch pin of the administrative system.

CONTROL

We have shown how the idea of an adult literacy campaign emerged in 1973. In the summer of 1974, the Government decided to allocate £1 million for adult literacy work between April 1975 and March 1976 and ALRA was set up with an expected life of one year only. Throughout the whole period 1975 to date, there have been periods of morale-shattering uncertainty. Would ALRA continue? Would ALU continue? Would the BBC repeat programmes? At peak times? Would adult literacy work suffer if incorporated in a more general aim to offer basic education programmes for adults?

We have, therefore, to record a genuine innovative project, during which control was flexible and responsible to opportunities. In the period 1975 to 1976, the main concern was to cope with the numbers of students; by 1977 the size of the problem of adult semi-literacy had been proved, the administrative organisation had shown itself capable of dealing with the numbers that were being reached, and questions of quality came to the fore. There was, for example, a more questioning attitude to the role and value of volunteer tutors; the concern centred on the problems of monitoring and support, and the need for adequate paid staff to help the volunteers (cf. 'Perceptions of Adult Literacy Provision in 1979', Jones H.A. and Charnley A., ALU 1979). There has been a steady decrease in students being taught in homes (tutors' or students') and an increase in small classes and group tuition in which one-to-one attention is given. Thus supervision and quality control have increased at the most crucial point, namely at the student-teacher interactive level.

Nevertheless, the current restrictions on educational spending are damaging literacy schemes like other sectors of adult education. Although the new ALBSU has a promised life of three years, experience shows that this is too short for the establishment of an effective scheme and for the individual student to make real progress. Forward planning of a comprehensive service of basic education, in which literacy may well be the largest component, is imperative if the needs of the educationally disadvantaged are to be met. It must be remembered that the broadcasts of 'On The Move', which in effect precipitated the whole literacy effort, began in October 1975; but the BBC's decision to embark on the project was worked out in 1972-3 and David Hargreaves's detailed account of its progress shows how tight was the time-table even so.

RESOURCES

Staffing in the local educational authorities in England and Wales by 1978/79, totalled 157 full-time staff, 512 part-time organising staff, 306 full-time staff partly responsible for adult literacy and 3,608 paid part-time teachers. As there were 104 local educational authorities, it is perhaps more interesting to average the figures per authority. The crucial figure is the 157 full-time staff: 1½ per authority. As an example, to assess the adequacy of that level of supervisory staff, consider that it takes a full hour to drive from the education office in Cambridge to that in Peterborough, both cities being within the same local educational authority. In metropolitan areas, distances are less but travel may still take equal amounts of time. In 43 of the authorities the full-time and other staff had to share existing secretarial provision: the ALRA report for 1978/79 draws attention to the general inadequacy of secretarial support. So one may go on: 41 of the full-time and 303 of the part-time staff were funded by the Manpower Services Commission (ALRA report, 1978/79, p. 7). But in 1980 the MSC has also suffered financial limitations and so this has been cut.

Yet the work continues. In 1978/79 the number of volunteers engaged reached 37,356; and of students, almost 70,000. But in an increasing number of areas the students are being charged fees, where previously tuition was free. How long it will be possible to sustain a volunteer service when the recipients are required to pay is open to question. In one area during the first year of the scheme serious opposition was expressed by some volunteer tutors to the idea of continuing to give their service when the LEA was charging for it.

Broadcasting costs for the period 1975/76 to 1977/78 were £1,024,200; the Adult Literacy Support Services Fund absorbed a further £201,600, mainly for the Referral Service, making a total of £1,225,800.

Between 1975-78, ALRA disbursed about £3 million; in April 1978, ALRA's disbursements to local education authorities ceased, but the Rate Support Grant Settlement for 1978/79 was adjusted to take in the additional costs of adult literacy work estimated at £1.3 million. Local education authorities are not however legally bound to spend any part of the Rate Support Grant on specific purposes, so there were differences in the exercise of financial support from that date. ALRA's successor, ALU, received £300,000 per year from April 1978, to April 1980, and its successor ALBSU has received £500,000 for the year 1980/81, with funding guaranteed until 1983/84, though at an unspecified level.

Taking into account the estimated local education authority expenditure, and the expenditure of the Manpower Services Commission, it is probable that some £7 million were spent on adult literacy in the period 1975/78 and since 1978 at least a further two million, making a total of some £9 million by 1980/81 for England and Wales alone. To these figures, we must add expenditure for Scotland and Northern Ireland. They must dispel the notion that a service staffed mainly by volunteers can be laid on for little cost.

But looked at in another way the above figures show an average annual cost - including broadcasting, ALU, LEAs and voluntary bodies - of approximately £1.8 millions 'in toto'. In 1979/80 there were 37,356 students registered in England and Wales. This means that for each registered student the annual cost is less than £50 and in that figure no allowance is made for the educational spin-off for the general public and for the volunteer tutors, whose own learning - about the nature of literacy, about the demands of our society, about the effects of educational disadvantage, and about the life-styles of people from different milieux - is in the eyes of some observers one of the most notable achievements of the whole literacy project. Indeed, if one classes the volunteers as learners too, then the £1.8 millions provided valuable education for over 110,000 participants in 1979/80 and the annual per capita cost comes down to £16. We would argue that there are no other sectors of education that can show cost-effectiveness of that order.

Such per capita costs are surprising and they prompt questions as to why no greater provision is found possible for this area of grave disadvantage. Yet we cannot but be encouraged that society in the UK has recognised the problem of semi-literacy and has found the political will to allocate resources to their alleviation. What the history of the adult literacy project shows is that

— outreach to a submerged and disadvantaged population is feasible
— the combination of broadcasting and other forms of tuition is possible and highly effective
— there is a great reservoir of voluntary goodwill waiting to be tapped for socially desirable ends
— a substantial initial investment can bring about a notably cost-effective service
— a national multi-media enterprise can be created in which full play can be given to the personal need and circumstance of the individual student
— a project of this kind can have widespread influence on the public mind about a particular form of social and educational deprivation.

Notes and References

1. H.A. Jones and A.H. Charnley, 'Adult Literacy: a Study of its Impact' (National Institute of Adult Education, Leicester, 1978), pp. 12-19.
2. Jones and Charnley, pp. 14-15.
3. Local Literacy Schemes which have produced publications for students include:
   - Cambridge House Literacy Scheme, (131 Camberwell Road, London SE5)
   - Canning Books, (73 Canning Street, Liverpool 8)
   - Friends' Centre, (Ship Street, Brighton, E. Sussex)
   - Gate House Project (c/o ICI Blackley Works, Waterloo Street, Blackley, Manchester 9)
   - Hackney Reading Centre, (136 Kingsland High Street, London E8)
   - Peckham Publishing Project, (13 Peckham High Street, London SE15)
   - Pen Friend Scheme, ALSSF, (252 Western Avenue, London W36)

Chapter 6

DANISH FOR ADULTS
DANMARKS RADIO

Peter Olaf Looms

ORIGINS

Needs leading to Establishment

The needs leading to the establishment of the Danish for Adults ('Dansk for Voksne') project were by no means exclusively educational. Two aspects in particular merit attention:
- the decision-making process which led to a decision to embark on the Danish for Adults project and
- the institutional context - adult education and educational broadcasting for adults - in which this process took place.

The Decision-Making Process. The origins of Danish for Adults can be traced back to a speech given by the then Minister of Education, Ritt Bjerregaard, to the National Council for Youth and Adult Education on September 24th, 1975.

In her speech, the Minister drew attention to the shift in priorities which had taken place in the education system in the course of three decades. Whereas resources had been concentrated on the expansion and development of the school system during the fifties and the sixties, the early seventies had seen an increasing interest in, and awareness of, the educational needs of adults in general, and of adults suffering social and educational deprivation in particular. Mention was made of UNESCO's 3rd World Conference of Adult Education in 1972, at which these 'forgotten groups' had been the subject of considerable attention.

In connection with the provision of a system of continuing education, the Minister felt there was a potential danger of aggravating educational inequality, if the recipients were to be those who had already received the lion's share of educational opportunities. To combat this danger, it would be necessary to implement changes on two fronts: to develop existing adult and further education provisions to ensure that those

145

seeking a second chance could do so, and to work with outreach activities aimed at the large forgotten group, who previously had not felt the need to avail themselves of adult or further education, or to take part in cultural activities of any kind.

It was in the context of continuing education that Ritt Bjerregaard asked the Council to commission a number of pilot projects aimed at these groups. In addition to outreach activities, attention was also to be paid to the content of, and methodologies underlying, educational provisions which could meet the felt or latent needs of these deprived groups. Ritt Bjerregaard outlined three models for pilot projects. Models I and II concerned various kinds of outreach activity, and pilot projects based on these two models were carried out by a number of adult education associations from 1976 to 1978. A consolidated report on these projects was published by the Council in 1979.[1]

Model III, which forms the basis of Danish for Adults, was described by the Minister as follows:

"Model III - co-operation between adult education bodies and the mass media - should be primarily an educational option for those with a limited educational background, and as a consequence would be a complex project. It would be advisable to limit the geographical extent of the pilot study. The aim should be to test the necessary co-operative mechanisms:
– co-operation among adult education bodies themselves,
– co-operation between the mass media and adult education,
– outreach educational activities
and the content, level, organisation and methods required in large-scale compensatory adult education."

In reponse to this request, a working party was set up in November 1975 to prepare a pilot project based on this model.

A proposal was submitted to the Minister in June 1976 which included recommendations concerning the target population, geographical extent, core content, organisation and evaluation of the project.

The proposal was adopted in a modified form by the Minister in December of that year. In the light of the evaluation findings described later in this chapter, some of the modifications were to be of crucial significance, hinging as they did on the question of formal versus real competence.

It is therefore of interest to note the wording of the working party recommendation and the version adopted by the Minister. The working party suggested that the common core

". . . should be of immediate value to the participants, giving them a real competence or benefit in connection with later study or work".

The curriculum was to be open-ended, taking into account

". . . the experience and initiative of the individual participants, enabling the work of a given group to lead in directions dictated by their circumstances, attitudes and intentions . . . The accent should be on the training of communicative skills, i.e. to make oneself understood and to understand communications of others in the mother tongue, in mathematics and in one or more foreign languages."

In her reply dated December 20th 1976, Ritt Bjerregaard thanked the Council for its proposal which

" . . . outlines new means for an understanding of the concept of competence.

However, I am of the opinion that the mere fact that radio and television are to be employed in an attempt to reach a wider range of social groups with established educational opportunities leading to formal qualifications - in this case lower and upper secondary examinations in individual subjects - involves such imposing challenges as regards the division of work, co-operation on the part of local adult education centres and the media that the project should be limited to the dissemination of this educational opportunity in the first instance."

The emphasis in the Minister's reply was on the development of existing educational provisions, on an existing curricular framework and on formal qualifications, whereas the working party proposal emphasised a student-centred curriculum leading to communication and numeracy skills of immediate value to the individual.

Following the adoption of the modified proposal, the Council set up a planning group including representatives from the county education authorities of Bornholm, Sønderjylland and Aarhus, Danmarks Radio, the Danish Employers' Confederation and the Danish Trades Union Congress, under the chairmanship of Johannes Nymark Jensen, a senior inspector from the Ministry of Education.

The pilot project was split into two phases: phase 1 concerned local initiatives using existing materials in a number of subjects, and phase 2 concerned Danish for Adults.

The Institutional Context. The Danish for Adults project involved five partners:
–   the education authorities and the further education centres of the counties of Bornholm, Sonderjylland and Aarhus
–   the Ministry of Education
–   the educational broadcasting department of Danmarks Radio.

In its final form, the project concerned the teaching of Danish to adults under the provisions of existing legislation, the Act on Single Subject Teaching preparing for an Examination 1977. This Act covers further education provisions leading to the lower secondary school leaving examinations (referred to here by their Danish abbreviations FSA, FSU) and the higher preparatory examination (HF). For a more detailed account of the Danish education system, see the English language edition of the Danish Central Council of Education report 'U-90' [2].

The conception, planning and implementation of the project took place over a five-year period (1975-1980), during which a number of significant developments took place in adult education and educational broadcasting.

It is important to note that co-operative ventures of this kind have a considerable lead-in time, during which the partners themselves undergo changes in response to variations in the political, economic and social climate. As will be seen from the following outline of the changes which the partners to Danish for Adults underwent, the co-operative framework for such a project has to allow for developments of this kind:

1. Legislative changes affecting the teaching of Danish to adults.
   The provision of courses for adults leading to examinations was introduced in 1958. These courses were run by adult education associations under the provisions of the Leisure Time Adult Education Act. The very idea of introducing examinations in the field of liberal adult education was felt by many to

be contrary to adult education traditions in Denmark.

The provision was changed in 1968, at which time the principle of a modular, or single subject, system was introduced. Participation in these courses rose from 0.1% of the adult population in 1960 to 1.5% in 1974.

In 1977, further education and liberal adult education parted ways, further education coming under the Act on Single Subject Teaching preparing for an Examination, and liberal adult education continuing under the Leisure Time Adult Education Act.

2. Developments at county level.

As a result of the 1977 Act, further education became the responsibility of the county education authorities, and the new county-run Further Education centres experienced considerable administrative problems in 1977 and 1978 during the running-in period.

After almost a decade of rapid growth, further education began to feel the impact of declining economic growth in the course of 1979, the year Danish for Adults was to start. There was a fair degree of uncertainty as to the likely impact of media-based outreach activities. In some quarters it was feared that television could give rise to a large increase in student intake on Danish courses at a time when education budgets at county level were either being frozen or cut back.

As regards audio and video cassette recorders, the copying and distribution of taped materials, teaching materials in general, and teachers' salaries, none of these required new legislation or special funding.

3. Developments in curricula and the role of the Ministry of Education.

Curricular guidelines for both lower secondary schools and further education courses leading to the two lower secondary examinations (FSA and FSU) were changed as the result of legislative reform in 1975, and new curricula were introduced in the 1976-77 academic year.

The provision of a tutor system in connection with Danish for Adults required a ministerial circular. This was forthcoming in June 1979 and allowed for such provisions in the three counties concerned. The circular was later revised, extending the provisions to the whole country for the 1980-81 academic year.

Finance for activities not covered by county education authorities or Danmarks Radio was borne by the Ministry: extraordinary educational counselling, extraordinary publicity materials in the three counties and expenses arising from meetings of the planning and management committees of the project. The Ministry also contributed to the evaluation of the project.

4. Developments in educational broadcasting

In the course of the Danish for Adults project, responsibility for educational broadcasting changed hands. Prior to April 1st 1977, schools broadcasting and educational broadcasting for adults was the sole responsibility of Danmarks Radio. Since that date, the educational broadcasting department has been wholly financed by the Ministry of Education. Proposals for adult education series are discussed with an advisory committee for adult education under the National Institute for Educational Media and are then submitted to the Minister of Education for her approval. Responsibility for educational broadcasting thus rests with the Minister, whereas it lies with the Broadcasting Council for all other broadcasting in Denmark.

Changes in the Danish Copyright Act as of July 1st 1977 provided for the off-air use of educational radio and television programmes by educational institutions for a period of four academic years after the first transmission date.

As the result of this change, most county educational media centres provide copies of radio and television programmes usually on a loan basis, and provisions for adult education are being expanded to match those for schools.

Analysis and Definition of Needs.

The analysis and definition of needs were closely related to the political goal behind the various projects commissioned by the Minister in 1975.

150

Danish for Adults

The overall aim was to provide compensatory adult education - in this case in the mother tongue - for those with a limited educational background in an attempt to bridge the 'educational gap' between the younger and older sections of the population.

In a recent study of adult education in Denmark conducted by the National Institute of Social Research, the authors, Bunnage and Hedegaard, concluded that:

"... the study indicates that the present situation within the field of adult education, insofar as it might be attributed the objective of compensating or equalizing earlier disadvantages especially for the educationally and occupationally poorly equipped - falls far short of the goal. On the contrary, inequalities are accentuated. Innovation in the form and content of adult education is required if the achievement of less educational inequality is to be a real political goal."[3]

The most widely-used yardstick for educational deprivation is the number of years of school education. Whereas all school children today receive a minimum of nine years of primary and secondary school education, more than half (54%) of the adult population went to school for seven years or less, as shown in Table 6.1 below:

Table 6.1: Level of School Education

Proportion of a given age group having received 7 years of school education or less.

AGE GROUP	MALE	FEMALE
20 - 29	19%	16%
30 - 39	51%	46%
40 - 49	68%	63%
50 - 59	76%	74%
60 - 69	77%	81%
TOTAL %	55%	53%

Source: 'Levevilkaar i Danmark' ('Living Conditions in Denmark'), Copenhagen, Danmarks Statistik/Socialforskningsinstituttet 1980, Table 5.1, page 107. All figures for 1976.

151

Not everyone in this category - those having studied for seven years or less - was felt to be in need of basic education in Danish, but obviously a significant proportion might benefit from the opportunity to 'catch up' on education which had not been available to them when they were of school age.

Initially the analysis and the definition of needs of the target population was conducted by a small working party ('the Danish working group') consisting of a teacher from each of three counties, a shop steward from SID, the Danish Federation of Semi-skilled Workers, David Bunnage from the National Institute of Social Research, and staff from Danmarks Radio.

Later in 1978, these inputs were supplemented by thirty or so case studies prepared for Danmarks Radio by social workers and employment counsellors in two of the three counties. Each case described the educational, social and working background of an adult from the target population. Also included were the individual's and case writer's assessment of needs 'vis a vis' Danish, in particular communication skills.

In order to assess the feasibility of participating in a Danish for Adults course - either conventional classroom instruction or the distance learning option - the case also included a description of the study environment and study resources available at home, as well as indications of the family's and workmates' attitudes to adult and further education.

Social workers and employment counsellors were chosen in preference to professional interviewers for a number of reasons:
-   the difficulty of getting subjects with, in many cases, an unsuccessful school background to talk freely about themselves
-   the need to establish an atmosphere of mutual trust in which data for individual and anonymous case studies could be collected
-   the subsidiary aim of promoting better long-term contacts between social welfare and educational services in the area concerned.

Why a Mass-media Distance Learning Solution?

In Danish for Adults, distance learning was adopted as one of several options from which adults could choose. Three main types of option were offered:
-   a conventional course based on classroom instruction

– a course comprising both classroom instruction and distance learning
– a course comprising distance learning and tutorials

The distance learning option was primarily for the following categories of adults:

– those with working hours which preclude their attending courses at a given time on a particular day on a regular basis (15-20% of the adult population fall into this category)
– young adults with children for whom baby-sitting is a problem
– those with physical handicaps limiting their mobility or those with handicapped members of their family
– those for whom the travelling time to and from the nearest Further Education centre is prohibitive.

The use of radio and television to support learning activities had the following specific aims:

1. The drama documentary TV programmes (broadcast prior to the start of Danish courses) was to have an informative and a recruiting role, giving a first-hand impression of some of the problems to be tackled prior to enrolling in a Further Education course.

2. The broadcast schedule, by covering the whole course period, should contribute to a reduction in the drop-out rate for Danish for Adult courses compared with conventional Further Education courses in Danish.

3. Distance learning students should be able to receive much of their instruction via the media at home and/or use television and radio materials off-air at the local Further Education centre at times convenient to themselves.

4. Television and radio materials should be an aid to teachers of conventional courses, facilitating, in particular, individualisation.

TARGET GROUPS

The target group for Danish for Adults comprised adults with a limited educational background who have not previously taken part in adult education, and those who have been prevented from following existing courses in Danish due to the inflexible nature of such provisions.

An analysis of the case studies mentioned above indicated a considerable variation in the felt needs, educational background and study skills of potential participants.

Those mentioning the mother tongue and their requirements in daily life tended to emphasize the formal aspects such as spelling and punctuation.

MATERIALS, MEDIA, AND METHODS

Three Basic Options

As mentioned above three main types of option were offered:

Classroom Instruction, supported by coursebooks, and radio and television programmes (usually on cassettes) in the class.

Variant A, the standard course, comprised 192 hours of instruction from late August/early September to May the following year. Variant B, the concentrated course, comprised 120 hours of instruction normally over the same period. In this case, the media were to be used primarily for review or revision purposes. Variant U, the extended course, comprised 320 hours of instruction over one or two academic years.

It was anticipated that the majority of those enrolling for courses would follow Course A. It was thought that those who had not previously participated in adult education and/or had limited study skills would require a lot of support initially which could best be provided in a more familiar classroom context. Course B was for those who had previously attended adult education classes, and Course U was for those with limited pre-requisites.

A Combination of Classroom Instruction and Distance Learning. This option comprised one-fifth classroom instruction and four-fifths distance learning, in that 38 hours of instruction with a teacher were provided. Outside classroom sessions, those following Course C were expected to work with the course books, and the radio and television programmes at home (on-air in the case of television) or at the local Further Education centre (off-air use of radio and television).

The teacher responsible for classroom instruction was also able to correct and discuss individual work as on Course A, although there was no provision for tutorials as such.

Course C was intended for those with well-equipped study skills who would not need much assistance.

'Self-Service' Distance Learning. This option, Course D, comprised counselling prior to the course and a combination of distance learning and tutorials. Provision was made for telephone and face-to-face tutorials, supplemented with monthly group sessions for those wishing to participate.

Each individual had, on average, 16 hours of tutor time. In terms of resources this is equivalent to one twelfth of the teacher hours for Course A, twelve being the minimum number for starting a class of that kind.

Materials

The following materials were produced by Danmarks Radio for the Danish for Adults project:

1. A twenty-minute introduction to the project, transmitted during peak evening viewing on August 20th and 25th 1979 and linked to telephone referral services in the three counties.

2. Six twenty-five minute drama documentaries broadcast every evening from August 12th to 17th focusing on the lives of two families. In the course of the series, one of the women, an unemployed semi-skilled worker with teenage children, decides to take a Further Education course, in order to get the necessary entry requirements for a vocational education and training course. We see a number of events leading up to this decision, and the (mixed) reactions of her family and friends. The series had two aims: to further an awareness of the sort of problems facing those who wish to follow an adult education course for the first time, not just in the target .population but also in the population at

large, and to act as 'non-written' texts in further education classes of Danish. The series was repeated.

3. Eighteen 'instructional' television programmes (15 minutes each). The first programmes dealt with skills of use in Danish courses: taking notes, making summaries and informal minutes, making full use of public lending library facilities. Examples in these programmes were taken from the drama documentaries or from other well-known television programmes, such as the main evening news. The series also included short interviews with contemporary authors whose works were included in the course books.

4. Eighteen radio programmes (15 minutes each). These programmes attempted to cover ground not dealt with in the television programmes and in the course books, especially topics such as music and archive materials where the medium could be fully exploited.

5. Five course books of 40-50 pages each, built around a central theme in each case. There was also a grammar book, and a user's guide to the material, suggesting course plans for the various options.

The materials outlined above formed the 'common core' of the project. In a classroom setting, the teacher and students were recommended to select texts and programmes from the package, supplementing them with other materials as required. Provision was also made at county level for the production of supplementary written and taped materials. In the case of distance learning, detailed study plans were to be worked out for each student, taking into account the fact that their requirements and interests would differ from individual to individual, and that some of the participants would be starting later than others.

Influences on the Nature of the Materials and Courses

As the project involved further education leading to the lower secondary leaving examination (FSA) in Danish, it was perhaps to be expected that the most significant influence was the 'backwash' effect of the examination and, to a lesser extent, the curricular guidelines for the subject.

The role of certificates should also be mentioned. Danish and Mathematics examinations at FSA level are almost universal entrance requirements for a number of short vocational training courses. There has also been a tendency in Denmark to increase the minimum formal entrance requirements for both vocational courses and higher education in the last ten years. Whether this reflects a general raising of standards, or an administrative response on the part of those faced with the demanding task of selecting candidates from increasing numbers of applicants is a moot point. The 'cuckoo' effect, i.e. applicants with formidable formal qualifications displacing applicants for vocational courses with practical, rather than theoretical qualifications, has also had an impact on the importance of certification. For a number of participants in further education, especially the unemployed who number approximately 11% in the Danish for Adults project, this continual raising of minimum requirements elsewhere in the education system makes for a lot of uncertainty about future admission and employment prospects.

At the institutional level, the 'backwash' effect of the examination was very clear in the requests made by teachers of Danish in the three counties regarding materials. Genuine concern on the part of teachers that their students should pass the examinations often overshadowed the felt communicative needs of the students themselves. At this level, too, pressures were often in conflict with each other. When discussing a pilot version of one of the course books, teachers asked for broader margins to allow room for student notes, whereas principals and county education authorities later pointed out that the five course books would have to be re-useable. Similarly, teachers and educational counsellors were strongly in favour of splitting the printed materials into five books, rather than publishing the same materials in one thick volume. The increase in the total cost of a set of five - thin - course books meant that in one county the price was about D Kr 10 (approximately £1 sterling) more than the average 'per capita' materials allowance.

As television and audio cassettes could be copied and distributed by the county educational media centres, and as audio cassette recorders were readily available, the only significant constraints regarding the electronic media concerned the number of video units available at each Further Education centre and their availability to distance learning students. Although timetabling at these centres ensured that almost all Danish classes could use video as and when it was relevant, this was not the case for the 'self-service' students. Plans to allow access to video on demand (in the evenings and at weekends) ran into practical difficulties: who was to be responsible for the equipment and cassettes, and lock up when the student was finished? These problems had been foreseen but were not resolved during the first year (1979-80).

One of the pressures - the decision by the county of Aarhus to standardize video equipment - greatly eased in-service teacher training. In the course of the first year, the lack of technical breakdowns probably contributed to the greater utilisation of video in that county compared with Sonderjylland, where both the VCR and U-matic standards were in use, and where there were several different models.

Student pressures regarding the contents of the courses were taken into consideration by the course book writers, all of whom were teachers of Danish at Further Education centres. Thus formal aspects of language use (punctuation, spelling, grammar) were dealt with early in the course along-side study skills. A conscious attempt to 'sell' a broader conception of language and communication was made from the start.

CREATION, PRODUCTION, AND DISTRIBUTION OF MATERIALS

Materials Creation

The overall framework of the Danish for Adults project was altered several times during the planning of the project. Initially, the hope had been to limit the role of television to outreach activities, the assumption being that sufficient audio-visual materials relevant to adult courses of Danish already existed. Courses in Danish based on programmed instruction had already been run for several years in the county of Sønderjylland, so the assumption that suitable materials for distance learners could be found was quite reasonable. A closer examination of the existing materials stock for adult learners revealed, however, that those which did exist could not be used in Danish for Adults.

The Danish working party mentioned in the 'Origins' section, having worked on the needs of the target population, then looked at a course framework which could meet these needs. By May 1978 they were discussing the synopsis of a drama documentary series which was to be the mainstay of the project. At this stage it was felt that a modest production of radio programmes and printed materials would be needed to supplement the series.

At a meeting held in early June 1978 the project steering committee added to its demands regarding the contribution of the media, and the framework proposed by the working party had to be altered accordingly. It was stressed that the media and printed materials should form the mainstay of the course, enabling those who had no other alternatives to follow it on their own and take the examination if they chose to do so. It was only at this point that the importance and requirements of a distance learning option were stressed. Danmarks Radio subsequently approached the National Institute for Educational Media, which in turn asked for a change in production plans for 1979, to allow for the production of eighteen instructional television programmes and a similar number of radio programmes.

At this stage, the drama documentary series had a dual role. It was to help create an awareness of the problems facing those wishing to participate in adult education, and it also had to provide suitable examples of communication successes and problems in the course itself. Having been transmitted 'in toto' for the former role, it was then to be repeated as the lead-in to one of five modules. A module would thus consist of an episode from the series, a course book which exploited in depth a theme from the episode in question and three instructional television and radio programmes.

The theme of the module was to be further developed in the three instructional television and three radio programmes for that module. Examples were to be taken from the drama documentaries, or from the media themselves. The framework at this stage could be termed a highly integrated multi-media course, in which course books and drama documentaries were the dominant elements.

The extent to which the components of the course formed an integrated whole was modified when course book writers took over from the Danish working party. The course book writers felt reluctant to commit themselves exclusively to themes or topics dealt with in the drama documentaries, so for this reason the link between the two became more limited in the final version of the course. An additional reason was that the scripts were written consecutively, not concurrently. Scripts were prepared for the drama documentaries and were approved before the course book writers had begun work.

159

Drama Documentaries. The series was entitled 'Ugen Ud' (the translation being 'a whole week'). The synopsis was discussed with the Danish working party in the spring of 1978, and scripts were produced in the autumn. Production began on location in February 1979. The first two episodes were available for discussions with teachers in May, and the remaining four in July.

Course Books. The Danish working party came up with modified proposals for the course books and the instructional materials in the summer of 1978. Some specimen units were written by the teachers in this working party, and these were assessed by a number of subject specialists including advisors at the Ministry. In November 1978, two teachers of Danish at a Further Education centre and a professor of Danish at the University of Copenhagen were invited to write the course books. Following discussions with Danmarks Radio and the social workers in the county of Aarhus who had prepared case studies, this team outlined a model on which they felt the course materials should be based. With one substitute, this team started work on the course books in February 1979 and produced scripts for the five books in five months. The producer responsible for both the instructional television programmes and radio programmes and the course book writers held frequent meetings from March to July 1979.

Instructional Television Programmes. These were designed to support material covered in a given course book. Television scripts for a given module could first be written as and when the scripts for the appropriate course books were available. Television scripts were the work of one of the two presenters in the programmes, who was also a former colleague of the three course book writers. Originally, plans had been made to pilot the first module of the course in conditions approximating to a normal course and normal distance learning situation.

Even though two pilot television and radio programmes were prepared along with a sizeable chunk of one of the course books, it proved impossible to try out these materials in a normal course setting, and piloting was limited to screenings for a variety of groups (members of the Semi-skilled Workers Union branch in Glostrup, at a merchant marine school, members of a housewives' association and students of Danish enrolled at a Further Education centre).

160

Radio Programmes. Scripts for the first ten radio programmes were written by a team consisting of the television script writer, another teacher of Danish from Aarhus and the producer. Radio production took place concurrently with the instructional television programmes.

User's Guide. This was written by all those involved in script writing, following the in-service teacher training courses for all Danish teachers involved in the project. Feedback and suggestions from the teachers involved were fed into the User's Guide, which was published a month after the courses (i.e. in early September), before the transmission of the course proper. The eighteen instructional television programmes and the User's Guide were revised in 1980, for transmission in 1980-81.

Materials Production

The course books were written by the writers' team described above. The television and radio producer acted as materials co-ordinator, and the physical production of the course was done by in-house graphics and text designers from the publications section of the educational broadcasting department. The head of this section acted as editor. The books were printed by one of a number of commercial printers with which Danmarks Radio works on a regular basis. Thanks to the working routine of the publications section and the printers, the very demanding deadlines for the course books were met. Final copies or proofs of all the course books were ready by early August 1979 in time for the in-service teacher training courses.

Production problems and the need to drop the piloting of the project were due exclusively to the late date on which the script writers were engaged.

Materials Distribution

Danish for Adults was fortunate in having a distribution system which had already been developed, so problems in this area were very limited.

Written Materials. These were available from the publications section of Danmarks Radio or through bookshops all over the country. Orders placed by institutions directly were despatched on the same day, so delivery time was commonly 24-72 hours, subject only to the workings of the parcel post system. Students enrolled at a Further Education centre (both class students and distance learners) were given the materials free of charge on a loan basis.

'Spontaneous' distance learners and classes of Danish being run under the Leisure Time Adult Education Act bought the course books singly or in sets, depending on their requirements.

Drama Documentary Series. The six episodes were transmitted every night for six nights in August 1979 and were then re-broadcast at monthly intervals (Tuesday evenings at 7.00 p.m.) for on-air users. The series was available to institutional users from all three county educational media centres on a loan basis, or recorded on the institution's own video cassettes. This service was free of charge.

Instructional Television Programmes. These were transmitted on Tuesdays at 7.00 p.m. with a repeat the following Saturday afternoon. The series was available on the same terms as the drama documentaries. As the institutional television programmes were broadcast for the first time throughout the year, off-air use was limited by the transmission schedule.

Radio Programmes. The first ten programmes were broadcast 'en bloc' on August 13th 1979 and were available for off-air use as audio cassettes after that date from the county media centres or from the National Institute for Educational Media. Further Education centres lent cassettes to distance learners as appropriate, and in some cases cassette recorders were also supplied for the duration of the course. For on-air use, the programmes were transmitted throughout the year on Tuesdays at around 8.00 p.m.

Operational problems. A number of book parcels despatched by Danmarks Radio were crushed in the automated sorting equipment at the Post Office terminal in Copenhagen, in spite of the fact that the books were packed in Post Office-approved boxes. The project coincided with the running-in of the sorting equipment, and postal delays also affected a few per cent of books despatched.

The copying of video cassettes was relatively trouble-free. Recording quality was consistently high, but some users of the VCR-standard cassettes experienced tracking problems. U-matic-standard cassettes were consistently reliable.

The distribution of video and audio cassettes at county level sometimes created difficulties. In some areas there was a weekly delivery, so users sometimes had to wait up to eight or nine days after the first transmission date for a cassette.

In one of the counties, use of video was delayed as the necessary hardware was not delivered on time for the start of the course.

Radio programmes on audio cassettes ran into unforeseen difficulties. In Aarhus, a technical error when recording the first ten programmes broadcast 'en bloc' resulted in poor quality cassettes, and the source of the problem was not identified for several weeks. It took an additional month to get hold of a working master from which new cassettes could be copied. Cassettes for dictation recorded by a team of teachers in Aarhus for use in the county did not suffer from this problem.

Delays of up to a fortnight were experienced on occasions when ordering cassettes from the National Institute for Educational Media.

Teachers and media centres were unanimous about the advantages of having all the video and audio programmes transmitted 'en bloc' before the course. This would enable a more flexible exploitation of the materials, freed from the limitations of the transmission schedule, and would also make it possible for teachers to see/hear programmes prior to their being used in class or by distance learners. Although block transmission of radio programmes in Denmark presents no problems, daytime or night block transmission of television programmes is not a feasible proposition.

PUBLICITY AND ENROLMENT

The project employed a combination of central and local information channels to attract potential students.

Central Initiatives

Folders and Posters. 30,000 folders and 6,800 posters were prepared for use in the three counties by a graphics designer and staff at Danmarks

Radio. The materials were prepared at the request of the project steering committee and were funded by the Ministry of Education.

The project's name, 'logo' and the Danish flag, the 'Dannebrog', were used throughout.

The folder addressed itself specifically to those with seven years of school education or less. The text mentioned examples to illustrate the importance of Danish in everyday life. The folder stressed that Danish for Adults was a project flexible enough for just about anyone to follow. Mention was made of the fact that those wishing to do so could take the secondary school leaving examination (FSA) in Danish. A space was provided on the back of the folder for Further Education centres to stamp their name, address, telephone number and opening hours.

Folders and posters were given to the Further Education centres for distribution. From there they were distributed via trade union offices, employment exchanges, social welfare workers, doctors' and dentists' waiting rooms and filling stations.

Television. The drama documentary series 'Ugen Ud' has already been described. Following the drama documentary, the twenty-minute introduction to the project (transmitted on August 20th at peak viewing time with a repeat on Saturday) attempted to outline what Danish for Adults was all about. Following a brief introduction in which a well-known television presenter talked about feeling uncertain, and the use of Danish in every day life, information was given about the range of course options on offer in three counties. To give viewers an impression of the course contents, extracts from some of the materials were shown, to demonstrate that the teaching of Danish is a lot more functional than it used to be. The programme ended with a brief account of how to make use of the referral and counselling services set up in conjunction with the project. Three telephone numbers were shown, one for each of the three counties, and for those outside the counties involved, viewers were invited to contact Television Centre in Copenhagen.

Press Conference. On April 3rd 1979, the Minister of Education, Dorte Bennedsen, and representatives from the education committees of the three counties involved held a press conference with reporters from the national and local press. As a result there were a number of articles about the project, in particular in August while 'Ugen Ud' was being broadcast.

Local Initiatives

County Brochures. Danish for Adults was mentioned as a separate course in county broch res about Further Education. These brochures were delivered to all households in April or August.

Advertisements. Advertising space in local newspapers was bought by the counties and, in some cases, by individual Further Education centres. Mention was made of the project and in some cases of the referral service and television introduction linked to it.

Press Releases. The county education authorities involved prepared press releases with details of activities in their area. This led to a number of articles before and during the course, a number of which were based on interviews with students.

Local Radio ar.d the Nation-Wide Regional Affairs Programme 'Landet Rundt'. 'Landet Rundt' interviewed a number of women taking part in the warm-up to Danish for Adults, and this was seen by a number of people in Sønderjylland, the county where the interviews were recorded.

Local radios in the three counties gave the project coverage in their news programmes, which usually contained interviews with local counsellors or teachers involved in the project.

Personal Contacts. Educational counsellors and/or the county education authorities briefed in a number of instances at county or municipal level about the project. Where possible, employment counsellors and social welfare workers were contacted, as were counsellors at other educational establishments, and in some cases trade union shop stewards.

Enrolment Procedures

Two main procedures were used, the main differences being the extent of educational counselling prior to enrolment.

The normal procedure at Further Education centres is that as the result of reading about a course in the county further education brochure, having been referred to the centre by the social welfare system or an employment exchange, or just having previously attended a course at the Further Education centre, the individual concerned contacts the centre. The enrolment procedure is quite brief, involving the filling-in of a form. Further Education courses and materials used on these courses are free.

In some cases, filling in this form, or a postcard containing the same data, is the only requirement, although since 1979 there has been a general tendency to provide a minimum of counselling (discussing the individual's wishes and requirements before enrolment).

The extraordinary procedure adopted in connection with Danish for Adults involved counselling for all those who contacted the Further Education centres as the result of extraordinary publicity activities. In reality this involved all those who expressed an interest in Danish and who had not previously attended a course at a Further Education centre.

The hypothesis behind this investment in counselling was that the majority of those responding to the television introduction and other extraordinary activities would know little or nothing about the various adult education opportunities in their area. A fair proportion of them would require either a course in Danish other than Danish for Adults, or a course in a completely different subject or discipline, not necessarily provided by a Further Education centre. The aim was therefore to help each individual find the most appropriate course in his area.

Nearly three-quarters (72%) of those who went through the extraordinary procedure were recruited via the television introduction programme and the telephone referral service. Those ringing the referral service number, which was usually the number of the county hall in question, were asked to give their name, address, telephone number (if any) and times at which they could be contacted within the next week. They were then told that a counsellor from the nearest Further Education centre would contact them in connection with Danish for Adults. People continued to ring the referral telephone number up to three weeks after the introduction to the project on television. After the first week or so, the county hall in question often gave the telephone number of the nearest Further Education centre to save time, as the closing date for enrolments was approaching.

The referral service procedures were based on advice and suggestions given to the project by colleagues in the United Kingdom who had worked on the referral service for the Adult Literacy Campaign (see Chapter 5). This was also the reason for choosing county hall numbers for display on the television screen during the introduction to the project, as they commonly have twenty to forty incoming lines all with the same 'star' number. On the evening/afternoon of the television programme, educational counsellors themselves manned the incoming telephone lines. The switchboard operators and counsellors were requested to keep each conversation as brief as possible, as callers tended to ring immediately after the number for their area had been shown on the screen. During the days that followed, incoming calls to the referral service were dealt with by the regular staff of the county education authority at county hall.

Records System. The evaluation of the outreach activities of the project and the extraordinary educational counselling went hand in hand, data necessary for counselling being recorded for project evaluation in a manner which protected the individual's identity.

Each person was interviewed by a counsellor at the Further Education centre, but on occasions interviews took place in the person's own home or over the telephone.

The interview procedure was divided into a general section (which was for all those interviewed) and a specific section (for those wishing to enrol in a Danish for Adults course).

Each section began with a number of exploratory questions, to enable the counsellor to get to know the subject. Among the questions which were asked were the following:

–   how did you come to learn about the existence of Danish for Adults?
–   for what reasons would you like to study Danish? Do you need the examination, and if so, for what purpose?
–   working and educational background?
–   previous participation in adult education in its broadest sense?
     (the interviewee was shown a list of educational opportunities)

Following this exploratory phase, the counsellor then began to discuss what there were in the way of relevant choices. Where appropriate, the counsellor was encouraged to describe special education courses for those with word blindness and the like, courses for immigrants (7% of those contacting the centres were foreigners), short courses in Danish under the Leisure Time Adult Education Act and courses for those at a higher level at Technical and Commercial Colleges or at the Further Education centre itself.

Finally, the counsellor and the interviewee were to agree on the most appropriate action. If this was a course in Danish at lower secondary level at the centre itself, the counsellor went through a new exploratory phase to elicit data as to the person's expectations and personal background, in order to suggest the most appropriate option.

During the interview, notes were taken by the counsellor on a yellow checklist. Data was later transferred to a questionnaire. Each questionnaire consisted of a cover sheet with the individual's name, address and telephone number and, sometimes, notes from the person in the referral service who had taken the call. This sheet and the following one had a serial number printed on it. On completing the questionnaire, the counsellor detached the top sheet and filed it for the rest of the year. The evaluators received the questionnaire without this personal data. In May and June 1980 a further questionnaire was filled in for all those who had enrolled in a Danish for Adults course, regardless of whether they had been given counselling prior to enrolment. At this point, counsellors added the serial number from the first questionnaire for those who had been to counselling, which facilitated cross-tabulations for the two sets of data.

We were fortunate enough to be able to process all our questionnaires within a fortnight of the last one being returned. It was therefore possible to provide counties and individual courses with feedback during the first part of the course about the effects of the extraordinary recruitment activities and the counselling.

The materials and questionnaires used in this connection can be found in the appendices to the final evaluation report of Danish for Adults[4].

SUPPORT FOR STUDENTS

Support Before Enrolment

Counselling for potential students prior to enrolment was felt to be of considerable importance, both in human, educational and economic terms. Finding the most appropriate opportunity - not necessarily

Danish for Adults - was likely to ensure a higher course completion rate for those receiving counselling, giving rise to fewer frustrations and less waste of resources.

The extent to which counselling could help an individual find the most appropriate opportunity depended in part on the counsellor, and also to some extent on the nature of the Further Education centre itself. In some respects, centres in large towns like Aarhus were at an advantage. The centres there were so large that they offered between them the whole range of Danish for Adult course options, and for classroom options, there was often the chance to choose among morning, afternoon and evening courses. For those for whom Danish for Adults was not the most appropriate, the two Aarhus centres could suggest a number of related opportunities at other institutions.

At the other end of the scale, small centres in rural areas often offered just two or three courses, with a limited choice of options. Here bigger compromises were needed, because there were often no other alternatives in the vicinity.

Support After Enrolment

Participants Receiving Classroom Instruction Only (Options A, B and U). Participants on these courses could draw on support from their teacher and from the educational counsellor concerned with lower secondary courses. The counsellor was able to assist with matters concerning the course in general, but also with other matters such as applying for study loans or enrolling for vocational courses.

For such students it was felt that the on-air use of the media would have a supportive function, in that they could provide additional opportunities to refresh or expand on work done in class, helping those who had missed a class work on something similar. Furthermore, by making the course 'transparent' to the population at large, it would be easier for students to gain the support of their immediate surroundings.

Participants Following Options C or D (the combination of classroom instruction or the 'self-service' distance learning option). In these two options, tutoring rather than teaching formed a part of the course. The emphasis of the tutor's work was on the animateur function, to enable to learner to work independently.

169

Support included a briefing on the materials available, decisions as to the objectives to be pursued, training in study and analytical techniques of relevance to the study of Danish, and feedback on written work sent into the tutor at regular intervals. Students were encouraged to come to group meetings held every three weeks or every month. For distance learners (course option D) face-to-face tutorials and/or telephone tutorials were available on an 'ad hoc' basis.

A number of tutors worked actively to promote co-operation in small groups in the intervals between group meetings. The idea here was that shy pupils would often prefer to discuss difficulties with a fellow student before asking the tutor, and that if students could be encouraged to help each other as and when the need arose, this could help break down the feeling of isolation which is often experienced by distance learners.

Counsellor In-service Training

In March 1979, counsellors from Further Education centres in the two biggest counties, Aarhus and Sonderjylland, were invited to a one-day briefing and planning meeting in their area.

The chairman of the steering committee outlined the aims for extraordinary counselling in connection with the project. The counsellors present then discussed the project and their role in it, in particular the organisation of the recruitment and counselling. As the evaluation of the outreach activities involved the counsellors and the counselling procedure adopted, a small working group in each of the counties worked with the two evaluators from Danmarks Radio to plan and try out the interview procedure involved and the questionnaires to be used for each individual.

Some of the counsellors attended a second briefing session for counsellors and teachers/tutors in May 1979. When the interview procedure and the associated questionnaires were ready in early August, they were distributed to counsellors in the three counties, complete with a short guide.

One of the difficulties encountered was the late selection of some of the counsellors who were to work with Danish for Adults.

Teacher/Tutor In-service Training

Prospective teachers in the Danish for Adults project were invited to county briefing sessions to discuss the course options and the materials being developed. The first of these were held in May 1979.

In June 1979 a teacher training group consisting of a tutor/counsellor, a county education officer and one of the Danmarks Radio evaluators planned a five-day in-service training course for all the teachers and tutors in the Danish for Adults project. Two courses based on this course plan were held simultaneously from August 6th to 10th 1979.

Following a brief review of the overall aims and structure of the project, the materials available were presented. Then followed a session to train teachers in the use of video equipment and efficient use routines. Also included was a session on basic fault-finding. The hardware supplier simulated a range of possible faults on the video units and taught the teachers to make the necessary diagnosis, which also included the possibility of ringing to the service man for help! The final two and a half days involved group work. Tutors from different courses worked together on the writing of a basic student course plan, while classroom teachers from Further Education centres of the same size looked into the exploitation of the material in the classroom. At this stage, all six episodes of the drama documentary, nine of the instructional television and nine of the radio programmes were available, as were three of the course books in their final form, and three in the form of proofs.

Further one-day sessions were held in November 1979 and April 1980 at which work that far could be discussed and assessed by the teachers and corrections in working procedures made.

ASSESSMENT AND EVALUATION

The principal aim of the project was to test the necessary co-operative mechanisms between the media and adult education, and the content, level, organisation and methods required in large-scale compensatory adult education. The intention was to provide experience which could be used to help plan a wide range of educational opportunities for adults with a limited education background.

As the project also led to the secondary leaving examination (FSA) in Danish, summative evaluation was also involved, but this aspect will only be touched on here.

Initially an external evaluation of the project had been envisaged, but the funds available from the Ministry turned out to be inadequate for the evaluation procedures required. Danmarks Radio then contributed much of the man-power and most of the funds for the evaluation of the project in 1979 and 1980. In spite of the ethical problems involved in asking two employees of one of the parties to the project to conduct the necessary studies, the steering committee actively supported this solution.

A detailed proposal for the evaluation procedures to be used was prepared in February 1979.[5] The plan included the following:

1. Target group research. The preparation of case studies by social workers and employment counsellors.

2. Pre-testing of printed materials and the instructional television format.

3. Statistics regarding participation in Danish courses in 1978-79 (the year prior to Danish for Adults) and statistical data regarding general trends in further education provisions at lower secondary level.

4. A national interview survey concerning public awareness of the Danish for Adults project along the lines of a similar survey conducted for the Adult Literacy Campaign in the U.K.

5. Statistics regarding enquiries following extraordinary publicity activities and the television series, counselling, recruitment, participation and drop-out and examination grades for those participating in Danish for Adults courses in 1979-80.

6. A student evaluation of the course. Initially a questionnaire was planned, but this was changed to a combination of classroom observation and interviews with participants. One of the 'self-study' students kept a detailed log of her feelings about the course from August 1979 to June 1980.

7. A teacher evaluation of the project. This was based on interviews and questionnaires at the end of the in-service training course,

teacher meetings in November 1979 and April 1980 as well as a series of logs or diaries kept by teachers and tutors covering the whole period of the course.

8. Counsellor evaluation of the project, especially the counselling based mainly on meetings and interviews.

In 1980 this was expanded to include statements from each of the parties involved as to their perceptions of the co-operative venture.

The first course co-ordinator was originally to have assisted with the project evaluation, but he experienced a number of difficulties when attempting to plan the statistical aspects, as Danmarks Statistik (the Danish Bureau of Statistics) was unable to deliver the data required at the agreed time. The second project co-ordinator worked closely with the two staff members of Danmarks Radio with project evaluation from July 1979 onwards and is currently involved in a more limited evaluation of the Danish for Adults project in 1980-81.

The evaluators had been involved in the project for almost a year at an informal level before it was officially decided that Danmarks Radio should support the project evaluation. This meant that they had a first-hand knowledge of the planning stage of the project, and were allowed to sit in on both steering committee and management group meetings as active members. The nature of the procedures employed allowed for evaluation results to be fed back into the forward planning of the project, so in that respect the evaluators did not remain passive and neutral during the project.

Self-assessment played a surprisingly limited part in the project when one considers the importance attached to this form of evaluation in other fields in Scandinavia.

Project Evaluation Results

The following paragraphs are a brief summary of the conclusions of the final evaluation report.

Co-operation. The partners to the project generally felt that this feature of the project had been satisfactory, largely due to the fact that a clear division of responsibility and labour had been agreed upon initially, and this was consistently followed throughout the life of the project. Where co-operation among the partners concerned gave rise to minor difficulties, they could usually be traced back to ambiguities in this agreement.

Another significant feature was the hiring of a project co-ordinator who commanded sufficient respect among all the partners that he could also act as 'slave-driver', reminding people of impending deadlines and taking necessary action where potential problems were developing. A co-ordinator of this kind for large-scale projects like Danish for Adults seems to be essential.

The importance of keeping information chains to those involved in the project as short as possible also became evident. Wherever possible it would seem to be a good idea to send materials to teachers and counsellors directly rather than making unreasonable demands of the county and Further Education administrations.

Expectations. The report then went on to deal specifically with difficulties which had arisen at Ministerial level, at county council level, at the Further Education centres and at Danmarks Radio. The crucial problem facing the project seems to be that of 'bedarf' and 'bedurfnisse', the dialectic between external expectations and demands and the individual's felt needs. In many cases, it was clear that individuals expect and require help in the more formal aspects of language and its use, i.e. correct spelling, punctuation, writing letters and the like. They find it difficult to relate to what appears to be a large, somewhat diffuse course of approximately two hundred hours in a subject, Danish. Although moderately successful in providing a flexible framework for following a Further Education course, Danish for Adults lacked in appeal because the content was subject, rather than functionally-orientated, and that the commitment required in terms of study hours was greater than most adults with a limited educational background felt necessary.

The differences of perception between the individual and the system also apply to the question of the final examination. Of the reasons given for wanting to follow the Danish for Adults course, one quarter (25%) concerned vocational needs and the need for a formal qualification. 40% of the reasons given involved real competence, the wish to acquire a knowledge of or skills in Danish and a further one in six (15%) concerned a general wish to keep up. Three times as many of those who were recruited via television completed the course without taking the examination as those recruited by conventional means (9% compared with 3% of those enrolling). This finding would seem to have implications for any similar project aimed at the educationally underprivileged.

Television. As regards the use of television as a medium for outreach activities, it seems that television introductions with associated activities like the drama documentary and more conventional publicity campaigns in the printed media seem to be good at bringing a project to the attention of the adult population, although less good at imparting information. It now seems likely that the 70% increase in participation in Danish courses in the three counties involved in Danish for Adults was largely due to television. Although television recruited a broader and more representative sample of the adult population than other media (which generally tend to attract the well-educated) it was not significantly better at attracting those who had never previously taken part in any adult education course. Only social welfare workers and employment counsellors were able to reach people of this kind in a significant proportion. It seems likely that a course of this kind appeals to the minority of the educationally deprived who have previously participated in adult education and those in need of a formal qualification. A more functional course in smaller modules would probably be more effective in reaching the majority of the target group.

Students. Those recruited to Danish for Adults tended to be older than for conventional courses and the bias in favour of women was less pronounced. Course options with a limited number of class hours or the 'self-service' option attracted a far higher proportion of those employed. At the same time the project showed that those with a demanding occupation, either in terms of the nature of the work itself or the variable working hours and conditions, also needed some degree of social contact and considerable tutor support. The self-service option made participation in a Danish course possible for a number of people who would otherwise have had to spend a prohibitively large amount of time travelling to and from the Further Education centre.

Counselling. Taken as a whole, the extraordinary counselling did not lead to a significant increase in the proportion of course completions. The only increases noted were for young adults and for women. Among the problems which were not solved in connection with counselling were the following:

— the late recruitment of some of the counsellors and their subsequent lack of knowledge of the project and its aims

— instances of counsellors not spending enough time at the exploratory phase of the interview to get to know the student in question

— a reluctance on the part of some counsellors - sometimes under pressure from colleagues or principals - to inform about and refer people to other related educational opportunities at other institutions

— the lack of real alternatives for counsellors to refer to in rural areas with few adult education institutions and few courses on offer.

There were also findings as regards the contents and methods followed and the reasons for course completion and drop-out.

ORGANISATION AND ADMINISTRATION

As mentioned earlier, there was a multi-tiered organisational structure:

Council for Adult and Youth Education	Responsible for the setting-up of the steering committee. Responsible to the Minister of Education on matters of educational policy.
Project Steering Committee (Planlaegnings-Gruppen)	Responsible to the Council for the planning and implementation of the Model III project, including Danish for Adults. Decisions at strategic level regarding aims, objectives, resources etc. Comprised representatives of the three counties, the Ministry of Education, labour market representatives and the National Institute for Educational Media, Danmarks Radio and the co-ordinator.

Management Group (Styrings-Gruppen)	Responsible to the project steering committee for the day-to-day planning and co-ordination of the project. Comprised members of county education authorities, principals from Further Education centres, Danmarks Radio and the chairman of the steering committee.

Danish Working Party	Coursewriter Team	In-service Training Group
Responsible to steering committee for course framework	Responsible to Danmarks Radio	Responsible to management group

At various stages in the planning of the project there were informal contacts with BBC Further Education (now Continuing Education), the referral service which supported the British Adult Literacy Campaign, and the Dutch Open School project (see chapter 7). The importance of these contacts is difficult to quantify, but it is certain that the television programmes, counselling provisions and the referral service would have been organised in different ways had these contacts not been made.

RESOURCES

Broadcasting
Broadcasting costs for 1979-80 were in the region of 2½ million kroner. This covered the production and transmission costs of the various television and radio programmes. Costs were met from the normal budget of Danmarks Radio for adult education. The Danish for Adults course was regarded as a priority within Danmarks Radio's normal educational provision.

County Level Expenditure
The major items under this head were:
- teachers' and counsellors' salaries
- acquisition of hardware, books and tapes
- publicity, briefing and training meetings

These were not extraordinary costs on the project since counties have a statutory obligation to make provision for adult education. Neverthe-

177

less the number of students following Danish courses increased by 70% as a result of this course being offered. And this had considerable financial implications. The three counties had to find an additional 2 million kroner to fund the project at a time when their budget for adult education had been reduced by 3% in real terms.

Cost of Evaluation

Between 1978-80 a thorough evaluation of the Danish for Adults course was carried out. The Ministry of Education made a small grant towards this but the substantial cost (250,000 kroner) was met by Danmarks Radio.

Miscellaneous Costs Borne by the Ministry of Education

These included such items as meetings of the steering and management groups, the publication of an information folder (30,000 kroner), extraordinary counselling (200,000 kroner).

Unit Costs

One thousand students participated in the pilot project hence unit costs per individual were very high. Such a consideration needs, however, to be offset by the following factors:
- materials exist for use over the next four to five years for the whole country
- the spin-off value for other collaborative projects
- the infra-structure of support centres e.g. wider use of video in teaching
- benefits derived by the eavesdropping public.

Notes and References

1. K. Mørch Jacobsen, 'Erfaring fra - og Praksis i - Forsøg med Opsøgende Virksomhed. Uddanddelserådat for Ungdoms - og Voksenundervisning m.v. (Undervisningsministeriet, Copenhagen, 1979).
2. Central Council of Education, 'U - 90: Danish Educational Planning and Policy in a Social Context at the End of the Twentieth Century' (Ministry of Education, Copenhagen, 1980).
3. D. Bunnage and B. Hedegaard, 'Voksenuddannelse...' (Teknisk Forlag, Copenhagen, 1978).
4. E. Anker Olsen, P.O. Looms and F. Kjaerum, 'Dansk for Voksne: Rapport om Projektet' (Danmarks Radio, Copenhagen, 1980).
5. P.O. Looms and E. Anker Olsen, 'Paedagogisk Planlaegning og Evaluering i Forbindelse med Model III Fase 2 (Dansk for Voksne) i 1979' (Danmarks Radio, Copenhagen, 1979).

Chapter 7

OPEN SCHOOL
NETHERLANDS

Lies Vellekoop *

INTRODUCTION

The planning and development of the Dutch Open School has been so complex that it was felt appropriate to depart in this instance from the case study format which has been adopted for the other projects and initiatives described in the book.

The Dutch Open School case study is arranged as follows:

1. Open School: a pilot project

2. Five questions which the Open School Advisory Committee wished to be answered through the pilot project:
    - What is the best way to reach people who have participated very little or not at all in existing forms of adult education?
    - What use of mass media is possible, and what combination of media produces the best results?
    - What is the potential of a curriculum which enables students to make their own choice of what they learn and how fast they learn?
    - How can people learn from and by their own experience and that of other group members?
    - How can a future Open School in the Netherlands be established and organised?

3. Changes introduced after two experimental years

4. Towards a future Open School

* Edited by Keith Harry

OPEN SCHOOL: A PILOT PROJECT

The Open School Committee

During the early seventies, ideas relating to 'éducation permanente', recurrent education, and educational leave gained currency in many European countries, including the Netherlands. Several Dutch congresses on continuing education and the use of mass media were held. By 1971 the Ministers of Education and of Culture had already reported to Parliament on instructional radio and television. The Ministers accepted that the education of adults requires more than instructional broadcasting alone, and that it would be accompanied by other facilities and means of learning. Printed materials, tutors and locally organised support, and group work should be available as well as broadcast programmes.

At the Agora congress on new developments in mass media, one of the topics for discussion was the concept of 'open school'. The experience of the British Open University strongly influenced the group which formulated the following two principles central to a Dutch open school:

– The Open University was not reaching the 'forgotten millions' whose basic education was very limited. An open school by contrast should be available to everyone
– The media selected for use by an open school should be employed in such a way that they would benefit to the maximum people not used to formal education

After the Agora congress, the group developed an initial outline of an open school and recommended the setting-up of a state committee to advise the Government on the development of an open school system in the Netherlands. This Open School Committee was established in 1974.

For more than ten years, 'éducation permanente' has been accepted policy for governments regardless of political persuasion. In 1974 the Minister of Culture stated in Parliament that the development of an 'Open School system' would be linked with other developments in adult education. The Open School from the very beginning was intended to be a 'multi-media' institution, making use of various media including radio and television. The further developments to which the Minister referred were the provision of adequate local educational networks to support adult students, and paid educational leave to provide wider opportunities for participation in adult education.

In fact, three separate advisory committees on the three different subjects were instituted. Each Ministry involved in adult education was associated with one committee. The Open School became principally the responsibility of the Ministry of Education and Science, the Ministry of Culture, Recreation and Social Welfare became responsible for educational networks, and the Ministry of Social Affairs for paid educational leave.

This division illustrates the principal problem which has always affected adult education in the Netherlands. The problem is the existence of barriers between three types of education:
—   formal, diploma-orientated education
—   informal education, and education directed at self-development and at greater awareness of society
—   vocational training
Each of these three types of education has its own history, principles, method of enrolment, privileges and administration.

The task of the Open School Committee was to advise the Minister of Education and the Minister of Culture on the best way to establish an Open School system. Shortly after its work began in 1975, the Committee published its first report, which recommended the setting up of a pilot project, to be called 'De Proefprojecten Open School'.

The members of the Open School Committee were appointed by the Ministers of Education and Culture. A wide selection was made so as to obtain a sufficiently broad range of expertise within the Committee. Many of the members were closely involved with adult education, but they were not appointed as official representatives of the organisations with which they were connected.

In this way, organisations responsible for correspondence courses, evening classes, womens' equal rights, and broadcasting, as well as organisations for informal education, all influenced the output of the Committee. In addition to contributing their expertise, Committee members could also express the principal concerns of the major organisations whose individual interests might have conflicted with those of the large group of potential students which stood to benefit from a soundly-based Open School system. But the Committee was required to act independently, and members were also to act independently without being involved in consultations with their individual organisations. For this reason, trades unions and employers' organisations were not represented on the Open School Committee.

The Pilot Project

The aims of the proposed project were to discover:
- The best way of reaching people who until now have not participated at all, or have participated to only a very limited extent, in the existing forms of adult education. Most of these people (around 30% of all Dutch adults) had received no more than six years of education.
- What use of media is possible, and what combination of media produces the best results.
- What possibilities are presented by a curriculum which enables people to make their own choices about what they learn and how quickly they learn.
- How can an Open School system be established and organised in the Netherlands?

Certain decisions were made before the project began:
- The project could only be successful if systematically observed and evaluated. Therefore only a limited student population could be admitted.
- A decision was made regarding the educational level of the target group. The Open School Committee was aware (probably earlier than any other body in the Netherlands) of the prevalence of illiteracy. But at that time (in 1975), little was known about the identity and the problems of the illiterate or semi-literate members of the community. It was considered that the establishment of a literacy programme would require more time than was available; the Committee would have expected to meet with many complex and previously unforeseen problems.

The Government accepted the proposal for a two-year pilot project. The experience gained during the project would be employed in the creation of the Open School. Every adult would eventually have an opportunity to participate, wherever he or she lived, whatever qualifications he or she possessed, whatever the required educational level and the time available for study, and whatever the objective of studying.

182

The project was not yet in operation when the Open School Committee decided that the Open School was not to be organised by a separate institution, nor was it to form a new framework for adult education. In the future, Open School was to comprise a combination of provision offered by different institutions, with available personnel and expertise being utilised.

As far as possible existing structures would be used, and the Open School might fill gaps in provision where necessary. On the other hand the Open School might co-ordinate and stimulate work done by others. However, the Stichting Proefprojecten Open School (Open School Pilot Scheme Association) was created to administer the Open School while it retained the status of a pilot project.

Existing institutions were concerned specifically either with formal education, informal education or vocational training. Open School would not simply provide one of these types of education, but would be involved in all three types simultaneously - the creation of a separate institution was therefore inevitable. The distinction led to two different uses of the expression 'Open School'; the first referred to the pilot project and its organisation, and the second to a plan for the future introduction of a new way of learning for adults who had previously lacked educational opportunities.

The Target Group

The identification of the target group accorded with the desire to give priority to those groups whose chances of profiting from existing educational provision had been minimal. The minimum educational level required from adults was the equivalent of five to six years of elementary education, and the maximum was set at a total of eight years of education.

The target group was divided into three sub-groups. Each of the sub-groups was very clearly defined so as to maximise the effectiveness of research studies. For example, participants were required to live in a particular town or area, or to be within a specific age group. The sub-groups were:
- (Married) women over 30 years of age, in eight locations throughout the country (Groningen, Amsterdam North, the areas of Haaksbergen, Schagen, Utrecht, Roosendaal, Venlo, and the

183

islands in the South of Holland). Cities were selected as well as rural areas. In some of these locations an educational infrastructure already existed, whereas in others virtually no provision existed.

- Young (working) adults between 17 and 30 years old living in three towns (Emmen, Leiden, Tilburg).
- Working or unemployed people over 30 years old living in three rural areas (Zeeland, Limburg, Friesland).

In each location an Open School working group was formed. A good deal of exploratory work was carried out by people who were involved in the local institutions dealing with education, social work or administration. The working groups also selected the tutors who were able to establish the vital relationship with participants.

But, in addition, a great deal of preparation had to be done at the central Open School office in Zeist. Very little ready-made study material was available; it was clear from the beginning that special written materials must be created. Another decision which had been made beforehand was to make use of the open television and radio networks. Working in basic groups was intended to be the central element in the system with radio and television used as a support to group work, but a high degree of integration was anticipated.

The use of mass media in a multi-media educational project aimed at adults was in many respects innovatory; little documented evidence was available which was related to experience in other countries.

The Open School project officially began on September 1st 1977. Many preparations had been made before that date, and some groups were already functioning by the summer of 1977. Other groups were busy preparing until the beginning of 1978.

The story of the project is a story of such complexity that it is difficult to describe it either chronologically or theme by theme. The next section returns to the original aims of the project and describes how, during the first two years, Open School staff and participants attempted to provide answers to the questions which had been asked.

FIVE QUESTIONS WHICH THE OPEN SCHOOL ADVISORY COMMITTEE WISHED TO BE ANSWERED THROUGH THE PILOT PROJECT

What is the best way to reach people who have participated very little or not at all in existing forms of adult education?

The Open School Committee and the Committee on Local Educational Networks estimated that some 10% of Dutch adults participated in adult education (taking into account all types of courses of whatever length). Earlier research had already shown that relatively few participants in adult education were from the less educated sections of the community.

The Committee wished to work towards an Open School system which would create opportunities for those adults for whom the step up to conventional courses of education was too high. The project had to attract less motivated people as well as enthusiastic adults eager to take advantage of a second chance for further education. Research on a group composed entirely of strongly motivated participants would not be valid for the entire target group.

The strict limitations on target groups resulted in more people applying for places than could be accepted. On the other hand, however, various kinds of outreach work were carried out to motivate potential participants who would require more persuasion than an article or an advertisement in the local newspaper to enrol with the Open School.

Social workers, ministers, school teachers, doctors and union officials were all asked to guide possible participants to the Open School working groups. The group members went to community houses and organised neighbourhood meetings.

After twelve months, Open School participants were asked whether they would have joined the project if their only source of information had been the newspaper, or a leaflet sent by post. 40% of participants answered in the negative; most of them enrolled because they were told about the Open School by friends or relatives who had already attended.

The Publicity Campaign. Before the start of the project, a one-hour television programme was broadcast several times. The programme was not designed to recruit participants; it explained what the Open School was going to be, and why only a restricted number of people could enrol during the first years as a pilot project.

A small book could be ordered which contained information about the Open School as well as about other existing schools and courses for adults. After one year, groups other than the 'official' ones, and individuals, were allowed, with restrictions, to order the printed material. From the very beginning, the Open School Committee argued that more people belonging to the target group, in addition to those officially enrolled, should be able to take advantage of the radio and television programmes and the printed materials, all of which had been specially produced for this large group of people whose opportunities had been so restricted. It was made possible for people to subscribe individually or in groups. This extension of the Open School project was publicised through several television programmes. However, these programmes were not particularly successful. The groups which sprang up spontaneously were initiated locally, and the participants were also recruited locally. Only 30% of the members of these 'spontaneous groups' appeared to have been attracted by, among other things, the television programmes.

The relatively small publicity campaign produced only a few hundred individual participants. The enrolment regulations were complicated, the costs were rather high (because this part of the project was not subsidised) and at this stage the television programmes were not very attractive. The programmes which were produced after the second year were a good deal more entertaining, and it was not long before people began ordering the printed materials which accompanied them.

Spontaneous Groups. Over 300 Open School groups sprang up spontaneously. At first they were not subsidised by the national government. They had to adhere to a variety of regulations, the most important of which was that the members of a group were required to be from the target group. Adherence to the regulations entitled the groups to order and purchase Open School material. The groups' tutors received some support, but it was several months before training conferences were organised for them. A newsletter was produced in the meantime to provide the necessary information.

This support was provided by the NCVO; the Open School Pilot Scheme Association was not at first permitted to give support, either through the central office or the local working groups. Many groups did not take the trouble to obtain official recognition. If they required printed materials, they copied the required books and pamphlets from other groups. It is therefore not easy to estimate the number of unofficial groups which existed.

The registered groups have been surveyed; the members of these groups appear to be on a higher educational level than the participants in the official Open School project. They are also on a higher level on socio-economic scales and are more strongly motivated towards further education than the participants in the official project originally were.

With some reservations, the conclusion may be drawn that the outreach work carried out in the Open School project worked well. The training of tutors in the area of counselling, and the time, energy and money expended, had a positive effect. But at least as important were the content of the curriculum and the way in which the Open School programmes was presented to participants.

The project had to operate within strictly defined limits because it had only pilot status and because money was not available to establish this expensive system on a larger scale. In the future the objective of ensuring that the Open School system reaches beyond the tip of the iceberg may be in conflict with the objective of substantially increasing the Open School population.

What use of mass media is possible, and what combination of media produces the best results

The Open School project, which started in 1977, was a product of at least two different developments. One was the widespread discussion about 'education permanente', and the other was the development of mass media and its supposedly infinite potential. In the early seventies, new ways of transmitting pictures and sound by video and cable were introduced on a large scale. Even earlier, the influence of television on patterns of behaviour had greatly impressed Dutch intellectuals and politicians as well as their counterparts worldwide. On the other hand, television could also be a 'window on the world', a window which needed to be opened on behalf of the millions who until that time lacked knowledge about the world. In addition, education through mass media was believed to be cheap.

When the Open School was instituted by the Minister of Education, its mandate stated that the Open School was to make use of the open broadcasting networks in combination with group work, printed materials, self-instructional study, and with other media such as film, audio and videotapes. Before the Project began operation, the first 'Onderwijs en Vormingsplan' ('Education Framework Plan') of the Open School was drawn up.

In the Framework Plan, working in groups was regarded as being of central importance. Each group comprised between ten and fifteen participants together with one or two tutors. During the first years there were about one hundred of these official Open School groups. The tutors were teachers with experience in conventional institutions and in community education. In the working groups which were formed at each of the fourteen locations, they made one another acquainted with the different methods and objectives peculiar to their own disciplines, diploma-orientated teaching on one side and community education on the other.

The basic group was designed to perform several functions, the exchange and accumulation of experience, practising social skills, and seeking to fulfil objectives set by the participants themselves. A developing activity which became characteristic of the Open School system was group work based around subjects of interest chosen by the students.

Printed Materials. During the first year of the project a great deal of printed material was produced. It consisted of small booklets designed to enable the student to study without professional assistance. These booklets (known as 'onderwijs leer eenheden', 'education modules') were intended to be worked through in four to six hours. For every school curriculum subject which was taught, lessons were produced at four levels. A considerable quantitiy of material on particular themes was written so that a wide choice of subjects outside the school curriculum was available for study.

Many of the printed texts which were produced at the beginning of the project were never used. Often the material, even if intended for the lowest level, was too difficult. Open School participants were required to have completed at least five years of primary education, but in practice, they often appeared to have lost knowledge since their schooling ceased.

Another problem encountered in using the printed booklets was that they sometimes arrived too late to be available when required by the group or by an individual group member working on a specific level of a formal course. The time taken to produce materials had been underestimated. Professional correspondence course writers, who often had little acquaintance with the target group, wrote the materials. Special groups ('klankbordgroepen', literally 'sounding-board groups') comprising members of the target group and tutors working for the Open School project, were asked to test the theme-orientated materials and to give their opinions. Inevitably, this process was time-consuming. In addition, the drawing-up of contracts for the writers and for the correspondence teaching institutions which employed them proved to be more complex than had been anticipated. A further significant factor was shortage of funds; the creation of a totally new curriculum was an expensive task to undertake. The production process early in the project was straightforward; many of the booklets were printed in black and white with line illustrations. But the printing process also took more time than had been expected. Open School tutors began to create their own materials and when these came into use the centrally produced and distributed materials became less and less attractive to students.

Radio and Television. The problems encountered with the use of radio and television programmes were in some respects comparable to those experienced with printed materials. Radio and television were originally intended to be used as part of an integrated system involving various other media and methods in support of students working in groups with themes and individually with formal courses.

The aim of integrating the use of mass media into the Open School system did not work during the early years when the original Open School concept was still adhered to. The full potential of the media was not exploited in the first radio and television programmes, and there were additional problems:
- Many of the television programmes were pitched at too high a level
- Programmes were presented according to a strict schedule requiring sequential study. To be able to understand lesson 8 it was essential to have previously mastered, for example, lesson 5 or 3 or 7, or perhaps all of them.
- Transmission time was 6.00 p.m. or 6.30 p.m. This is one of the busiest times for many of the female students with families.

– There was an inbuilt contradiction in the functioning of two separate parts of the system. On the one hand a strong emphasis was placed on the importance of students or groups of students being able to decide for themselves how quickly they wished to learn. On the other hand, the use of the open broadcasting network requires adherence to a strict time schedule. Decisions made by the groups always took precedence over pre-conceived attempts to integrate the different media.

Additional Media. From the beginning of the Open School project the term 'media' has been used more broadly than in many educational contexts. It includes working in basic groups as well as printed materials and radio and television broadcasting. Other important media employed by the Open School include excursions, video and data banks. The data banks are designed primarily for use by students, who are seeking ideas for projects they might work on, or are tracing materials suitable for their use.

– Excursions comprise visits to experts in subjects being studied, trips to a library, a mill, or a farm. Some groups have visited countries whose language they have been studying.
– Video-cassettes have been used to enable replay of programmes broadcast at inconvenient times, and also to enable programmes replayed to groups to be stopped to discuss particular points. The latter type of usage has been taken into account during the production of some television programmes. Every Open School group, whether belonging to the official project or not, has access to tapes of all programmes. The central office at Zeist maintains a collection of recordings of all radio and television programmes. Some, but not all, of the problems of working with the open network have been eliminated through the employment of replay facilities. An important factor is that programmes made specifically for the Open School target group did not make a significant impact although they were transmitted nationwide. After two years of Open School broadcasting the objectives of radio and television production have been drastically revised.
– Data banks. The proliferating amount of available printed material has been produced not only at the Open School central office and the various locations. Other projects working with comparable target groups have also produced useful material for using with

190

adults. In addition, new methods have been devised by study projects operating at Dutch universities. Data about available Open School material and other tested project material has been selected and arranged for access by potential users. Video and audio tapes are included in the data bank as well as printed materials.

What is the potential of a curriculum which enables students to make their own choice of what they learn and how fast they learn?

In designing the most appropriate curriculum for the Open School project, the Committee inclined towards an open rather than a closed system. Members of the basic group, or the group as a whole, should be able to decide for themselves what was to be studied. Nevertheless, some structure and guidance was essential because the students had little study experience, and even this might have been acquired many years previously. An important aim of the Open School programme was to eliminate the separation described above between formal and informal education. In one programme adults should be able to study subjects from the school curriculum and obtain the appropriate qualifications, and also be involved in community education. Courses in areas such as acquiring job skills, raising children, and hobbies were foreseen as part of the Open School programme but their development has varied from location to location. During the first years the most successful course in this area was 'How to Learn'. Before the project began operation it was anticipated that Open School students would study and learn in two ways, with the theme-orientated part of the curriculum reflecting the aim of increasing social skills and knowledge and the subject-orientated part offering the opportunity of acquiring basic knowledge and skills of a more formal kind. In fact, although courses are divided into theme and subject areas, this separation did not occur on the level of student learning. Knowledge relating to social orientation is gained from every book, every project, every course and every programme.

Theme-based Courses. The original concept of the Open School theme-based courses was as follows:

A new theme is presented every eight weeks, for example, Living and Housing (other themes included Health, Working, and Money). A

television programme introduces the participants to some of the many aspects of the subject:
- Buying or renting a house
- Taking out a mortgage
- Home decorating
- Apartment buildings or one-family houses
- Obtaining a playground for children

The group visits an experimental community project and a specialist is invited to talk to the group. Following the general introduction of a theme, the group can sub-divide, with each sub-group selecting for study a particular aspect of the theme. Several booklets are available which provide additional information.

Further material or information may be obtained from a local library or through interviews with local councillors or estate agents. In the first years of the project, the theme was completed by the presentation by the sub-groups to the basic group of a paper or a summary of work done.

During the course of the project this pattern has evolved so that themes are not any longer centrally prescribed, and groups can decide for themselves for how long they study a particular subject. In addition, more formal studies developed from students' work on themes. During the Living and Housing project, for example, participants wrote a letter to the town council seeking improved facilities in the locality.

It had emerged that a common problem of participants, and particularly of those who had recently enrolled in the project, was spelling. The identification of the needs of students was regarded as particularly important. Students identifying their own needs tended initially to refer back to subjects remembered from their school years. Only after some experience of the Open School curriculum did they recognise the importance of other aspects of learning which related to their social life. Social skills which have developed through Open School experience include confidence in expressing a particular point of view, and improving performance in interviews.

Subject-based Courses. As well as working in a basic group on a theme-based course, each student had (and still has) the opportunity to study all the subjects which are taught at secondary school: Dutch, Mathematics, English, French, German, Geography, Biology, History and

Arithmetic. Another course open to all students is 'How to Learn'.

It was intended that these formal courses should be presented at four levels, some of which were accompanied by radio and television programmes. Each student was tested at the beginning of a course to determine the most appropriate level at which he or she should begin, and another test was administered at the end of the course. A satisfactory result in the final test of the highest-level course gave the Open School participant the opportunity to begin study in that particular subject at the second grade of secondary education for adults. This means that the level which can be reached in the formal, subject-based courses of the Open School is comparable to the end of the second grade of secondary education for children (MAVO).

At the beginning of the Open School project, several problems had to be solved. One problem concerned the intake of students. In order that a satisfactory evaluation of results could be undertaken, students were subjected to a rigorous test of their 'knowledge'. The members of the working groups in the fourteen locations were required to ask students a long list of questions, some hard to answer or even to understand. Thus while the tutor was on the one hand assuring the newly arrived participants that the Open School was not too 'difficult', on the other hand the detailed and complex questionnaires made them feel inferior or lacking in education. After administering the initial test on a few occasions, the tutors refused to continue using them and another way of assessing students at the commencement of their studies with the Open School had to be introduced.

Another problem was related to the delivery of subject-based printed materials. Producing each subject course at four different levels was so time-consuming that at the beginning of the project only the materials for the lowest level were available, and even these often appeared too difficult for the students. Of the courses offered, Dutch, English, and Mathematics were most frequently selected for study; only a few participants wished to study some of the other subjects. After two years the printed materials were revised and re-written according to the wishes of the participants. The three most popular subjects were the first selected for revision.

At first, most participants asked to study the subjects they remembered from school, but after a few months the theme-based work was regarded as being of greater value. The Open School system of learning was so much appreciated that on the completion of their courses, and

193

their permitted period of study, many participants wished to continue studying in a similar way, but unfortunately provision was not available outside the Open School project.

The certificates awarded to participants on completion of their studies indicate the themes which have been studied, the skills which have been taught, and to what level formal school subject courses have been followed. These final certificates are currently being analysed to make as much use as possible of the information they contain.

How can people learn from and by their own experience and that of other group members?

In designing a scheme for adults who want to learn, and in creating a curriculum for them, it is essential to take into account the differences between adults and children. One notable difference lies in motivation. Children, although not always happy to do so, learn in order to benefit themselves in the future rather than to immediately improve their current situation. For adults, the reverse is often true; the less closely a course is related to a particular function or a particular job, the more the adult student may learn in relation to his or her life and preoccupations. In general, adults are more influenced than children by their social environment and their social situation. Although there are fewer barriers between social classes in the Netherlands than in, for example, England, and although relative freedom of social mobility exists, it was still possible in the mid-1970s to hear the view expressed that 'Studying is not for our sort'. This view could be heard most frequently in those sections of the population in which the Open School anticipated finding its target group.

But adults have far greater experience than children, and although members of the Open School target group may have no paper qualifications, they may well have learned a good deal from life.

Learning from Experience. Much of the knowledge which is gained by an adult through experience as worker, parent, or member of a particular social class or group is not necessarily recognised as 'knowledge' by the individual concerned. One of the objectives of the Open School project was to utilise accumulated knowledge for the mutual benefit of participants in the Open School. This was in fact one of the reasons why the basic group became the central focus of the project.

Teaching and learning through mutual exchange of experience could also be achieved through the use of radio and television, provided that the editor and members of the production team could establish a satisfactory relationship with the tutors and the students. Although there were successes in the initial programmes, this concept proved difficult to put into practice. The making of a television or radio programme always remains to some extent an individual process. The utilisation of the experience of Open School students therefore depended on the readiness of editors to listen to those students who could best articulate their knowledge. The programme makers would then transform this knowledge in such a way that it would appeal to a mass audience.

To carry this process into practice required staff who were not only familiar with the possibilities and the limitations of mass media, but who also understood the problems of the target group, had a wide knowledge of education, and would pay close attention to the working of groups. The Open School project was fortunate enough to find such staff. Learning from one another and teaching one another were important functions of the basic group. The role of the tutor was to participate in this process and to provide support. Initially the process was considered difficult; students entering Open School expected to find the kind of school which they remembered from their days of formal education. As Open School became better known, this initial difficulty decreased, both in established and new groups.

The fact that students' experience was central to the theme-orientated group work placed greater responsibility on individual students than they had previously known. They selected the subjects to be studied, expressed their own wishes and needs, and voiced their opinions on subjects about which they had never before been asked. The recognition that other peoples' problems and experiences were similar to their own enabled students to extend their own experience.

The Work of WOVO. During the first years of the project, a special group (WOVO, Werkgroep Ontwikkeling Van Onderop) was working on the developments of methods of learning by experience. Theories of Freire and Negt, where appropriate and where the support of tutors and students was obtained, were applied to Open School methods.

WOVO stated that learning through experience, generally accepted

195

as a starting point for Open School, could not exclude learning through new experiences as an individual, as a member of a group, or as a member of a social class. WOVO considered that learning through experience was only a step away from social action.

The nature of WOVO's philosophy determined that no method could be imposed from outside on the basic groups or the students. The method of working adopted by the Open School required time to evolve, and the final results of the evaluation of learning through experience have not yet been made available. In the meantime this aspect of the project has already made an impact on Dutch adult education; many institutions involved with the education of adults, in addition to the Open School groups (those working with WOVO and the remainder) recognised the fact that 'ervaringsleren' (literally 'experience-learning'), learning through experience, includes more than simply using examples from everyday life.

How can a future Open School in the Netherlands be established and organised?

When it was first established, the Open School was intended to represent a new, different and independent approach to educational provision for adults. It was new not only because there was little existing provision at the level at which it was to provide educational opportunities, but because the Open School in the long term was to cater for all adults and young people, to enable them to study according to their particular needs. The Open School was different from existing institutions principally in terms of its employment of a variety of media, each to be utilised to the maximum benefit, and to be integrated as effectively as possible.

The Open School represented an independent approach to educational provision for adults because it was to offer a form of education which combined diploma-orientated education, education to develop individual and social awareness, and vocational training; in 1974, no other institution in the Netherlands offered such a combination. Three different administrative systems for adult education existed, and responsibility for educational policy was divided between three Ministries. This division has been maintained while the number of students engaged in the different areas of adult education has increased.

The Ministry of Education and Science was responsible for the evening schools for adults which replicate provision for children in day schools. Community education was the responsibility of the Ministry of Culture, while the Ministry of Social Affairs controlled adult vocational training, which was related to policy affecting the labour market. But in practice, this separation of responsibilities could create problems. For example, the evening schools, while offering formal education in the evening, also opened their doors to women students during the day. In order to respond to the needs of its day students, the evening schools wished to offer non-academic courses. In addition, English and Dutch language courses were taught in community centres, and trades unions advocated the inclusion of courses on the social system and on labour organisation in vocational training programmes. These kinds of development indicated to the Open School Committee that in the future, adult education provision might well require greater flexibility between the areas which had previously been separated.

The second report of the Open School Committee departed from the original recommendation for the establishment of an independent organisation. The reasons for this change have never been analysed, but they are in fact particularly interesting in view of later developments which have threatened the existence of the Open School system and prevented a large-scale expansion of its activities.

1. During the lifetime of the Committee (which ended in 1980) it appeared that several existing institutions were in favour of integrating different areas of adult education and supported the implementation of the concept of learning through experience.

2. Several organisations represented on the Committee might well have suffered in competition with a strong and attractive Open School.

3. The economic situation deteriorated. At a time of financial retrenchment it was unlikely that a proposal for a new organisation funded by national government would receive a favourable response. A much more economical solution was to make use of the facilities of existing organisations and to seek additional state funding.

4. The Open School was reckoned to be expensive; during the first

two years the average cost per student was estimated to be at least 3000 guilders per year. This figure is based on an average attendance for 'classes' of six hours per week.

5. The centralised organisation of the project was strongly criticised. The project was based on a central office at Zeist, was funded by the national government, and was subject to restrictions and limitations imposed by the Ministry of Education, for example on the use of centrally produced printed materials. Tutors employed in the official projects as well as tutorial staff of other, similar, groups were of the opinion that the Open School should be as far as possible decentralised. The majority of Open School employees may not have shared this opinion, but it was nevertheless widely publicised.

The reasons stated above account for the Committee's decision to establish a decentralised Open School system; no body comparable to the Open School Pilot Scheme Association was to be established, and no additional substantial superstructure created. The national Open School organisation would co-ordinate, stimulate and act as a service institution for existing institutions and for local initiatives. The Committee strongly emphasised the lack of existing provision for the large number of men and women who comprised the target group.

The work of the Open School Committee ended before the result of the pilot project could be evaluated. The Committee was however able to make indirect use of various aspects of experience obtained through the project in the ten reports which it published on different areas of adult education. Its experience in relation to the pilot project enabled the Committee to address questions not only on curriculum, organisation, and reaching the target group, but also on policy making and politics.

While the project was in progress the Open School Committee reported on the following topics:
− Open higher education (progressing towards an Open University)
− Research on the Open School project
− Use of education in preparation for old age
− Financing adult education
− Illiteracy
− Development of the expertise of teachers and tutors in adult education

The follow-up to the Open School project (in relation to students, local projects and the national organisation)

The reports published on the last-mentioned subject are of the greatest interest to the current study and of greatest significance to the future of the Open School. They were written following the first two years of the project; shortly before the end of the second year it was decided that the pilot project should continue for another one year. Further time was required because of the complexity of the problems encountered at the outset and because adequate planning for the follow-up had not been completed. But the result of the first two years of operation was that public opinion recognised the project as offering a chance to those who previously had lacked educational opportunities; to close the Open School would be out of the question.

CHANGES INTRODUCED AFTER TWO EXPERIMENTAL YEARS

The Open School pilot project was to continue as a pilot project for one further year. After this third year it was intended that other groups and organisations should benefit from the knowledge and experience gained during the project. Efforts were therefore made to improve the work being done in the fourteen locations.

Radio and television outputs were re-planned in the light of the failure of the attempt to integrate the use of mass media with the work of the basic groups. New ways had to be discovered to exploit radio and television both to meet the needs of Open School students and to reach the wider Open School target group.

Working In Groups

In the third year of the project the central role of the basic group was reaffirmed. Initially the working schedules as well as the subjects of the themes to be studied were prescribed from Zeist (after testing by the 'sounding-board groups'). But in the third year the Open School groups decided for themselves the themes for study and the amount of time to be devoted to each theme. Students were thus enabled to determine their own programmes of study to a much greater extent than during the initial stages of the project.

Printed Materials

The print theme-orientated materials were adapted to the revised system of study. The form and content of each booklet had to be such as to enable it to be used independently of the others; no new courses were produced requiring sequential study. Each booklet could be taken off the shelf and used separately as a source of information on a particular topic.

The clear distinction between theme-orientated and subject-orientated materials was not maintained. New printed materials for subjects from the school curriculum were produced according to the same criteria as the theme-orientated materials. For example, if a group working on the theme 'health' required additional information on 'food', this information could be obtained from a booklet which formed part of the biology course. In the first years of the project, the subjects most frequently studied were Dutch, English and Mathematics. The printed materials relating to these subjects were the first to be revised.

In order to meet the revised standards of the project, the printed materials were required to fulfil a different function. They were rewritten and tested by people experienced in working with the target group so as to ensure that they could meet the needs of the Open School students.

Evaluation

Evaluation was always regarded as a vital function in the pilot project. When the first method of evaluation, which involved the application of tests to new students from the very beginning of their Open School studies, was rejected, an alternative method had to be devised.

Students had at first been regarded as objects for research. The evaluation process hindered the development of self-awareness and the evolution of the group. Following discussions within the project, several decisions were made:
–   all the information which could be obtained from the project should be used not only for the final report but for effecting

improvements in the project
- tutors and students were to be subjects as well as objects
- the importance of determination of processes was emphasised. This involved the description of the working of groups rather than the measurement of effects.

The last decision was instrumental in the appearance of a series of reports describing the processes which were observed in the groups. A considerable quantity of valuable information was obtained and made available in all the study locations.

Radio and Television

To some extent Open School group work and Open School radio and television programmes have become disengaged after the first two years of the project. They retain a common target group, adults who have completed only five, six or seven years of primary education. The vital factor in the separation lies in the difference between reaching students in a group once or twice per week, and reaching students through broadcasting.

The new radio and television programmes were presented in a magazine format, under the title 'Open School Time' ('Open School Tijd'). The revised format was devised in the light of the following departures from earlier policy:
- The target group for Open School broadcasts was extended to include not only students (in official groups, in spontaneous groups, and a few individual students) but also general television and radio audiences
- Each programme was required to be able to stand independently from other programmes, so that sequential study was excluded. Any viewer or listener who tunes in to 'Open School Time' should be able to benefit from it. Each broadcast should be regarded as potentially the first step towards regular viewing of or listening to 'Open School Time', and should be planned and produced accordingly.
- The materials produced through each of the various media employed by Open School should be usable individually as well as in combination with materials produced through other media.

Radio. Almost all the broadcasting companies in the Netherlands are involved in the production of Open School radio programmes. Most companies represent one particular religious or political viewpoint; it was the wish of the Open School Committee that all main stream opinions current in the Netherlands should be represented in the Open School.

In the third year of the project the broadcasting companies were granted greater freedom in the selection of subjects for programmes. They were still required to bear in mind the needs of the target group, to produce printed materials to accompany broadcasts, and to ensure that Open School tutors and students were represented on the supervisory production team. The various companies produced fifty hours of radio during the year, broadcast nationally on Monday afternoons with repeats late on Monday evenings.

A special radio course entitled 'How to Learn' dealt with learning problems of individual students and also discussed more general barriers to learning, and prejudices which prevent people from studying.

A regional radio station in Friesland (Radio Fryslan) began production of a short weekly Open School programme specially designed for this northern province with its own language. The radio station and the Open School project in this province (Heerenveen) provided one another with feedback. For various reasons, including changes of policy, the involvement of different authorities, and the uncertainty about the continuation of the Open School project, this experiment in co-operation between a local project working with basic groups, and a regional radio station, has lasted only a short time. The evaluation of the experiment has not yet been completed, but its relative success or failure will be only one factor in determining the planning of future experiments. Another major factor is the creation of a network of regional radio stations covering the entire country. The debate on who will pay for regional radio (and in the future, television) is currently under way.

Television. Teleac (the Television Academy) produces twenty six hours of television per year for the Open School. The hour-long programmes are transmitted on Sunday afternoons, preceding a weekly family programme. The repeat transmission is on Wednesday mornings.

Initially the Open School Time' format comprises four elements:
- a language element dealing with one Dutch spelling problem every week (15 minutes)
- a theme element, on, for example, insomnia, money, death,

- immigration (25 minutes)
- mathematics and arithmetic (15 minutes)
- information on opportunities and provisions in various areas of adult education, one area being covered each week (5 minutes)

After one year of broadcasting according to this format, the mathematics and arithmetic element has been removed. This element had been included in the television programmes because of the popularity of the subjects with Open School students during the first two years of the project. In fact, television proved to be not a particularly suitable medium for these subjects, and other courses were introduced in their place, including courses on politics and on justice.

One of the most popular subjects offered by the Open School was English. A course entitled 'A Little Bit' was broadcast on radio, and the internationally-produced television course 'Follow Me' was adapted for a Dutch audience and broadcast by Teleac. Since the course was not produced according to Open School requirements it was neither adopted by the Open School Pilot Scheme Association nor broadcast under the auspices of the Association, but was transmitted purely as a Teleac course.

Open School television programmes have an estimated total viewing audience of between 400,000 and 500,000, which in the Netherlands is considered a high figure. The programme's popularity is also demonstrated by the sales figures of the printed materials produced to accompany the courses; 15,000 copies of the material produced for the most popular course, Dutch language, have been sold.

The distribution of printed Open School materials was organised by the central office at Zeist. At the Teleac office in Utrecht, a telephone number was available where answers could be obtained to questions raised in radio and television programmes.

TOWARDS A FUTURE OPEN SCHOOL

By the time that the end of the pilot project was in sight, at the end of the third year, the Open School was held in high public regard. But the provisions which should have been made to adopt on a national scale the learning system tested in the pilot project had not been made. The plan for the incorporation of the Open School system into existing adult education institutions was not completed.

The Open School Pilot Scheme Association had designed a new Framework Plan; this new Plan recommended that formal and informal education provision for adults, previously separated, should be integrated. Learning through experience and learning in small groups were key elements in the system. Further time was essential to enable existing adult education institutions to comply with these and other requirements laid down in the Framework Plan. The matter was discussed in Parliament with the result that the project was enabled to continue for a fourth year to bridge the gap until the local authorities (municipalities) could assume responsibility for the project. New students had to be recruited, and the Open School's tutors, whose jobs had almost been lost, were required to begin a recruiting campaign. They requested a guarantee, which was granted, that new students could study with the Open School for a period of at least two years. The Minister of Education also guaranteed continued employment to the tutors employed by the Open School Pilot Scheme Association. This was in fact a difficult guarantee to honour because the funds made available for the continuation of Open School in the thirty planned locations (which included the fourteen existing locations) were scarcely sufficient to pay all the tutors. In addition, the national organisation was scheduled to close on August 1st 1981 and other institutions, organisations and authorities were free to select and employ their own staff.

The active co-operation of the local authorities was essential if the mass of experience accumulated during the years of the pilot project was to be fully utilized. The employees of the Open School organisation and the Ministry of Education have worked hard to obtain this co-operation, and their efforts have achieved considerable success in all fourteen locations, although not all the tutors can be retained in the future.

Because of the decreasing financial resources of the local and of the national government, the municipalities had little opportunity to raise the level of funding of Open School provisions above that which had been paid by the national government during the previous four years. In many cases it proved necessary to curtail activities in other areas of adult education in order to continue Open School activities.

The spontaneous Open School groups and other groups comparable to Open School also suffered from government financial restrictions.

The climate which favoured the continuing expansion of a flourishing Open School seems to have disappeared, which is regrettable in view of the results produced by the project. But this conclusion must inevitably be drawn from the hesitation shown by policy-makers engaged in designing an adult education system which provides compensatory education for those whose basic education is limited.

A New Structure

The Advisory Committees on the Open School, Educational Networks and Educational Leave advised on a policy which covered all aspects of adult education. The responses from the various Ministries involved in adult education have been greatly delayed because of internal differences of opinion and because of the complexity of existing structures. A report on adult education will however be presented to Parliament in 1981. In the meantime a policy has been formulated which is intended to stimulate activity on five aspects of adult education:
- literacy
- education for cultural minorities
- educational networks
- introducing Open School
- basic vocational training

In these five areas, specific projects could be proposed by local authorities or were initiated by the national government. In each specialist area a Project Group is being formed, which will co-ordinate professional support, advise on common problems, and also advise on the development of future policy. The projects are intended to last for three years, by which time it is hoped that a clearer structure will have emerged and a system of funding will have been developed.

The presidents of each Project Group, together with half a dozen independent experts on different aspects of education policy, form a Co-ordinating Committee. The president of this Committee (Coordinatigroep Projecten Volwasseneneducatie) is Professor R.A. de Moor. The Committee's office is in Zeist, in the same building which the Open School Pilot Scheme Association occupies until the middle of 1981.

The Committee is intended to carry fewer responsibilities than the current Open School organisation, and is taking over only a proportion of the tasks which were allocated to the Open School Pilot Scheme

Association during the years of the project. Some of the remaining tasks are transferred to other authorities and organisations, but others are not allocated at all. The following paragraphs describe briefly the planned future continuation of the different aspects of the work of the project.

Organisation and Administration. The Open School was an employer, it rented buildings, purchased and supplied materials and equipment, and was a partner in contracts of various kinds. From 1981 these activities will be the responsibility of local authorities subsidised annually for three years by the national government at the level of the salaries of two full-time employees together with a maximum of 100,000 guilders for additional costs. Other facilities must be provided by organisations participating in the projects, of which there will be thirty.

Course Creation. The Open School Framework Plan will guide the development of the new projects. The actual arrangements for the future creation of printed materials have not however been completed. Radio and television programmes will continue to be made, and a special Programme Advisory Committee will advise on their content. The Minister of Culture has recently proposed the setting up of a Federation of Educational Broadcasting, in which educational as well as general broadcasting organisations would be represented; a decision is expected in the near future.

Distribution of Materials. One of the most urgent, unresolved problems at the time of writing is the allocation of responsibility for the distribution of existing materials.

Support to the Projects. During the years of the project the Open School organisation had to cope not only with the problems involved in planning, developing, producing and distributing courses, but also with organisational problems arising from, for example, the scattered geographical locations of the project's activities. Experience gained during these years will certainly be of value in the future, but it must be anticipated that a different order of additional problems will occur due to the involvement of many different organisations and authorities in the new structure.

206

Support relating to the content of courses will be given by two existing national organisations on formal and non-formal education respectively. The Open School Project Group will advise on general organisational problems, but a great deal of reliance must be placed on the solution of local problems at a local level.

Co-ordination. The Open School organisation has until now co-ordinated the activities of the various local projects; co-ordination will in the future be the principal task of the Project Group. The proposed creation of a Federation of Educational Broadcasting may assist one of the most difficult aspects of the task, establishing a satisfactory relationship between the different media and methods employed, in particular between the working groups and the mass media. It is possible that the various Project Groups mentioned above may each be allocated the task of co-ordinating that part of educational broadcasting which is aimed at the particular target group with which it is concerned. The Co-ordinating Committee mentioned above would also have a role in the Ministry of Culture's proposed Federation.

CONCLUSION

The period when this case study was being written (the first half of 1981) has been a time of almost continuous debate on the future of adult education in the Netherlands. In the near future further potential evidence will be available in the form of the evaluation of the Open School project, carried out by the Open School Pilot Scheme Association. Those people who have been involved on the project are already convinced however that Open School is effective in providing new educational opportunities for men, and in particular for women, and that as many people as possible should be enabled to take advantage of the benefits created by this innovatory system.

Chapter 8

RADIO ECCA
CANARY ISLANDS

Luis Espina Cepeda *

INTRODUCTION

Radio ECCA is a very special institution, a radio broadcasting station converted into an educational centre.

'ECCA' stands for 'Emisora Cultural de Canarias' ('Cultural station of the Canaries'), since the initiative began and is still based in Las Palmas. But 'ECCA' is now also the t:ademark of the educational system created by this station, a system which is currently operating in the mainland Spanish provinces and in several Latin American countries.

The licence to transmit from Radio ECCA was granted by the Spanish Ministry of Information on December 10th 1963. The new station broadcast its first lessons on February 15th 1965 after more than a year of preparatory experimenting and testing.

The body which owns Radio ECCA, the Society of Jesus, granted the Spanish Ministry of Education the use of all the property of the station for 'adult education and experiments in distance education'. Thanks to this concession, the Ministry of Education was able to set up in the station itself a permanent state centre for adult education. The management and administration of Radio ECCA is entrusted to the body ultimately responsible for the station, the Society of Jesus.[1]

During the sixteen years of its existence, Radio ECCA has enrolled 175,000 students from the Archipielago Canario, which represents approximately 11.5% of the Islands' total population.

Various Spanish institutions have introduced the ECCA system of teaching into their respective provinces by means of collaborative agreements with Radio ECCA. In this way the total enrolment of ECCA students in Spain (including the Canary Islands) reached the figure of 28,505 for the academic year 1979/80. Nine Latin American countries have also introduced the ECCA system, through collaborative agreements with Radio ECCA.

* Translated by Geoffrey Pucci and edited by Keith Harry

The present study deals with Radio ECCA and its educational system, except in those instances where specific references are made to other provinces and countries, the study is confined to the experience of Radio ECCA in the Canary Islands.

WHY THE INSTITUTION CAME INTO BEING

Radio ECCA was created in order to provide education for the adult population. The founder of the station, Francisco Villen Lucena S.J., decided that the first task should be to provide socially deprived sections of the community with cultural opportunities. Having learned about the methods of Radio Sutatenza, which was already teaching by radio in Colombia, he set about creating a Spanish equivalent. Although Radio ECCA and Radio Sutatenza both use radio as a teaching medium, their educational systems are now very different.

Radio ECCA's first priority was to teach reading and writing, thus providing deprived sections of the population with what they most urgently required. Its principal focus of attention was, and still is, the poorest classes of society. But this section of the population, and all others, also require educational provision at a more advanced level, which since its inception, Radio ECCA has striven to provide. ECCA's courses have diversified, and continue to reflect the needs of the population to which they are addressed.

Although its efforts are concentrated in the formal area, Radio ECCA does not exclude non-formal education altogether. It presents some courses which result in an academic award and others which do not. Above all, its unswerving aim is to raise the cultural level of the population with a view to bringing about greater individual freedom and a progressively increasing share in public life.

Radio ECCA works on the basic premise that only the progressively more educated person can preserve his freedom and participate to the full in the life of today. In addition, to educate the weakest is the best way to put an end to the excessive social and economic inequalities which still exist.

For these reasons, Radio ECCA's purpose is the education and the raising of the cultural level of the people to whom it is directed.

WHO FOR ? DESCRIPTION OF THE STUDENT BODY

Although Radio ECCA focuses its attention on the educational difficulties of the lowest strata of society, it does not exclude the higher
strata from its student body.

Radio ECCA has provided real evidence to support the theory that
education by radio ('enseñanza radiofonica') can teach individuals and
groups of people who, through personal circumstances, would not be
able to benefit from conventional education.

It would have been impossible for the 175,000 adults who have
studied in the Canary Islands during the last sixteen years to have
attended conventional educational centres.

The Spanish educational budget for the region could not have met
a demand for adult education on this scale. In addition, these people
would not have been able to attend the conventional centres with any
regularity. Age, location of homes, and other aspects of the social
situations of this massive 'student population' would have made it
impossible to fulfil their educational requirements by traditional
methods.

The following data serve to illustrate the above remarks:

Ages of students of Radio ECCA

above 45 years	15%
from 26 to 40 years	47%
from 20 to 25 years	28%
from 14 to 19 years	10%
	100%

Places of residence of ECCA students

Islands' capital	32%
Towns with town hall	27.4%
Villages or small towns without town hall	33%
Houses in the countryside	7.6%
	100%

Occupations of ECCA students

Professional occupations	2.3%
Construction workers	3.1%
Tomato crop workers and other rural occupations	16.1%
Clerks, shop assistants, etc.	20.4%
Students in other educational institutions	16.8%
Housewives	31.3%
	100%

The last two tables originate from a survey carried out in 1972 so they are not recent, and by this time there will be some alterations in the various statistics. In general the population of the Canaries has become more urbanised than previously, but the predominantly 'popular' character of the student body has nevertheless survived since 1972.

Radio ECCA has thus succeeded in reaching the public for which it was brought into being. Without the use of radio, this public would have been able to study in no other way.

WHAT MATERIALS ? ACTIVITIES CARRIED OUT BY RADIO ECCA

It has already been asserted that Radio ECCA aims to address itself to the educational needs of the population which it serves. ECCA's educational activities are centred on three areas:

1. The broadcasting of courses leading to an academic qualification. Initially, situated in 1965 in the Spanish province with the highest percentage of total illiterates (10.4% during the 1960s), ECCA's focus was on literacy education. In the series of six courses, the total illiterate had the opportunity to progress towards the 'Certificado de Estudios Primarios', which was at that time an essential pre-requisite for employment. When alterations were made in the Spanish education system in 1973, Radio ECCA modified and extended its academic curriculum. There are at present a series of five 'Popular Culture' courses, including the

211

first stage towards literacy, followed by three courses which prepare students for the 'Titulo de Graduado Escolar', which represents the final stage of basic education (or primary education) in Spain. In these academic courses it is intended that students should not only strive to obtain a qualification but should also broaden their horizons, working progressively towards full personal development. In 1980-81, as part of its programme offering a second opportunity to the adult population, Radio ECCA has also introduced courses leading to the 'Bachillerato', beginning with the first stage.

2. Formal teaching and academic courses for adults are not receiving a good press at the present time. Not for this reason, but in order to meet the most urgent needs of its public, Radio ECCA has since its foundation provided non-academic courses (not leading to qualification) aimed at improving both quality of life and job performance. Thus, courses have been provided for some years in English, and Accountancy and Commercial Mathematics, and there is in addition a 'Parents' School' ('Escuela de Padres') which aims to help parents in the task of educating their children. ECCA is continuing to develop non-academic courses; courses currently in preparation include a course for the training of group leaders, courses on techniques of evaluation (for teachers), on preventive medicine (for a wide popular audience), on techniques of management at an elementary level for small traders, and even on photography. Through the ECCA system it is possible to teach virtually any subject by radio; it is therefore essential that the station retains its sensitivity to the general educational needs of the people it serves.[2]

3. The third area of activity is less clearly defined but no less important. During those times when its education programmes are not being transmitted (i.e. three hours per day on working days and all day on holidays), ECCA's broadcasts are devoted to entertainment. The station has a considerable listening audience, one of the largest of any station in the Canary Islands, due to its expertise in presenting entertainment programmes and to the fact that it does not use commercial advertising. Educational elements are sometimes slotted into the entertainment programming; campaigns

have been mounted to encourage a positive attitude towards self-help or towards study, and towards wider objectives such as community development, the necessity of being well-informed on election issues, and promoting awareness of consumer pressures at Christmas time. It is impossible to determine accurately the degree of penetration of these campaigns. since no kind of evaluation is carried out, but they appear to be successful. Their potential for penetration is enhanced by the credibility which ECCA enjoys in the community as a result of its educational work and its frequent contact with the public via its entertainment programmes.

Through its frequent use of the telephone and the recorded interview, Radio ECCA attempts to become the voice of the people, especially of those whose views are not usually heard. The people consider ECCA to be their station and they take notice of its suggestions. In its turn, ECCA treats its audience with great respect; it does not base campaigns on controversial issues but promotes programmes of clear positive value to the community. However, this third area of cultural activity is much less precisely defined than the other two, a factor which makes it difficult to evaluate.

WHAT MEDIA AND METHODS ?

ECCA describes its teaching system as 'un sistema tridimensional'; it is based on three elements frequently found in combination in distance education: print materials, radio, and face-to-face tuition.

Every ECCA lesson is centred upon a 'lesson master sheet' ('esquema') The teacher has a copy of the lesson master sheet in front of him while he broadcasts over the radio, and the student follows his own copy simultaneously in his own home. This specially produced printed material, prepared by ECCA's educational staff and printed in its own workshop, fulfils the function of worksheet, blackboard or slate.

The student is required to respond to the radio teacher by writing on the lesson master sheet during the course of the broadcast. The master sheet is therefore the means of maintaining both continuous attention of the student and the necessary communication between

213

teacher and student. In addition, a full set of master sheets comprises a student's text book. Exercises are included on the back of each master sheet; these are designed to be completed after the student has listened to the radio broadcast. The student will receive assistance from the exercises in consolidating his learning, and ECCA uses the exercises as part of its student evaluation process. The lesson master sheet therefore fulfils a number of different functions.

Full comprehension of an ECCA radio lesson cannot be achieved without a lesson master sheet. In addition, the master sheet is supplemented by various other types of printed material produced by ECCA for its students, notes or technical memoranda ('notas o apuntes tecnicos') on difficult topics, synoptic tables, special exercise sheets, complementary texts, etc. The nature of the course to be presented determines the type of printed material which is produced to complement the indispensable lesson master sheet.

The second element of the ECCA system is the 'radio lesson' ('clase'), which resembles neither a lecture nor any other traditional type of radio programme. It might perhaps best be described as a detailed explication of the content of the lesson master sheet. The student listens to the radio lesson not seated in his armchair as he would normally listen to the radio or watch television, but seated at a work table, pencil in hand, carrying out the teacher's instructions. ECCA's radio lessons are above all student-active, since the student is constantly at the 'blackboard'. In addition, radio lessons are highly personalised; the teacher, although he has thousands of students, always talks directly to one, utilising all the resources of radio to achieve personal contact. The objectives of ECCA's specially designed radio lessons are to stimulate interest in the theme covered in the master sheet, to explain the content fully and clearly, and to encourage the student's involvement in private study.

ECCA's radio lessons are not scripted; the team of teachers who present the lesson are well prepared to improvise before the microphone and the lesson master sheet, just as a teacher would improvise when talking face-to-face with a group of students.

The third element of the ECCA system, complementing the lesson master sheet and the radio lesson, is the 'tutor' ('profesor orientador'). If the learning process ended with the class simply listening, then the ECCA system would be relatively easy to organise. The complexity and the particular quality of the system arises from the personal contact

214

which all students must maintain each week with a tutor. ECCA students are each attached to a tutorial centre ('centro de orientacion') as near to home as possible; the centre is the venue for the weekly meeting between student and tutor.

The tutor's duties are as follows: he hands out the booklet of lesson master sheets for the following week, collects work completed in the previous week, guides the student and tries to resolve difficulties which have arisen. He also explains the most difficult points covered in the previous week's work, makes on-the-spot evaluations, and, most important of all, seeks to motivate and encourage the student. In addition, the tutor collects the student's weekly fee payment.

A great number of activities are carried out on a one-to-one basis, but groups of students may also meet together for one or two hours at a time, so that there is the possibility of considerable flexibility within the system. The nature of the different courses dictates whether the one-to-one or the group alternative is chosen. Finally, by reporting to ECCA on the progress of his students, the tutor is able to provide feedback.

The ECCA system comprises these three elements or dimensions, whose interrelationship provides enormous educational potential. The carefully planned integration and synchronisation which characterises the ECCA system is the reason for its effectiveness in teaching and motivating adult students. The three elements are integrated into the whole, the system could not function if any one element was absent, and similarly no one element could function separately from the other two. But success is not cheaply bought; the success of the system is ensured by a great expenditure of personal and organisational effort.

COURSE CREATION

The major technical difficulty presented by the creation of an ECCA course (and of any distance education course) lies in the fact that the creative act of teaching is divided and is carried out by different teachers. At ECCA, teaching is performed by:
- a teacher, or a team of teachers, who devise the course, create the printed material and plan the integration and synchronisation of its various elements;

215

– a team of two teachers, a man and a woman, who record the radio lesson, always synchronising it with the previously prepared lesson master sheet; and
– the tutor, who meets the students in person every weekend.

All these teachers have to work with the knowledge that the whole operation encompasses a single teaching act, albeit that the individual parts are separately created. It is essential that the common plan of action should always be followed so that the student is not distracted by an awareness that the different elements of his course are not properly integrated.

The first stage of this divided teaching process is the formulation of the course. Radio ECCA has a Pedagogical Department ('Gabinete Pedagogico') whose function is to devise courses. It has two sections, one responsible for academic courses and the other for non-academic courses. In each of these sections the teachers work in their own specialist areas. This creative work involves a broad study of the subject material which is to be taught, the determination of the objectives of the course and an account of its outline, detailed planning of the content to be included and the activities to be devised.

Only when this work is completed can the work of creating the printed materials be undertaken, materials both for the student and for the tutors and the teachers who are involved in recording radio lessons. Course creation in distance education is a slow process which must be carried out systematically; every detail must be planned in advance.

The creation of a course of this kind requires knowledge of the students for whom it is intended. Before presenting its first radio lessons in 1965, Radio ECCA piloted lessons for more than a year with a group of students whose immediate reactions were taped so as to enable amendments and improvements to be made to the lesson master sheets and the radio lessons. This time-consuming experiment shaped ECCA's technology significantly. Recently, before launching the first stage of the 'Bachillerato' course, ECCA spent one year testing it with a group of students. The teachers who work in this area have generally come from other work groups which have direct contact with students.

Feedback works in ECCA through the transmission of information from students back to the Pedagogical Department, so that the courses are continually reshaped. Planning for new courses is not only concerned with the subject material to be taught, but also takes into account the students' requirements as expressed in feedback. If it was to ignore feedback from students, the Department's work would be doomed to failure.

COURSE PRODUCTION: PRINTING OF MATERIALS AND RECORDING OF LESSONS

Radio ECCA possesses its own print workshop which handles all its printed materials. A special department, organised and run by teachers, is responsible for page preparation; the subsequent printing is by offset litho. The drawing of illustrations and the layout of printed text are regarded as tasks for teachers and as part of the ECCA integrated educational process because the educational effectiveness of the lesson master sheet depends to a great extent on how well or how badly the information it contains is presented. The fact that the print workshop belongs to ECCA is particularly important in view of the considerable number of courses which are produced and of the many students requiring materials. More than 20 million sheets are printed every year in the workshop.

It is important to note that course creation and printing of materials are carried out at the ECCA headquarters in Las Palmas not only for the Canary Islands but for all the Spanish provinces. Significant savings are made by centralising the printing of course materials, but all the other processes and activities which characterise the ECCA system are undertaken separately by each mainland province.

In its headquarters at Las Palmas, Radio ECCA has facilities for the production and recording of radio lessons. The lessons are always pre-recorded to avoid inaccuracies and to ensure precise timings. Recording is carried out live one or two days before transmission. Radio lessons are not used from year to year but are newly recorded every year so as to effect maximum communication with the student. The lessons are recorded by teams comprising one man and one women teacher, and not merely by radio presenters. Well-prepared teachers find room for improvisation in the radio lesson so that the best possible use can be made of available time and the greatest possible assistance given to students.

Whereas printed materials are produced centrally and then distributed throughout the whole of Spain, ECCA encourages the recording of radio lessons locally. In this way, local language variations can be incorporated and the educational effectiveness of the lessons can be increased by their adaptation to local needs and environment. The total system is considered less effective in provinces where there are relatively few students so that local recording is not considered feasible. The production of radio lessons is undertaken after the creation of printed materials, sometimes by a matter of weeks or months.

COURSE DISTRIBUTION: THE TWO-WAY WEEKLY COMMUNICATION BETWEEN ECCA AND THE STUDENT

Part of the ECCA distribution system involves the establishment of a weekly communication channel which follows the pattern

$$ECCA \rightarrow Tutor \rightarrow Students \rightarrow Tutor \rightarrow ECCA$$

The setting up of this two-way communication is straightforward in theory, but can in certain cases prove to be the most problematic aspect of the whole system. The fact that communication is weekly makes the task more difficult, but it also offers so many advantages, assisting the students in following courses and facilitating the feedback process, that ECCA does not wish to reduce its frequency.

The weekly communication channel is used for the distribution of printed materials to students. Each week ECCA sends to its tutors the printed material to be distributed to students on its various courses. The week-to-week delivery cycle is important in motivating students; it helps to maintain continuous interest and to reduce the tendency to drop out which commonly occurs in other systems if all the materials for a course are delivered at once.

In order that the distribution mechanism should function as smoothly as possible, the tutor sends to ECCA a 'bulletin' ('parte') containing complete details of student enrolments and drop-outs. In return, ECCA sends the tutor a detailed list ('relacion') of all the materials to be distributed to students.[3]

The package sent by the tutor (containing only a simple list) is much smaller than that sent out by ECCA, which contains all the materials for distribution to students. Additional information will be transmitted when tutors report on students' progress and assessment. The student usually follows the course in his own home, tuning in to ECCA's transmissions at certain times. The frequency of radio lessons varies according to the course, ranging from one per week to one per day. In certain Spanish provinces where the transmitter is not sufficiently powerful for the student to tune in to it, successful experiments have been carried out using audio cassettes. The delivery and distribution of cassettes has been arranged weekly through the radio station-tutor link.

STUDENT ENROLMENT

A perennial problem in adult education is how to persuade the potential student to enrol on a course. There is little point in creating a good course if adults are not motivated to study it. The enrolment campaign therefore plays a vital part, and Radio ECCA has the invaluable advantage of being able to exploit its own broadcasting facilities. Since it does not transmit commercial advertising, the full strength of this powerful medium can be focused on cultural themes.

During the time when radio lessons are not being transmitted, ECCA's output is very much orientated towards publicising its educational activities. Using different techniques such as repeated slogans, surveys, interviews, short features and even complete programmes, ECCA mounts its publicity campaign to persuade adults that they should study. Variations on the basic message, 'You should study', 'It is never too late to study', 'Don't say "I don't know" ', are frequently repeated. A few months before the beginning of the courses, the station intensifies its campaign. It tries to motivate the people to study, very often using the voices of those who are studying or have studied; it also broadcasts details of how, when and where it is possible to become a student. The insistence with which the message is presented has earned ECCA the affectionate nickname 'Radio Jaqueca'[4]. Once the courses are under way, the station turns its attention to retaining its students by encouraging them to persevere in the task which they have undertaken.

Radio ECCA's strongest message is in fact its own continuing existence; it motivates through what it does ('por lo que hace') rather than by what it says ('lo que dice'). The persuasive powers of a radio station devoted exclusively to educating the people are somewhat difficult to quantify, but are nevertheless of vital importance. The public image which a station of this kind creates is its principal means of motivating the people.

Various other means of persuasion are employed, such as posters, leaflets, letters to potential students and to persons or institutions capable of motivating people to study, press announcements, broadcast announcements on other radio stations and on television, and personal contacts with cultural organisations and associations. But these means only complement the most powerful motivator, the broadcast output of Radio ECCA.

The effectiveness of ECCA's campaign is clearly demonstrated by comparison with the results of the publicity mounted by commercial radio stations in other Spanish provinces using ECCA courses. These stations lack the sharp educational focus which ECCA can achieve, and as a result their student numbers are much lower.

The recruitment and enrolment of students necessitates an extensive infrastructure. The tutorial centres in the Islands, where the weekly meetings between students and tutors take place, are also used as enrolment centres ('centros de matriculacion'). ECCA has sited these centres throughout the Islands wherever their transmissions reach. More than 600 enrolment and tutorial centres serve the 1.5 million inhabitants of the Canary Islands. The multiplicity of centres enables the student to enrol without having to travel far from his home.

In addition, ECCA has a duty to provide courses which cater for the fundamental needs of the Islands' population. If these needs were not respected, the enrolment campaign would be pointless. The massive response to ECCA by the people of the Canaries is the best proof that its courses and its total approach are answering the real needs of the population.

STUDENT SUPPORT

This section places emphasis on the importance of personal, direct support of the student. It was stated above in the 'Course Creation' section that printed material and radio lessons form two of the elements of ECCA's 'sistema tridimensional'. The third element involves the student attending his local tutorial centre every week to meet his tutor and other students.

The tutorial centre has a clear educational function which is defined by the methodology of each course. In general it is the place where students can clear up doubts, receive additional information on difficult points covered in the course, and complete practical exercises. The second, separate, function of the centre is to maintain and if possible increase the student's motivation.

It is vital that the adult student should realise that a person exists, whose surname and first name he knows, who knows him personally and who is familiar in depth with his work. By this means the impersonality which is often a characteristic of distance learning systems, by which the student deals with an anonymous organisation or a name whose face he never sees, is eliminated. For its students, ECCA always has available the surname and forenames of the tutor. The influence of the tutor on the student is of paramount importance, in fostering the commitment to study, providing encouragement in moments of despondency, inspiring confidence, and generally bringing a human touch to the educational process. This boosting of morale is also assisted by regular contact with the other adults at the tutorial centre.

In order to fulfil these objectives and the specifically educational objectives described below, Radio ECCA employs a network of more than three hundred teachers responsible for supervising the six hundred or so centres currently functioning throughout the Islands. It will be evident that for so many teachers to work in so many different places with one common methodology is not an easy task, and indeed it is a task not always successfully carried out.

It was mentioned in the 'Course distribution' section that ECCA communicates regularly with its tutors by various means: a weekly circular, additional pedagogical information, occasional extra printed materials for specific purposes, and regular meetings for teachers of each course and each region. Induction courses are also held for new tutors, a particularly important factor in mainland provinces where ECCA courses are being introduced for the first time. Adequate preparation is essential in such a complex integrated system.

ASSESSMENT AND EVALUATION

In the ECCA system of education by radio it is possible to apply an assessment procedure for individual students which is very similar to that used in conventional full-time study centres. This is made possible by students' weekly attendance at their tutorial centres. A description follows of the assessment procedure used by ECCA in courses leading to an academic qualification. The remaining courses use all or some of these elements according to circumstances.

One of the most important moments in the assessment process is when the student comes along to enrol and is placed on a course. As each course has specified objectives and pre-determined content, it is possible to assess which course is appropriate for the new student. For this purpose the tutor administers an entry test to each student who wishes to enrol. Once the student is placed on the most appropriate course his further progress depends on his own efforts.[5]

The function of the lesson master sheet has been described in the section 'What media and methods?'. On the reverse side of each sheet are exercises which the student is required to complete after the radio lesson in order to consolidate and to apply what has been learned. These daily exercises provide a broad base for the student assessment process.

In the first stage courses, the tutor corrects the master sheet exercises. He collects them from the students each week and returns the corrected exercises at the following week's meeting, with whatever written comments he feels are appropriate. In more advanced courses the daily exercises are corrected by the student himself with the help of a self-correction master sheet supplied for the purpose. The tutor nevertheless oversees the student's work and his self-corrected exercises. Students who correct their own work are required in addition to complete a two-part weekly assessment sheet, one on Arts and one on Sciences, the answers to which do not appear on the self-correction master sheet. The sheet is collected by the tutor for his assessment and is returned to the student the following week. These completed assessments provide the tutor with an additional guide to the work of the student.

In addition to the regular completion of exercises, students also take part in three assessment sessions during each course, held either at the tutorial centre or at another place where all the students on the course can conveniently meet. During these sessions, each student has to complete a number of written texts, the contents of which are not made known to him beforehand. The results of these written tests provide the main basis for the student's marks. The mark obtained in the final and most difficult test of the course is set against the average mark of the assessment tests completed during the year, to produce the student's final mark. This final assessment is not worked out with mathematical rigidity, but takes into account the tutor's direct personal knowledge of the student, ECCA headquarters staff may also be involved in the calculation of the final assessment. The three partial assessments and the final assessment are all recorded in ECCA's student files, which are created at the beginning of each course.

The ECCA system offers much the same opportunity for assessment as a conventional institution and the entire procedure is organised with great care. Any arbitrary assessments made during the course will come to light when the partial assessment marks are compared with the mark for the final assessment test. The normal outcome of this comparison is a mark somewhere between the partial and final assessment marks, which seems to indicate that the procedure works well.

ORGANISATION AND ADMINISTRATION

In common with other Spanish radio stations, Radio ECCA has a number of personnel under direct contract to undertake management, administrative, technical and secretarial tasks. But the specialised nature of ECCA's activities requires that its contract staff of nearly thirty also carry out duties in connection with the print workshop and with the storage and distribution of printed material.

In its capacity as a state teaching centre, ECCA also has nearly fifty teachers who have been appointed by the Ministry of Education and Science, just as they could have been appointed to any other state centre operating a conventional system. The Ministry appoints these teachers at the proposal of ECCA following a competitive examination, the results of which remain confidential, which attempts to discover in candidates the specific qualities required by teachers working for ECCA.

ECCA attempts to achieve unity in the operation and development of its broadcasting and educational functions by maintaining a single management structure for the whole system. The highest governing bodies of ECCA are:

1. the Management Council ('Consejo de Direccion'), appointed by the Society of Jesus, the organisation with ultimate responsibility for the station, and

2. the Board for Educational Advancement ('Junta de Promocion Educativa'), supreme governing body of the teaching centre, comprising representatives of the Ministry of Education and Science, of the Society of Jesus, and of the teachers appointed to ECCA.

The internal operational structure of ECCA is of particular interest. Although the teaching staff on the one hand and the personnel contracted to ECCA on the other hand have separate, specific responsibilities, the work and the people are in fact distributed and organised in accordance with a rationalised structure of the functions to be carried out. The organisation chart derived from this structure is not static since it is subject to alterations imposed by the active development of these functions.

From 1980-81, in addition to the other operational structure, the work of ECCA will be organised into two departments or divisions which will be separately housed:

1. A production centre ('Centro de Produccion'), responsible for all central services to the provinces which teach ECCA courses and also responsible for the co-ordination of ECCA delegations located in the provinces of mainland Spain.

2. An experimental centre ('Centro de Realizacion'), responsible for services to students in the Canary Islands and for the collection of feedback on different courses to enable necessary improvements to be made in particular courses and in the whole system.

The current rapid increase in student enrolments, combined with the fact that a considerable number of functions of a very different order are performed in ECCA (those of radio station, teaching centre, educational publishing house, and print workshop), determine that its organisational structure is subject to constant change.

Radio ECCA

CONTROL: EVALUATION OF THE SYSTEM

The assessment of students and the provision of feedback to ECCA which are described in the 'Assessment and evaluation' section form integral parts of the system of overall evaluation. If feedback from the student assessment procedure is not channelled towards the evaluation and improvement of the system then the feedback is not being properly utilised.

Primary data which can be used to evaluate ECCA's teaching effectiveness are the results attained by students taking academic courses. ECCA students' academic results are in fact similar to those of students in conventional institutions. In the final general basic education examination, leading to the 'Titulo de Graduado Escolar', ECCA students throughout Spain have achieved the results set out in the table below. The question paper for these examinations is approved by the Ministry of Education and Science and the grades are awarded by a tribunal supervised by an expert inspector from the Ministry.

Percentage of Student Passes in 'Titulo de Graduado Escolar' (1979)

Province	Student Entries	Student passes	Percentage pass rate
Almeria	116	80	69%
Badajoz	231	96	41%
Caceres	252	101	40%
Cordoba	287	166	57%
Granada	756	465	61%
Jaen	155	96	61%
Lugo	141	54	38%
Madrid	1,176	740	62%
Murcia	351	195	55%
Palma M.	84	70	83%
Sevilla	648	371	57%
Vigo	537	339	63%
Canarias	659	365	55%
TOTAL	5,393	3,138	58%

Another piece of numerical data relevant to the evaluation of ECCA's teaching is the permanent nature of the students' interest.

225

In distance education it is notoriously difficult to maintain student interest, and the drop-out rate is often high. In ECCA, over 50% of students, and in some courses 70% or 80%, complete their courses.

More important than the numerical data which testifies to ECCA's success are the continuing contacts established by tutors with their students. Through meetings and interviews, and through telephone and personal contacts, the tutors have their fingers on the pulse of the system. Their reports back to ECCA on students' progress or lack of progress enable such factors as badly presented lessons or typographical errors to be consistently detected.

In order to fully utilize this flow of information, ECCA's courses are maintained in a state of continuous revision. Each year new materials are printed for certain courses and new radio lessons for all courses are recorded. This is the only way in which the course can be preserved 'live', in touch with reality and susceptible to change.

In spite of all that has been said so far, it has to be admitted that evaluation of the quality of teaching cannot be achieved mathematically and is therefore always somewhat imprecise. A better method of assessment at ECCA is the accurate numerical data on students which is derived from the system of student fee payment and remuneration of tutors. Tutors in fact receive a percentage of the weekly fee, amounting to 70 out of 100 or 150 pesetas. The tutor retains his share and passes the remainder to ECCA. The station therefore does not pay the tutor directly, but receives from him a number of fees equal to the number of his students. In turn, ECCA supplies the same number of copies of printed materials to the tutor, and therefore always knows how many students are following its courses. If a tutor informs ECCA that he has fewer students than have actually paid fees, he will not receive printed materials for those students whose existence he is concealing. If he informs ECCA that he has more students than have actually paid fees, he will himself have to pay the fees of the 'extra' students. The technical problem of ascertaining the exact number of currently enrolled students is conveniently solved through the two-way communication between ECCA and its tutors.

Perhaps the very best piece of evaluation data is the confidence which the people of the Canary Islands have placed in ECCA since its foundation. More than 175,000 people (approximately 11.5% of the total population) have been ECCA students during the sixteen years of its existence, which is surely a popular endorsement of the success of the station's system. The trust and affection which the people of the Islands display towards ECCA is its most valued testimonial and the most important factor in an evaluation of its overall effectiveness.

RESOURCES

ECCA's resources emanate from two sources:
- subsidies and state or institutional aid, and
- student fees.

In 1979 the latter accounted for 53.54% of the total income of the station. 42.96% was derived from the Ministry of Education and Science and from subsidies from other organisations, the Ministry of Culture, regional bodies and private persons. It is hoped that external funding will be increased so that students' fees may be maintained at the present level or even reduced.

Total costs (123,353,493.47 pesetas in 1979) were more than met from the total income of 127,186,273.90 pesetas; there was even a small surplus for investment and improvements. ECCA is a non-profit making organisation; because of its institutional nature none of its income may be removed for any other institution or purpose.

ECCA owns the buildings in the city of Las Palmas which house its offices and the radio production facilities, and also the print workshop located nearby, and the transmitter in the mountainous centre of the island of Las Palmas.

Radio ECCA does not have abundant means at its disposal and many necessary items must be provided using whatever means are available. Nevertheless ECCA has contrived not only to survive but to expand, making economically viable this individually evolved formula for popular education.

CONCLUSION

This account of ECCA has been confined to a technical description of the system and has not attempted to portray the warm relationship between the radio station and its audience. To obtain a full picture of

ECCA it is necessary not only to read this report, nor simply to visit the station's offices, but to go into the street and speak to the people, whether in the city or the countryside. It is the people of the Canary Islands who possess the key to Radio ECCA.

Notes and References

1. The agreement between the Ministry of Education and the Society of Jesus became public with Decreto (Decree) 145/1975 of April 10th ('Boletin Oficial del Estado', May 6th 1975). The classification and control of the 'ECCA permanent centre for adult education' was established later, by Orden Ministerial (Ministerial Order) of October 14th 1977 ('Boletin Oficial del Estado', November 16th 1977).
2. For each course a table is compiled which provides information on enrolled students.
3. The weekly information sent out by ECCA to its tutors is included in the 'Circular', which contains lists relating to all courses. Further pedagogical details appear in the 'Circular Pedagogica', which acts as a guide for the tutorial centre. The 'bulletin' ('parte') is the brief weekly report sent back by tutors to ECCA.
4. A play on the Spanish words meaning 'migraine' and 'prattle'
5. When the student enrols, the tutor fills out a form requiring students' personal data. The tutor retains a copy of this form and another copy is sent to the station's archives. When the student completes or abandons his studies, the tutor sends in his copy so that it can be matched with the archive copy. Upon enrolment, the student is also given an accreditation card.
6. The files for students of the final stages of the basic education courses are fuller than those used for students of the first stage courses. The weekly assessment sheets are adapted to the content of the course as prescribed by the syllabus.

Chapter 9

DIRECTORY AND SELECTIVE BIBLIOGRAPHY

Keith Harry

INTRODUCTION

This chapter contains one entry for each of the twelve countries of the enlarged Community. The information in each entry is presented in a standard format under the headings 'Adult education provision', 'Broadcasting' and 'Projects and initiatives'. Bibliographical information is generally confined to the 'Projects and initiatives' section.

The section headed 'Adult education provision' describes very briefly the nature of provision as it affects basic adult education. No attempt is made to describe in detail the structure of adult education provision in particular countries because the European Bureau of Adult Education has already undertaken this task in its *Directory of Adult Education Organisations in Europe* (third edition 1978, fourth edition scheduled for publication late 1981).

The 'Broadcasting' section describes, again very briefly, the ways in which radio and television broadcasting in individual countries are organised. Finally, the 'Projects and initiatives' section includes information on projects and initiatives which are not described in previous chapters, together with bibliographical details of the most important documents which have been produced by or about the projects which are the subjects of chapters 2-8. The bibliographical coverage is extremely selective; further coverage can be found in the Study Report to the European Commission.

BELGIUM

Adult Education Provision

The government department responsible for adult education for the Dutch community is the Ministerie van Nationale Opvoeding en Nederlandse Cultuur, Bestuur voor Volksontwikkeling en Openbare Lectuur-

229

voorziening (Ministry of National Education and Dutch Culture, Directorate for Adult Education and Public Libraries), Sainctelette-square 13, B-1000 Brussel. Contact: The Director.

The department responsible for provision to the French community is the Ministère de l'Education Nationale et de la Culture Française, Direction Générale de la Jeunesse et des Loisirs, Galerie Ravenstein 4, B-1000 Bruxelles. Contact: Henry Ingberg, Conseiller Adjoint, Responsable du Service Audio-visuel.

Broadcasting

Belgische Radio en Televisie (BRT) and Radiodiffusion-Télévision-Belge (RTB) are autonomous institutions responsible for Flemish-language and French-language broadcasting respectively.

BRT
Auguste Reyerslaan 52
B-1040 Brussel
Contact: Jerome Verhaeghe,
Head of Adult Education, or
Bert Hermans, Television

In 1975, BRT established an Adult Education Service which under the title 'Open School' organises courses. using a variety of different media, in the areas of vocational training and general education (secondary level)

RTB
52 boulevard Auguste Reyers
B-1040 Bruxelles
Contact: Holde Lhoest,
Chef de Service à la Direction
Générale

RTB established an 'Education Permanente' service in 1971 to provide vocational and other training programmes in co-operation with various agencies.

In addition to the national transmissions of RTB and BRT, television programmes are also widely distributed by cable by various private interests operating under license.

Projects and Initiatives

Canal-Emploi, 49 avenue des Tilleuls, B-4000 Liège. Contact: Fredy Jacquet.
This project is aimed primarily at unemployed in the Liège area, and seeks to reach its target audience through weekly cable-TV programmes

230

and through face-to-face workshops with specific groups. The project's publications include *Animation et Sensibilisation des Travailleurs de la Région Liègeoise* (1977), which states the objectives of the project, and *Operation de Remise a Niveau des Connaissances: programme des activites de formation* (1981), reviewing the needs of the target groups and the organisation and content of courses.

Formation pour l'Université Ouverte de Charleroi (FUNOC), 106 route de Mons, B-6031 Monceau-sur-Sambre. Contact: Paul Demunter or Christiane Verniers.

A collective/community action project which identifies, analyses and provides for basic education needs through group work. Plans are currently being developed for using the mass media to support group work. The development of the project is well documented, in the publications of the Direction Générale de la Jeunesse et des Loisirs, e.g. JEB 7/76, Demunter, P., Quevit, A. and Verniers, C. *Université Ouverte: Leçons des Experiences Pilotes* (1976), and particularly in FUNOC's own publications series, e.g. No. 8, Demunter, P. *L'Université Ouverte: un Projet Socialiste* (1980)

DENMARK

Adult Education Provision

Voluntary adult education is provided by county education authorities at further education centres under the direction of the Undervisnings-ministeriet Direktoratet for Folkeskolen, Folkeoplysning, Seminarien m.v. (Ministry of Education Directorate for Elementary Schools, Youth and Adult Education and Teacher Training Colleges), Frederiksholms Kanal 26, DK1220 København K. Contact: Knud Michelsen, Det Internationale Kontor (International Relations Division).

Two national bodies with a co-ordinating function whose activities are of importance to basic adult education are:

Dansk Folkeoplysnings Samrad (Danish Council for Adult Education) The Council is a joint committee representing all national adult education associations

Ny Kongensgade 4, DK1472
København K

Contact: The Director

Landscentralen for Undervisningsmidler (National Institute for Educational Media), Oernevej 30, DK2400 København NV	The Landscentralen, which is responsible to the Ministry of Education, co-ordinates activities in the field of educational media.

Contact: Mogens Elvius

A specialist library, financed by and linked to the National Library. which is responsible for materials relating to education and educational psychology, is Danmarks Paedagogiske Bibliotek, Lersoe Parkalle 101, DK2100 København OE. Contact: Mikel Soegaard-Larsen, Librarian responsible for adult education.

Broadcasting

Danmarks Radio (Untervisningsafdelingen) Islands Brygge 81, DK2300 København S	Danmarks Radio is a public corporation with a monopoly of sound and television broadcasting. Its Educational Broadcasting Department is entirely financed by the Ministry of Education.
Contact: Harald Engberg-Pedersen (Head of Educational Broadcasting), or Peter Looms	

Projects and Initiatives

Dansk for Voksne (Danish for Adults). The project is described by Peter Looms in Chapter 6. A major evaluation report has recently been published; this is Olsen, E.S., Looms, P.O., and Kjaerum, F. *Dansk for Voksne: Rapport om Projektet* (Danmarks Radio, Copenhagen, 1980).

The following projects are included because they were launched as co-operative undertakings using a variety of media:

232

Laere for Livet (Learning for Life). Contact: The Director, Dansk Folkeoplysnings Samråd. A two-year project designed to stimulate debate on the U-90 education plan (published 1978) for the development of Danish education up to 1990.

Et Bedre Liv (A Better Life). Contact: Harald Engberg-Pedersen, Danmarks Radio. A project on health education employing trained animateurs as well as television, radio and various types of printed material.

EIRE

Adult Education Provision

The Department of Education is responsible for general education and for vocational education, but a total of nine Ministries have some degree of responsibility for particular aspects of adult education. At local level, the county is the unit for provision of educational services.

AONTAS	AONTAS's corporate members are
National Association of Adult	voluntary and statutory adult educa-
Education	tion agencies; both types of agency
14 Fitzwilliam Place	play a vital part in adult education
Dublin 2	in Eire

Contact: Michael O Murchu, Director

Broadcasting

The Irish national broadcasting organisation is Radio Telefis Eireann (RTE), Donnybrook, Dublin 4. Contact: Liam O Murchu, Assistant to the Director-General.

RTE is a statutory autonomous corporation which does not run an adult education programme; its Education Department has however been involved in the creation of a series of radio programmes designed to help tutors engaged in the work of teaching adults to read. RTE's involvement is described in Kelleher, K., 'Helping Adults to Read',

Directory and Selective Bibliography

European Bureau of Adult Education Newsletter, no. 3/4 (1978), pp. 26-27.

Projects and Initiatives

None identified.

FRANCE

Adult Education Provision

The Ministry of Education is responsible for the provision of adult education in France through its network of educational establishments. It has created a number of institutions to support its policy at national and regional level, including the Centre National de Documentation Pedagogique (CNDP), 29 rue d'Ulm, 75230 Paris Cedex 05 (Contact: P. Guigue, Director Adjoint, or Viviane Glikman, Chef de la Division des Evaluations). CNDP is involved in the production of audio-visual material and the promotion of modern teaching techniques as well as in documentation work.

Another institution which is part of the Ministry of Education and is involved in all levels of education is the Centre National d'Enseignement par Correspondance (CNEC); Central Office, 60 boulevard du Lycee, 92171 Vanves Cedex (Contact: The Director). CNEC's correspondence teaching programmes include courses in basic adult education. (See Projects and Initiatives.)

Other Ministries and national organisations are responsible for provision in particular, specialised areas. A joint committee representing the Ministries engaged in adult education is responsible for policy decisions. Its directives are implemented by the Ministry of Labour and the Secretariat d'Etat chargé de la Formation Professionnelle, 55 rue St. Dominique, 75007 Paris (Contact: Alain Flageul). The Secretariat studies the implementation of vocational training policy, co-ordinates training programmes at regional level, and deals with requests for funds or accreditation.

In addition, voluntary organisations have traditionally been involved in many different aspects of adult education provision.

Broadcasting

The French radio and television broadcasting service operates nationally and regionally under the general supervision of TéléDiffusion de France (TDF). 21-27 rue Barbes, B.P. 518, 92542 Montrouge Cedex (Contact: A. Cayet, Bureau de Prospective).

One of the six organisations responsible to TDF is the Institut National de l'Audiovisuel (INA), 21-23 boulevard Jules-Ferry, 75011 Paris (Contact: M. Bezie, Director of Professional Training).

Projects and Initiatives

Association Nationale pour les Télécommunications du Littoral et de la Mer (Antelim) 50 rue Saint- Ferdinand, 75017 Paris. Contact: Yves Le Gall, Director. Antelim comprises a communications network providing training support and information to seamen working from French ports through radio, audio and video cassettes and some printed material. In 1978, in co-operation with INA and Radio France Internationale, Antelim produced its first major report, *Dossier sur la Communication des Gens de Mer et du Littoral.*

Centre de Télé-Promotion Rurale Rhône-Alpes-Auvergne (TPR) B.P. 47x Centre de Tri, 38040 Grenoble Cedex. Contact: Marc Girardin, Co-director. Girardin is the author of Chapter 2 of the present book. Many documents have been produced by TPR in addition to those quoted in Chapter 2; these include *L'Utilisation du Film T.P.R. pour l'Animation des Groupes Agricoles* (1977) and Hermerlin, C. and Cipra, A. *L'Expression Collective des Agriculteurs dans le Cadre de la Télé-Promotion Rurale* (1977)

Centre National d'Enseignement par Correspondance (CNEC), 109 rue Vauquelin, 31051 Toulouse Cedex. Contact: Hélène Vabre. CNEC's Toulouse office presents 'pré-Formation' courses in French and Mathematics based on correspondence texts but also using a variety of other supporting media. Accounts of various aspects of CNEC's work include Paasche, A. *Les Unités de Formation du C.N.T.E.* (CNTE, Paris, 1979) and Vabre, H. *Presentation du Projects de Préformation* (CNTE, Toulouse, 1980)

Radio-Animation-Peche (RAP), 54 avenue de la Perrière, 56100 Lorient. Contact: Jean-Yves Le Norcy, Director. RAP provides non-formal courses, using printed materials, radio and audio cassettes, on themes of particular concern to fishermen employed in the North West of France. An analytical survey of the work of RAP has been produced by INA, entitled *Radio-Animation-Pêche: Expertise Professionelle* (2 vols., INA, Paris, 1979)

WEST GERMANY

Adult Education Provision

The Länder have educational autonomy and their Ministries of Education and Culture and for Social Affairs have direct responsibility for adult education.

Throughout the Federal Republic is a network of Volkshochschulen, adult education centres of which most are run by local authorities. The Volkshochschulen are autonomous institutions which have formed regional associations which in turn have created the Deutscher Volkshochschul-Verband e.v. (DVV), Konstantinstrasse 100, D-5300 Bonn 2 (Contact: The Director at Bonn, or Gerd von der Handt, Padagogische Arbeitsstelle, Holzhausenstrasse 21, D-6000 Frankfurt am Main).

An organisation which develops curricula for distance teaching at various educational levels is the Deutsches Institut für Fernstudien an der Universität Tübingen (DIFF), Wöhrdstrasse 8, D-7400 Tübingen (Contact: Karlheinz Rebel, Director). DIFF has been involved in the preparation of materials for the Quadriga-Funkkolleg as well as in setting up the Zeitungskolleg (see Projects and Initiatives).

Broadcasting

There are two broadcasting systems in the Federal Republic: Arbeitsgemeinschaft der öffentlichrechtlichen Rundfunkanstalten der Bundesrepublik Deutschland (ARD), Bertramstrasse 8, P.O.B. 3111, D-6000 Frankfurt am Main (Contact: Ernst Emrich (radio) or Walter Flemmer (television), Bayerischer Rundfunk, Postfach 200 508,

D-8000 München 2). ARD is a union of broadcasting corporations transmitting regionally.

Zweites Deutsches Fernsehen (ZDF), Postfach 4040, D-6500 Mainz 1 (Contact: Ingo Hermann). ZDF is the only nationwide station producing and transmitting only television programmes.

Several broadcasting corporations are involved individually in multimedia adult education projects. For example, Norddeutscher Rundfunk (NDR), Gazellenkamp 57, D-2000 Hamburg 54 (Contact: Gerhard Vogel) has collaborated in the international planning and production of 'Follow Me', and with the Adolf-Grimme-Institut and Hessischen Rundfunk in course materials production (see Projects and Initiatives).

The Adolf-Grimme-Institut des DVV (AGI), Eduard-Weitsch-Weg 25, D-4370 Marl (Contact: Peter von Rüden, Director) was established in order to consolidate co-operation between adult education institutions and educational broadcasting authorities.

Projects and Initiatives

DIFF-Zeitungskolleg. Neckarhalde 55, D-7400 Tübingen. Contact: Jost Reischmann. Zeitungskolleg offers courses for adults, using series of articles printed in newspapers throughout the Federal Republic, supplemented by printed readers. An account by Jost Reischmann of the Zeitungskolleg from its establishment in 1977 up until 1980, entitled 'Zeitungskolleg: A New Way in Open Adult Education in West Germany' will appear in a forthcoming issue of *Distance Education.*

'Erziehen ist nicht Kinderleicht' ('Parenthood is no Child's Play'). A course designed by AGI to help parents of young children, making use of television and printed materials. Contact: Peter von Rüden.

'Un Ruhestand'. Another AGI course employing television and printed materials, addressed at the problems of elderly and retired people. Contact: Manfred Borchert, Karin Derischs-Kunstmann, or Margret Hamann.

GREECE

Adult Education Provision

Within the Ministry of National Education and Religion, as the result of radical reforms during 1976-77, a Directorate of Adult Education is entrusted with responsibility for Greece's extensive network of regional and local adult education provision. The Directorate implements the policies of the Central Committee of Adult Education.

Ministry of National Education and Religion, Adult Education Directorate, 15 Hermou Street, 4th Floor, Athens. Contact: P. Kehayopoulos, Director.

Broadcasting

Ethnikon Idryma Radiophonias Tileorassis (EIRT, the National Radio Broadcasting and Television Institute) is a state-controlled public body. There are several privately owned commercial radio stations, but EIRT is the only television broadcasting company. During the period of the Study it did not prove possible to elicit any information from EIRT relating to adult education provision.

Projects and Initiatives

None identified.

ITALY

Adult Education Provision

The Ministry of Public Education is responsible for adult education, but other Ministries undertake professional and technical training. Ministero della Publica Istruzione, Direzione Generale per l'Istruzione Elementare, Viale Trastevere, 00100 Roma. Contact: Michele Aurelio Sinisi, Director General.

Amongst the considerable number of initiatives in the area of social education, one of the oldest and best established is UNLA.

Unione Nazionale per la Lotta contra Analfabetismo (UNLA) Palazzo della Civilta del Lavoro 00144 Roma

Contact: Anna Lorenzetto, President, or Antonietta Leggeri

UNLA has established a wide network of adult education centres in Southern Italy and in the Islands; many cultural and educational activities are undertaken in these centres, including small-scale projects employing some audio-visual media but not mass media.

Broadcasting

In 1976, Radiotelevisione Italiana (RAI) lost its monopoly of radio and television broadcasting in Italy. The number of local radio stations had grown by 1979 to over 3,500, and there were also more than 500 television stations.

Radiotelevisione Italiana (RAI)	RAI, in spite of its success in the
Viale Mazzini 14	1960s with experiments such as the
00195 Roma	Telescuola instructional courses and,
	in particular 'Non e mai troppo tardi',
Contact: Daniele Doglio	has not introduced any further basic
	adult education courses.

Projects and Initiatives

None identified. A report specially commissioned for the Study, Doglio, D. *A Report on the Current Situation in Italy as regards the Use of Mass Media for Adult Basic Education* (1980), examines the reasons why no projects or initiatives relevant to the Study are currently operating.

LUXEMBOURG

Adult Education Provision

During the course of the Study it proved impossible to elicit information from the Education Ministry concerning adult education provision in the Grand Duchy.

Broadcasting

Both television and radio broadcasting are controlled by the privately-owned Compagnie Luxembourgeoise de Télédiffusion, known as Radio-Télé-Luxembourg, whose finances are derived from advertising revenues. There is no separate educational broadcasting department, and although certain programmes are aimed at groups such as immigrant workers and the unemployed, these take the form of information programmes rather than courses.

Radio-Tele-Luxembourg, Villa Louvigny, Luxembourg. Contact: Nic Weber, Directeur International, Direction Generale Presse et Publications.

Projects and Initiatives

None identified.

NETHERLANDS

Adult Education Provision

Formal adult education is overseen by the Ministry of Education and Science, as are correspondence education and part-time education for young workers. The responsibility for policy in the field of adult education provided by local educational centres for liberal adult education, by voluntary organisations, and by residential centres, rests with the Ministry of Culture, Recreation and Social Welfare. This Ministry also has final responsibility for broadcasting. Adult schooling and (re)training in relation to the labour market is the concern of the Ministry of Labour and several other Ministries. Three Ministries, of Culture, Recreation and Social Welfare, of Education and Science, and of Labour, work together in the Interdepartmental Steering Group on Adult Education under the direction of the Minister of Education and Science, who is also Co-ordinating Minister of Adult Education.

In practice, adult education programmes are conducted by autonomous, mostly private, institutions which are united in national co-ordinating bodies. One of the most important of these bodies is the Samenwerkingsorgaan NCVO, P.O. Box 351, 3800 AJ Amersfoort (Contact: The Director), which is an umbrella organisation for such institutions as folk universities, local centres for liberal adult education, folk high schools and other residential centres.

Broadcasting

Both radio and television broadcasting are carried out by private organisations and groups licensed by the government through the Ministry of Culture, Recreation and Social Welfare, and working together through an umbrella organisation,

Nederlandse Omroep Stichting (NOS)
P.O. Box 10
1200 JB Hilversum
Contact: Kees van der Haak, Head, General Broadcasting Policy Group, or Henk Jurgens, Secretary, Commission on Instructional Broadcasting

The broadcasting organisations, of which there are currently eight, are associations of listeners and viewers sharing particular cultural, religious or political interests. Each organisation is required to present a proportion of educational programmes.

Another institution with primarily educational objectives is the Teleac Foundation, Jaarbeursplein 15, P.O. Box 2414, 3500 GK Utrecht (Contact: H.J. van Schalkwijk, Director). Teleac produces television programmes with accompanying printed materials for various audiences, including the Open School.

Projects and Initiatives

Open School. Contact. Ger van Enckevort, General Secretary, Co-ordinating Group for National Projects in Adult Education, Laan van Vollenhove 3227, 3706 AR Zeist. Chapter 7 of the present book is an account by Lies Vellekoop of the Open School project. Many reports have been produced by the Open School, the majority of which are available only in Dutch, and further reports will be completed by August 1981. The final report on the project will be translated into English and will be published at the end of 1981.

From the experience gained during the Open School project phase, a new plan has been developed: Open School Pilot Schemes Association, *The Open School Framework Plan: a Revised Plan for Adult Education* (Open School, Zeist, 1980).

PORTUGAL

Adult Education Provision

Within the Ministry of Education, the Directorate responsible for adult education is the Direcção-Geral de Educacão de Adultos (DGEA), Avenida 5 de Outubro 35 7º, Lisboa (Contact: Lucas Estevão, Director, or Silva Pereira). DGEA is charged with implementing a National Plan for Literacy and Basic Education for Adults (PNAEBA).

A team of adult education specialists from Sweden have been engaged since the late 1970s in building up institutions for adult education at two Portuguese universities and in providing assistance to DGEA. The Portugal Project is based at Linköping University, Department of Education, S-581 83 Linköping, Sweden (Contact: Johan Norbeck)

Broadcasting

Radiodifusão Portuguesa, E.P. (RDP)
Avda Eng. Duarte Pacheo 5
Lisboa
Contact: President of the
Administrative Committee

Founded in 1975 after the nationalisation of nine radio stations and their merger with the existing national broadcasting company. RDP also broadcasts at regional level.

Radiotelevisão Portuguesa, E.P. (RTP)
Rua de S. Domingo a Lapa 26
Lisboa
Contact: President of the
Administrative Committee

Founded in 1956, RTP was nationalised in 1975.

Projects and Initiatives

For the purpose of the Study a special report was written, Melo, A. *The Mass Media and Distance Teaching for Basic Education: A Case Study on Portugal* (1980). The report describes the post-Revolution

242

activities of the DGEA. Melo has written a number of reports and articles on the Portuguese experience, including *Experiments in Popular Education in Portugal 1974-76* (Unesco, Paris, 1978) with A. Benavente, and 'Portugal's experience of reform through popular initiative', *Convergence*, vol. XI, No. 1 (1978), pp. 28-39.

The *Annual Reports* and other publications in the Portugal Project's Documents series provide detailed information of more recent developments in Portugal.

SPAIN

Adult Education Provision

A separate Department of the Ministry of Education is responsible for permanent education for adults and for education at a distance. This is the Gabinete de Educacion Permanente de Adultos y Educacion a Distancia, Paseo del Prado 28-8°. Madrid 14 (Contact: Francisco Moron Dominguez, Jefe del Gabinete). The Department administers adult education centres throughout Spain, and also publicly and privately run distance teaching organisations.

Broadcasting

The controlling and co-ordinating body for radio and television in Spain in Radiotelevision Española, Prado del Rey, Madrid 11 (Contact: Fernando Labrada, Jefe del Servicio General de Documentacion). Television Española is the only television company but there are many commercial radio stations. Radio ECCA (see Projects and Initiatives) is in the unusual position of being the only non-commercial radio station amongst the 40 stations comprising the COPE network.

Projects and Initiatives

Centro Nacional de Educacion Basica a Distancia (CENEBAD), Sagasta 27, Madrid 4 (Contact: Antonio Lopez Pavon, Director) is now in its second year of operation. It provides courses at all levels of basic education for adults as well as for children unable to attend schools. CENEBAD is developing printed materials and audio-cassettes, and may soon have the opportunity to produce radio programmes.

Radio ECCA, Av. de Mesa y Lopez 38, Aptdo 994, Las Palmas de Gran Canaria. Contact: Luis Espina Cepeda, Director. The Director of Radio ECCA has contributed Chapter 8 to this book. He is also the author of the most comprehensive document so far published on Radio ECCA, *Radio ECCA, Centro Docente* (Radio ECCA, Las Palmas, 1976). A considerable number of reports have been published on particular aspects of Radio ECCA's system and its effectiveness. These include Equipo de Investigacio Sociologica (EDIS) *Estudio Del Alumnado de la Escuela de Padres ECCA* (EDIS, Madrid, 1980) and Espina Cepeda, L. *Relacion Coste-eficacia de Radio ECCA.* Ponencia presentada en el Seminario sobre el Coste-eficacia en Enseñanza a Distancia, Buitrago, 28 enero 1980 (Radio ECCA, Las Palmas, 1980)

UNITED KINGDOM

Adult Education Provision

Local authorities and voluntary bodies provide adult education facilities and services in England and Wales. The government department primarily involved is the Department of Education and Science; the Department of Employment (through the Manpower Services Commission and its Training Services Division and Special Programmes Division) is also active in adult education.

Information Department, Department of Education and Science, Elizabeth House, York Road, London, SE1 7PH. Contact: Chief Information Officer.

In Scotland, the Scottish Education Department grant-aids approved associations concerned with educational and cultural activity. Adult education has been combined with the much more extensive provision of Youth and Community Work services. Local education authorities are responsible for adult education provision.

Scottish Education Department, New St. Andrews House, St. James Centre, Edinburgh, EH1 3SY. Contact: J.J. Farrell, Assistant Secretary, Community Further Education Division.

In Northern Ireland, the main providers of adult education are several university departments together with the Workers' Educational Association. A Council for Continuing Education has been established to advise the Department of Education.

Department of Education, Rathgael House, Balloo Road, Bangor, County Down, BT19 2PR. Contact: C.W.L. Graham, Principal Officer, Continuing Education.

Advisory Councils have also been established for England and Wales, and Scotland:

Advisory Council for Adults and Continuing Education (ACACE)
19b De Montfort Street
Leicester LE1 7GE

Scottish Council for Community Education
c/o Scottish Education Department
113, Rose Street, Edinburgh

Contact: John Taylor, Secretary

Contact: Sir Fraser Noble, Chairman

Two national bodies which promote co-operation, co-ordinate existing activities and operate as publishers and centres of information are:

National Institute of Adult Education (NIAE)
(address as ACACE)

Scottish Institute of Adult Education
4 Queensferry Street
Edinburgh EH2 4PA

Contact: Alan Charnley, Senior Research Officer, or Elaine Pole, Librarian

Contact: Vernon Smith, Director

Those organisations which were established to concern themselves with adult literacy now have a broader remit:

Adult Literacy and Basic Skills Unit (ALBSU)
Kingsbourne House
229-231 High Holborn
London WC1V 7DA

Scottish Adult Basic Education Unit
4 Queensferry Street, Edinburgh
EH2 4PA

Contact: Pablo Foster, Director

Contact: Alan Wells, Director,
or Elspeth Cardy,
Field Consultant.

Northern Ireland did not set up a special literacy unit because special funding was not provided. A working party (superseded by a Liaison Group) was set up by the Department of Education primarily to co-ordinate the work of the agencies already active in adult literacy.

Northern Ireland Literacy Liaison Group, c/o Department of Education (address above). Contact: Jean Whyte, Department of Psychology, Queens University of Belfast, Belfast, BT7 1NN.

Other organisations actively concerned with basic adult education include:

National Extension College 18 Brooklands Avenue Cambridge CB2 2HN Contact: Richard Freeman, Executive Director	A non-profit-distributing organisation which has been involved in the planning and production of a number of basic adult education courses, including Just the Job and 'Make it Count' (see below)
Volunteer Centre Media Project 29 Lower King's Road Berkhamsted Herts. HP4 2AB Contact: Mike Hodgkinson, Research Officer	Set up in 1977 to collect and disseminate information on initiatives in the general area of community involvement through TV and radio, to monitor activities and encourage research.

Broadcasting

Both the BBC and the independent companies with an IBA franchise have been involved in recent years in collaborative development with outside agencies of projects and courses relating to basic adult education. A selection of these projects and courses are described in the next section.

British Broadcasting Corporation (BBC) Broadcasting House London W1A 1AA	Independent Broadcasting Authority (IBA) 70 Brompton Road London SW3 1EY

Contact: Don Grattan,   Contact: Naomi McIntosh, Senior
Controller,   Commissioning Editor, Channel 4
Educational Broadcasting

Projects and Initiatives

This section contains references to only a selection of the many projects which are, or have been, operating in the United Kingdom, to demonstrate the range of subjects covered:

Adult Literacy Campaign. Contact: Alan Charnley, Senior Research Officer, NIAE, or ALBSU (addresses of both organisations above). The Campaign is described in Chapter 5 of the present book by A.H. Charnley and A.H. Jones, who have also written *Adult Literacy: a Study of its Impact* (NIAE, Leicester, 1978) and *The Concept of Success in Adult Literacy* (Huntington Publishers Ltd., Cambridge, now published by ALBSU, 1979). An official record is provided by the annual reports of the Adult Literacy Resources Agency, of the Adult Literacy Unit, and of ALBSU (all published by HMSO) and by the *Newsletter* which continues to be published by ALBSU. A further important document reflecting a different perspective is Hargreaves, D. *Adult Literacy and Broadcasting: the BBC's Experience* (Frances Pinter (Publishers) Ltd., London, 1980).

Just the Job Project. Contact: Barry Deller, Media Services Unit, National Extension College, 46A Fore Street, Ivybridge, Devon, PL21 9AE. Chapter 3 of the present book is an account of the Project by its first Director, Barry Reeves. Two evaluation reports on the Project have been undertaken, the first of which was written by Project staff and included in an interim report to the National Extension College in 1977-78. The second report, Gladstone, D., Etheridge, J. and True, C. *Just the Job: an Evaluation ...* (University of Exeter, Dept. of Sociology, Exeter, 1979) was submitted to the Manpower Services Commission. A comprehensive account of the Project is currently being written by the International Extension College. Already available is a report by the Volunteer Centre Media Project, *The Just the Job Project: a Multi-media Approach to Helping the Young Unemployed* (VCMP, Berkhamsted, 1978).

247

'Let's Go'. BBC television- and radio-based course for moderately mentally handicapped young adults and those who have to deal with them.

'Make it Count'. Numeracy project based on television broadcasts and print materials, launched by Yorkshire Television and the National Extension College and evaluated in Stringer, D. *Make it Count: a Report* (Independent Broadcasting Authority, London, 1979).

Open University Community Education Courses. Contact: Nick Farnes, Academic Co-ordinator, Community Education, The Open University, Sherwood House, Sherwood Drive, Bletchley, Milton Keynes, MK3 6HW or Judith Calder, Institute of Educational Technology, The Open University, Walton Hall, Milton Keynes, MK7 6AA. Chapter 4 of the present book is an account by Farnes and Calder of these courses. The Open University's involvement in community education is reviewed in Farnes, N. (ed.) *Community Education with the Open University . . .* Provisional edition (Open University PECU Community Education Section, Milton Keynes, 1979). The Open University's Community Education Evaluation Group has published a series of papers, including No. 11, Lilley, A. *The Local Radio Experiment: a Collaborative Community Education Programme between the Open University and Two Local Radio Stations* (1980).

'Other People's Children'. BBC television-based course with backup printed material, aimed at childminders, particularly those who were unregistered.

'Parosi'. BBC project based on television and supplemented by local radio broadcasts, designed to help and encourage Asian women to learn English. The project is described in Matthews, T. *Parosi: a BBC Contribution to Language Learning in the Asian Community* (BBC Education, London, 1978).

'Roadshow'. Television-based BBC project for young unemployed, written up in Volunteer Centre Media Project *Roadshow - an Evaluation of the BBC Television Series for Young People* (VCMP, Berkhamsted, 1980).

'Speak for Yourself'. BBC television- and radio-based course begun in 1980 which seeks to help all larger non-English-speaking racial groups in the United Kingdom with language and other social and educational problems.

APPENDIX I: CONTRIBUTORS TO THE STUDY

Listed below are the names of those who have contributed to the Study on which this book is based, through, for example, attendance at meetings and preparation of reports and case-studies.

Belgium	Mr. Fredy Jacquet, Canal Emploi
	Mme. Christiane Verniers, FUNOC
Denmark	Mr. Peter Looms, Danmarks Radio
	Mr. Mogens Elvius, National Institute for Educational Media
Eire	Mr. Liam O Murchu, Radio Telefis Eireann
France	Mr. Alain Flageul, Fonds de la Formation Professionelle et la Promotion Sociale
	Mr. Marc Girardin, Centre TPR (Grenoble)
	Mme. Hélène Vabre, CNEC (Toulouse)
W. Germany	Dr. Jost Reischmann, DIFF-Zeitungskolleg
	Mr. Peter von Rüden, Adolf-Grimme-Institut
	Mr. Gerhard Vogel, Norddeutscher Rundfunk
Greece	Mr. P. Kehayopoulos, Ministry of National Education & Religion, Adult Education Directorate
Italy	Dr. Daniele Doglio, RAI
	Professor Anna Lorenzetto, UNLA
Netherlands	Mr. Kees Jan Snijders, Open School
	Ms. Lies Vellekoop, Open School
Portugal	Dr. Alberto Melo, Université Paris Dauphine, Service Education Permanente
Spain	Mr. Luis Espina Cepeda, Radio ECCA
	Ms. Carmen Rodriguez Mederos, Radio ECCA
	Mr. Antonio Fabregat Conesa, CENEBAD

Appendix I: Contributors to the Study

United Kingdom   Ms. Frances Berrigan, BBC/Open University Productions
Mr. John Cain, BBC
Ms. Judith Calder, Open University
Ms. Elspeth Cardy, ALBSU
Dr. Alan Charnley, NIAE
Mr. Barry Deller, National Extension College
Mr. Nick Farnes, Open University
Mr. Richard Freeman, National Extension College
Professor H. Arthur Jones, CBE, University of
Leicester
Ms. Naomi McIntosh, IBA
Mr. Barry Reeves, formerly of the National
Extension College
Mr. John Robinson, formerly Education Secretary,
BBC

Study Team	Mr. Anthony Kaye	Distance Education
	Dr. Keith Harry	Research Group
	Dr. Kevin Wilson	The Open University
	Ms. Nazira Ismail	Walton Hall, Milton
		Keynes, MK7 6AA

Commission	Mr. Hywel Jones	Directorate-General for
	Ms. Karen Fogg	Employment and Social
		Affairs
	Ms. Henriette	EEC
	Bastrup-Birk	Rue de la Loi 200
	Ms. Deborah Gallo	B-1049 Brussels

| **European** | Mr. Blachette | European Youth |
| **Youth Forum** | | Forum, Brussels |

APPENDIX II: REPORTS PRODUCED FOR THE STUDY

Listed below are the main reports and other documents produced as part of the Study on which this book is based. They are available in mimeo from the Distance Education Research Group, Open University.

1. Project Case-Studies

* ESPINA CEPEDA, L. (1980) *Structure and Educational Technology of Radio ECCA* (in English and Spanish)

* FARNES, N. and CALDER, J. (1980) *A Distance Learning Contribution to Community Education* (UKOU)

* GIRARDIN, M. (1980) *L'Experience de Télé-Promotion Rurale* (in French and English)

* JACQUET, F. (1980) *Canal Emploi: Presentation d'une Experience: Perspectives d'un Project Intégré de Formation Permanente* (French)

* JONES, H.A. and CHARNLEY, A.H. (1980) *A Case Study of the Adult Literacy Initiative in the United Kingdom 1974-79*

* LOOMS, P.O. (1980) *Danish for Adults: A Case Study*

* MELO, A. (1980) *The Mass Media and Distance Teaching for Basic Education: A Case Study on Portugal*

* REEVES, B. (1980) *National Extension College/Westward TV 'Just the Job' Project*

* REISCHMANN, J. (1980) *Zeitungskolleg: A Mass Media and Distance Learning Project for Open Learning*

* VABRE, H. (1980) *The Pre-Training Scheme of the French National Centre for Correspondence Education* (in French and English)

Appendix II: Reports Produced for the Study

* VELLEKOOP, L. (1981) *The Dutch Open School Project: A Case Study*

* VERNIERS, C. (1981) *Presentation de l'Action Collective de Formation de Charleroi et Réflexion sur le Rôle que les Mass Media Peuvent y Jouer* (in French)

2. Special Reports

* BERRIGAN, F. (1980) *Access to Broadcast Media and Community Use of Media in Respect of Adult Basic Education Programmes*

* CAIN, J. (1980) *A Personal Report on the British Experience of the Use of Mass Media for Basic Adult Education*

* DOGLIO, D. (1980) *A Report on the Current Situation in Italy as regards the Use of Mass Media for Adult Basic Education*

* ROBINSON, J. (1980) *Organisational and Collaborative Frameworks for the Provision of Adult Basic Education using Multi Media Methods*

3. Study Report to the European Commission

* HARRY, K., KAYE, A.R. and WILSON, K. (1981) *The European Experience of the Use of Mass Media and Distance Methods for Adult Basic Education*

INDEX